M000248773

FEMINIST INTERPRETATIONS OF PLATO

RE-READING THE CANON

NANCY TUANA, GENERAL EDITOR

This series consists of edited collections of essays, some original and some previously published, offering feminist reinterpretations of the writings of major figures in the Western philosophical tradition. Devoted to the work of a single philosopher, each volume contains essays covering the full range of the philosopher's thought and representing the diversity of approaches now being used by feminist critics.

FEMINIST INTERPRETATIONS OF PLATO

EDITED BY NANCY TUANA

THE PENNSYLVANIA STATE UNIVERSITY PRESS
UNIVERSITY PARK, PENNSYLVANIA

Library of Congress Cataloging-in-Publication Data

Feminist interpretations of Plato / edited by Nancy Tuana.

p. cm. — (Re-reading the canon)

Includes bibliographical references and index.

Contents: Was Plato a feminist? / Gregory Vlastos — Plato, irony, and equality / Janet Farrell Smith — The politics of women's bodies / Monique Canto — The philosopher and the female in the political thought of Plato / Arlene W. Saxonhouse — Hairy cobblers and philosopher-queens / Elizabeth V. Spelman — Why women cannot rule / Natalie Harris Bluestone — The Platonic appropriation of reproduction / Page duBois — "Supposing truth were a woman" / Wendy Brown — Sorcerer love, a reading of Plato's Symposium, Diotima's speech / Luce Irigaray — Irigaray and Diotima at Plato's Symposium / Andrea Nye — Overcoming dualism / Cynthia Hampton — The presence and absence of the feminine in Plato's philosophy / Nancy Tuana and William Cowling.

ISBN 0-271-01043-6 (alk. paper) — ISBN 0-271-01044-4 (pbk.)

1. Plato. 2. Woman (Philosophy). 3. Feminist theory. I. Tuana, Nancy. II. Series.

B398.W5F46 1994

184—dc20 93-30521

CIP

Printed in the United States of America

Published by The Pennsylvania State University Press,
University Park, PA 16802-1003

It is the policy of The Pennsylvania State University Press to use acid-free paper for the first printing of all clothbound books. Publications on uncoated stock satisfy the minimum requirements of American National Standard for Information Sciences—Permanence of Paper for Printed Library Materials, ANSI Z39.48–1984.

For Christopher Tuana Carleton,
in joyful celebration of the love and the laughter.

Contents

Preface ix

Acknowledgments xiii

Part One: Plato on Women

Introduction 3

1 Was Plato a Feminist? 11
Gregory Vlastos

2 Plato, Irony, and Equality 25
Janet Farrell Smith

3 The Politics of Women's Bodies: Reflections on Plato 49
Monique Canto
Translated by Arthur Goldhammer

4 The Philosopher and the Female in the Political Thought of Plato 67
Arlene W. Saxonhouse

5 Hairy Cobblers and Philosopher-Queens 87
Elizabeth V. Spelman

6 Why Women Cannot Rule: Sexism in Plato Scholarship 109
Natalie Harris Bluestone

Part Two: Plato and the Feminine

Introduction 133

7 The Platonic Appropriation of Reproduction 139
Page duBois

8 "Supposing Truth Were a Woman . . ." : Plato's Subversion of Masculine Discourse 157
Wendy Brown

9 Sorcerer Love: A Reading of Plato's *Symposium*, Diotima's Speech 181
Luce Irigaray
Translated by Eleanor H. Kuykendall

10 Irigaray and Diotima at Plato's Symposium 197
Andrea Nye

11 Overcoming Dualism: The Importance of the Intermediate in Plato's *Philebus* 217
Cynthia Hampton

12 The Presence and Absence of the Feminine in Plato's Philosophy 243
Nancy Tuana and William Cowling

Select Bibliography 271

Notes on Contributors 275

Index 279

Preface

Take into your hands any history of philosophy text. You will find compiled therein the "classics" of modern philosophy. Since these texts are often designed for use in undergraduate classes, the editor is likely to offer an introduction in which the reader is informed that these selections represent the perennial questions of philosophy. The student is to assume that she or he is about to explore the timeless wisdom of the greatest minds of Western philosophy. No one calls attention to the fact that the philosophers are all men.

Though women are omitted from the canons of philosophy, these texts inscribe the nature of woman. Sometimes the philosopher speaks directly about woman, delineating her proper role, her abilities and inabilities, her desires. Other times the message is indirect—a passing remark hinting at woman's emotionality, irrationality, unreliability.

This process of definition occurs in far more subtle ways when the central concepts of philosophy—reason and justice, those characteristics that are taken to define us as human—are associated with traits historically identified with masculinity. If the "man" of reason must learn to control or overcome traits identified as feminine—the body, the emotions, the passions—then the realm of rationality will be one reserved primarily for men,[1] with grudging entrance to those few women who are capable of transcending their femininity.

Feminist philosophers have begun to look critically at the canonized texts of philosophy and have concluded that the discourses of philosophy are not gender-neutral. Philosophical narratives do not offer a universal perspective, but rather privilege some experiences and beliefs over others. These experiences and beliefs permeate all philosophical theories whether they be aesthetic or epistemological, moral or metaphysical. Yet this fact has often been neglected by those studying the traditions of philosophy. Given the history of canon formation in Western philosophy, the perspective most likely to be privileged is that of upper-class, white males. Thus, to be fully aware of the impact of gender biases, it is imperative that we re-read the canon with attention to the ways in which philosophers' assumptions concerning gender are embedded within their theories.

This new series, *Re-Reading the Canon*, is designed to foster this process of reevaluation. Each volume will offer feminist analyses of the theories of a selected philosopher. Since feminist philosophy is not monolithic in method or content, the essays are also selected to illustrate the variety of perspectives within feminist criticism and highlight some of the controversies within feminist scholarship.

In this series, feminist lenses will be focused on the canonical texts of Western philosophy, both those authors who have been part of the traditional canon, as well as those philosophers whose writings have more recently gained attention within the philosophical community. A glance at the list of volumes in the series will reveal an immediate gender bias of the canon: Arendt, Aristotle, de Beauvoir, Derrida, Descartes, Foucault, Hegel, Hume, Kant, Locke, Marx, Mill, Nietzsche, Plato, Rousseau, Wittgenstein, Wollstonecraft. There are all too few women included, and those few who do appear have been added only recently. In creating this series, it is not my intention to reify the current canon of philosophical thought. What is and is not included within the canon during a particular historical period is a result of many factors. Although no canonization of texts will include all philosophers, no canonization of texts that exclude all but a few women can offer an accurate representation of the history of the discipline as women have been philosophers since the ancient period.[2]

I share with many feminist philosophers and other philosophers writing from the margins of philosophy the concern that the current canonization of philosophy be transformed. Although I do not accept the position that the current canon has been formed exclusively by power relations, I do believe that this canon represents only a selective history of the tradition. I share the view of Michael Bérubé that "canons are at once the location, the index, and the record of the struggle for cultural representation; like any other hegemonic formation, they must be continually reproduced anew and are continually contested."[3]

The process of canon transformation will require the recovery of "lost" texts and a careful examination of the reasons such voices have been silenced. Along with the process of uncovering women's philosophical history, we must also begin to analyze the impact of gender ideologies upon the process of canonization. This process of recovery and examination must occur in conjunction with careful attention to the concept of a canon of authorized texts. Are we to dispense with the notion of a tradition of excellence embodied in a canon of authorized texts? Or, rather than abandon the whole idea of a canon, do we instead encourage a reconstruction of a canon of those texts that inform a common culture?

This series is designed to contribute to this process of canon transformation by offering a re-reading of the current philosophical canon. Such a re-reading shifts our attention to the ways in which woman and the role of the feminine is constructed within the texts of philosophy. A question we must keep in front of us during this process of re-reading is whether a philosopher's socially inherited prejudices concerning woman's nature and role are independent of her or his larger philosophical framework. In asking this question attention must be paid to the ways in which the definitions of central philosophical concepts implicitly include or exclude gendered traits.

This type of reading strategy is not limited to the canon, but can be applied to all texts. It is my desire that this series reveal the importance of this type of critical reading. Paying attention to the workings of gender within the texts of philosophy will make visible the complexities of the inscription of gender ideologies.

Notes

1. More properly, it is a realm reserved for a group of privileged males, since the texts also inscribe race and class biases that thereby omit certain males from participation.

2. Mary Ellen Waithe's multivolume series, *A History of Women Philosophers* (Boston: M. Nijhoff, 1987), attests to this presence of women.

3. Michael Bérubé, *Marginal Forces/Cultural Centers: Tolson, Pynchon, and the Politics of the Canon* (Ithaca: Cornell University Press, 1992), 4–5.

Acknowledgments

Gregory Vlastos, "Was Plato a Feminist?" is reprinted by permission of Stephen Vlastos from *Times Literary Supplement*, iss. 4485 (17–23 March 1989): 276, 288–89. Copyright © 1989 by Gregory Vlastos.

Janet Farrell Smith, "Plato, Irony, and Equality," is reprinted by permission of Pergamon Press and the author from *Women's Studies International Forum* 6, no. 6 (1983): 597–607. Copyright © 1983 by Pergamon Press plc.

Monique Canto, "The Politics of Women's Bodies: Reflections on Plato," is reprinted by permission of the publisher from *The Female Body in Western Culture: Contemporary Perspectives*, ed. Susan Rubin Suleiman, trans. Arthur Goldhammer (Cambridge: Harvard University Press, 1986), 339–53. Copyright © 1985, 1986 by the President and Fellows of Harvard College.

Arlene W. Saxonhouse, "The Philosopher and the Female in the Political Thought of Plato," is reprinted by permission of Sage Publications from *Political Theory* 4, no. 2 (May 1976): 195–212. Copyright © 1976 by Sage Publications, Inc.

Elizabeth V. Spelman, "Hairy Cobblers and Philosopher-Queens," is reprinted by permission of Beacon Press from *Inessential Women: Problems of Exclusion in Feminist Thought* (Boston: Beacon Press, 1988), 19–36. Copyright © 1988 by Elizabeth V. Spelman.

Natalie Harris Bluestone, "Why Women Cannot Rule: Sexism in Plato Scholarship," is reprinted by permission of Sage Publications from *Philosophy of Social Science* 18 (1988): 41–60. Copyright © 1988 by Sage Publications, Inc.

Page duBois, "The Platonic Appropriation of Reproduction," is reprinted by permission of The University of Chicago Press and the author from *Sowing the Body: Psychoanalysis and Ancient Representations of Women* (Chicago: University of Chicago Press), 169–83. Copyright © 1988 by The University of Chicago.

Wendy Brown, " 'Supposing Truth Were a Woman . . .': Plato's Subversion of Masculine Discourse," is reprinted by permission of Sage Publications from *Political Theory* 16, no. 4 (November 1988): 594–616. Copyright © 1988 by Sage Publications, Inc.

Luce Irigaray, "Sorcerer Love: A Reading of Plato's *Symposium,* Diotima's Speech," trans. Eleanor H. Kuykendall, is reprinted by permission of Eleanor H. Kuykendall and Georges Borchardt, Inc., from *Hypatia: A Journal of Feminist Philosophy* 3, no. 3 (Winter 1989): 32–44. Original French text. Copyright © 1984 by Les Editions de Minuit.

Andrea Nye, "Irigaray and Diotima at Plato's Symposium," is reprinted by permission of the author from *Hypatia: A Journal of Feminist Philosophy* 3, no. 3 (Winter 1989): 46–61. Copyright © 1989 by Andrea Nye.

Cynthia Hampton, "Overcoming Dualism: The Importance of the Intermediate in Plato's Philebus," is reprinted by permission of the State University of New York Press from *Critical Feminist Essays,* ed. Bat Ami Bar-On (Albany: State University of New York Press, 1993). Copyright © 1993 by the State University of New York Press.

Part One

Plato on Women

Introduction

> A most beautiful finish, Socrates, you have put upon your rulers, as if you were a statuary.
>
> And on the women too, Glaucon, said I, for you must not suppose that my words apply to the men more than to all women who arise among them endowed with the requisite qualities.
>
> That is right, he said, if they are to share equally in all things with the men as we laid it down.
>
> —*Republic* 540c

In the past two decades a surprisingly large number of articles have been devoted to the question of Plato's feminism. While the majority of feminists have concluded that Plato's philosophy is sexist, there has been persistent support for the view that Plato's proposals for social policy are feminist or at least consistent with feminist principles. The typical argument in support of Plato's feminism focuses on issues of sex equality concerning education and economic opportunity, as well as Plato's rejection of a generalized sex difference in human nature. Those who cast Plato's philosophy as sexist look at a variety of issues. Some question the extent to which Plato's social policies would in fact result in full participation of the sexes; others argue that even if the changes guaranteed equal opportunity, they would only do so for a small number of women. Still others emphasize that Plato continues to privilege those traits and roles that would have been viewed as masculine within Greek society. Another critique shifts the focus from Plato's social prescriptions to his metaphysics, maintaining that the dualism inherent to his worldview is essentially incompatible with feminism.

In this first section I offer a selection of texts designed to illustrate the variety of perspectives involved in this controversy. In the first article, Gregory Vlastos supports the idea of Plato as the first feminist while acknowledging aspects of his philosophy that might lead one to claim that Plato was antifeminist. Vlastos contends that there is controversy because Plato's position concerning women is multifaceted. He explains that although Plato's treatment of the guardian women in the *Republic* was feminist, his view of the remaining majority of free women was antifeminist. In addition, Vlastos acknowledges that Plato's personal attitudes toward contemporary Athenian women was decidedly misogynist. He also notes that Plato's alternative society (what Vlastos labels his "second-best society") depicted in the *Laws* is feminist in some respects and antifeminist in others.[1] Despite this variety, Vlastos argues that Plato's various responses to women involved no inconsistency.

Vlastos defends the feminism of Plato's views of guardian women by pointing out that Plato allocated rights to guardian women that were denied to Athenian women: the right to education, to vocational opportunity, to unimpeded social intercourse, to equal legal status, to sexual choice, to own and dispose of property, and to political participation. From his arguments we can infer that Vlastos is employing a liberalist definition of feminism in which the primary concern of feminism is the equality of rights between the sexes.[2]

Vlastos explains that Plato's many disparaging remarks concerning women, such as his categorization of people who desecrate enemy corpses as of "womanish and small intellect" (*Republic* 469d), refer to the traits of women "deformed and misshaped" by the corruptness of Athenian society. He contends that none of Plato's misogynous statements imply beliefs about woman's nature and thus do not speak to the possibilities for women in the ideal state.

Janet Farrell Smith's discussion of Plato's views on women augments that of Vlastos. Noting that Plato's focus was not the elimination of sex discrimination, but rather the conditions necessary for the development of a just state, and acknowledging that Plato's state would involve classes in hierarchical relations, Smith disagreed with Vlastos's characterization of Plato's views concerning guardian women as "feminist." Nevertheless, Smith points out that Plato advocated a tenet concerning sex roles central to contemporary feminist beliefs and supported by recent psychological findings: that Plato did not view sex roles as resulting from natural differences between the sexes, but rather believed them to be constructed in large part by cultural, social, and political factors. Smith attributes to Plato the tenet that the range of individual variations between women is greater than the variations between the traits and abilities of the two sex groupings, that is, between women and men. According to Smith's interpretation, Plato held the position that educating women to guardian status is both just and natural, that is, enables each person to perform the function she or he is best suited for by nature.

While Smith rejects the application of the label of "feminist" to Plato, Monique Canto enthusiastically embraces it. However, it would be a mistake to see her position as similar to that of Vlastos. Canto ignores the type of liberal feminist rights analysis offered by Vlastos and replaces it with an analysis of Plato's conception of otherness.[3] She argues that a feminist politics requires the actual presence of women in the public space and claims that this is exactly what we find in Plato's philosophy, that is, women's bodies, works, labors, and voices present in the polis. Whereas Vlastos ascribes Plato's feminism to the opportunities available to guardian women, Canto bases her claim upon the way in which Plato deals with difference.

Canto argues that women represent two conditions necessary for political life: procreation and desire. Reproduction requires difference, "for without difference the idea of the same and the idea of the other make no sense" (51). She sees desire as equally necessary, arguing that every political order must come to terms with the realm of the emotions, for pleasure and pain are the vital principle of the city itself, yet ones that threaten the city's very existence. A crucial decision to be made in organizing the polis is where this difference resides: inside or outside the city. Canto contends that Plato locates difference outside the polis in the *Republic*, but inside the polis in the *Laws*.

Plato's goal in the *Republic*, in Canto's view, is that citizens share all pleasures and pains in common. In order for this to be possible, women and men must hold all political functions in common, which in turn requires neutralizing what Plato sees as the enduring difference between the sexes: that the male "begets" while the female "bears." Thus Plato's "eugenics" program, which includes the practice of raising all children in common, with no parent being able to identify her or his offspring, is designed to solve this problem of difference. This for Canto is a politics for which procreation is the primary issue. In this way Plato directs the desire of all citizens to one object: the city. It is Canto's view that in such a city, the body of woman is neither the object nor subject of desire. In the *Republic* woman does not represent otherness; otherness is located outside the city.

In the *Laws* Canto sees Plato as applying the theory developed in the *Republic* to a real city that exists in time. She argues that in a real city, woman's otherness cannot be neutralized, it can only be regulated. Hence, otherness remains inside the city. In the *Republic* the image is of the political *identity* of women and men, but in the *Laws* the metaphor becomes that of "a well-compounded bowl" in which the political life of the city requires difference. According to Canto, the city of *Laws* constitutes itself by coming to terms with rather than eliminating the place of women. The *Laws*, being an adumbration of the *Republic*, requires that images of the feminine be regulated, since woman's otherness cannot be removed. In this Canto again deviates from Vlastos. Whereas Vlastos saw the *Laws* as feminist only in certain respects and antifeminist in others, Canto argues that the *Laws*, in making women the primary object and first principle of political regulation, is a true feminist political manifesto; within its vision of the polis women will negotiate "on their own behalf with the otherness which in part they represent" (62).

Arlene Saxonhouse offers yet a different interpretation of what Vlastos calls the complexity of Plato's views of women in the *Republic*. Like Canto, Saxonhouse depicts the guardian women of Book V as free from desire, claiming that they are neither the desired nor the desiring. However, Saxonhouse rejects Canto's depiction of Plato's vision of the polis as a feminist political manifesto and argues rather that Plato's attempt to de-sex women in the *Republic* results in a perception of woman as inferior to man.

Saxonhouse calls our attention to the image of women prior to Book V as provokers of sexual eros. Women are courtesans, mistresses, and objects of sexual desire. But the control of the bodily passions necessary for the founding of the Platonic conception of the polis requires that this image of woman be denied. Thus to allow woman into the polis Plato must de-sex her, must "make her void of any special erotic attraction or function" (70). Only in this way can sexual passion be trained to serve the need of the city.

In challenge to Canto's account, Saxonhouse argues that this banning of desire from the polis results in woman's denigration, for it denies to woman one area of her excellence, namely, the ability to bear children. By minimizing woman's reproductive role and thus overlooking her natural function in the physical preservation of the city, Plato makes women inferior to men. Women are destroyed as women in that their natures are perverted. This, Saxonhouse argues, is incompatible with the Platonic definition of the just society in which each follows her or his own nature. By reorienting woman to war, Saxonhouse claims that Plato denies one of her individual excellences.

Saxonhouse equates Plato's inclusion of woman into the polis with his introduction of philosophy and the philosopher into the political world. She argues that the philosopher, like the woman, must be "de-natured" in order to enter into politics. That is, just as Plato must pervert woman's body, so too must he pervert the philosopher's soul. Saxonhouse views the various metaphors in which Plato depicts the philosophic process as like that of the sexual experience of women, as a representation of the true nature of philosophy when not perverted by the demands of the polis. Both the philosopher and the woman must refrain from participation in the political realm in order to preserve their individual excellence, yet Plato's creation of the ideal political state demands the inclusion of both within the polis. Saxonhouse concludes that this tension is designed to illustrate the fundamental imperfectibility of politics.

Elizabeth Spelman develops the insight noted by Smith that Plato's model of the just state involves a hierarchy of classes. Like Smith, Spelman admonishes against labeling as feminist any position that would argue for equality between women and men of one class, but allow radical inequality between some women and some men, some women and some other women, and some men and some other men. Spelman employs Platonic philosophy as a cautionary illustration of how one can argue against sexism yet leave other forms of oppression intact.

Spelman would reject Vlastos's description of Plato as "unambiguously feminist" concerning guardian women. She bases her analysis on Plato's treatment of the soul/body distinction. She notes that the Platonic metaphysic treats soul and body as distinctly different types of things. Souls are invisible, eternal, and only contingently connected to visible, changing bodies. Furthermore, it is the nature of one's soul that determines one's capacity to be a guardian. Thus Spelman, like Vlastos, attributes Plato's ability to see beyond a person's sex to his treatment of the soul/body distinction. Whether a person possesses a woman's or a man's body is irrelevant to her or his capacity to rule, which is determined exclusively by the nature of one's soul.

Spelman's most important contribution to the controversy surrounding Plato's treatment of women is the realization that, for Plato, souls are gendered. Spelman illustrates that the "philosopher-queen" does not have a feminine soul, that is, a soul unable to resist the temptations of the body and unable to distinguish between appearance and reality. Spelman explains that the guardian woman has a manly soul: the kind of soul that true philosophers have. She thus reveals Plato's four categories of people:

1. manly soul/male body (the philosopher-king);
2. manly soul/female body (the guardian woman);
3. womanly soul/male body (the cowardly male soldier);
4. womanly soul/female body (the typical Athenian woman).

Spelman, like Vlastos, argues that the inconsistency between Plato's misogynistic remarks and his treatment of guardian women is only apparent. However, her explanation differs from his. Whereas Vlastos emphasizes the sociopolitical conditions in which the typical Athenian woman exists versus the idealized society of the *Republic*, Spelman's position is grounded on the contention that Plato uses the term "woman" ambiguously. Plato, Spelman explains, employs the term *woman*, particularly in the context of his misogynist remarks, to denote the combination of womanly soul/female body. However, when using the term "woman" to refer to guardian women, Plato intends the alternative combination of manly soul/female body.

Interestingly, although Spelman and Vlastos basically agree concerning the consistency of Plato's treatment of women, they diverge radically concerning Plato's alleged feminism. Whereas Vlastos allows that Plato is feminist concerning the guardian women, Spelman is troubled by a feminism that would permit such class hierarchy. Spelman also asks whether the kind of power and authority Plato ascribes to guardians is the kind of power and authority that feminists ought to embrace. Her response to these rhetorical questions is clearly no. Spelman would thus reject the categorization of Plato as a feminist on the grounds that the only women who are fully present in the public space are guardian women. What we learn from Spelman, and what Canto neglects, is that all the women Plato relegates to the "lower" classes, particularly slave women, are excluded from Plato's "feminist political manifesto."[4] This, for Spelman, is "the sad irony in the description of Plato as the first feminist philosopher" (88).

Natalie Harris Bluestone offers the important reminder that feminists must attend not only to prejudice against women within the Platonic corpus, but that we must also be vigilant concerning sexist bias within the scholarly translations of Plato's writings and the commentaries on them. Bluestone traces a history of hostility against Plato's plan for sexual equality within the guardian class.

According to Bluestone, the most common form of reaction to Plato's proposal of equal education and roles within the guardian class is the rejection of it as unnatural. Many of the most prominent and influential Plato scholars, including Ernest Barker, Allan Bloom, Benjamin Jowett, and A. E. Taylor, rejected Plato's premise that the biological difference that man begets while woman bears is irrelevant to woman's nature and thus to woman's individual excellences. Each argued that this difference had profound consequences for woman's desires and abilities that were ignored by Plato. Such commentators saw woman's biological difference as extending beyond the simple fact of bearing to include a natural desire and disposition to rear and nurture her children. Such commentators often associated this natural inclination to raise children with gendered differences in mind and feeling. The conclusion was that Plato was mistaken in viewing his ideal city as either desirable or realizable; to deny women's biological inclinations in this way in order to turn them into guardians would ultimately be unsuccessful or would result in women being turned into inferior men.

An interesting tension arises at this point in the anthology: the criticism that Plato's model of guardian women would result in a distortion of woman's nature that would ignore woman's particular excellence is one that is shared not only by the commentators Bluestone identifies as prejudiced, but is also found within the commentary of Saxonhouse, a professed feminist commentator. Is there a difference between Saxonhouse's admonition that Plato's proposal de-sexes woman by denying one area of female excellence, woman's ability to bear children, and the position of those commentators discussed by Bluestone that Plato was incorrect in stating that woman's ability to bear was irrelevant to her nature and ability? Both hold that woman's nature would have to be distorted to bring her into the polis and that doing so would result in her being inferior to man.

The articles in this section, while mapping out the major controversies surrounding the classification of Plato's philosophy as feminist, also demonstrate the inadequacy of viewing feminist analyses as uniform or unitary. The diversities of feminist theories and methods result in different focuses and perspectives on the questions of Plato's feminism. It is important that we as readers be sensitive to these differences in order to judge how they affect a theorist's interpretation.

Notes

1. While Vlastos does not elaborate upon this tenet, he depicts the *Laws* as a retreat on the part of Plato from his position in the *Republic* caused by "the more conservative philosophical and political outlook which comes over Plato with increasing age" (22).

2. For a clear discussion of the varieties of definitions and theories of feminism, see Alison Jaggar's *Feminist Politics and Human Nature* (Totowa, N.J.: Rowman and Allenheld, 1983) and Rosemarie Tong's *Feminist Thought* (Boulder, Colo.: Westview, 1989).

3. Canto is offering a version of what has been labeled "postmodern feminism."

4. Another valuable contribution made by Spelman is her identification of the tendency of feminists to fall prey to a similar exclusion of certain groups of women from full consideration within their theories by failing to recognize the importance of differences, in particular those of race and class, between women.

1

Was Plato a Feminist?

Gregory Vlastos

Was Plato a Feminist? Hot scholarly controversy has swirled around this question. Plato has been hailed as Ur-feminist by some, denounced as antifeminist by others. When we view such collisions between honest readers of the same texts we may suspect that not all of three desiderata have been fully met: clarity of definition; awareness of complexity; dispassionateness of judgment.

How should we define the term? For "feminism" the *OED* lists "advocacy of the claims and the rights of women," dating the entry to 1895. This is too loose. To tighten it up I borrow wording from the Amendment to the United States Constitution proposed earlier in the present decade (failing to pass, though strongly supported by feminists and favored by a majority of the American electorate): "Equality of rights under the law shall not be denied or abridged by the U.S. or by any State on account of sex." Dropping everything unessential for my purpose I get a shorter formula whose scope is wide enough to cover all personal rights that may be claimed for women—not just the legal ones envisaged by the Amendment, but social, economic, and moral rights as well: "Equality in the rights of persons shall not be denied or abridged on account of sex."

Does this give a defensible definition of "feminism"? I believe so. But I shall waste no time defending it. The focus of my interest is Plato, not feminism. It suffices for my purpose, making the question under debate entirely clear: Plato will qualify as a "feminist" if his ideas, sentiments, and proposals for social policy are in line with this norm.

Well, are they? When the question is put in that way any informed reader of the *Republic* and the *Laws* should be able to see that there is no simple answer. I would argue that it takes no less than four distinct propositions to formulate one that takes account of everything he says: (1) In the ideally best society outlined in Books IV to VII of the *Republic* the position of the women in its ruling elite, the so-called guardians, is unambiguously feminist. (2) In that same society the position of the great majority of its free women, composing its industrial and agricultural class, is unambiguously antifeminist. (3) In the alternative, second-best, society laid out in the *Laws,* the position of free women is a hybrid, feminist in some respects, antifeminist in others. (4) In his personal attitude to the women in his own contemporary Athens Plato is virulently antifeminist.

That Plato can run the gamut of these extremes will raise hackles of incredulity. It would take a whole book, a fat one, to allay them completely. All I can do here is to show that the initial impression of inconsistency between them is false. To do this I shall have to focus sharply on the first, short-shrifting the other three. For this is the eye of the controversial storm. Plato's feminism has been denied even here. Claiming that Plato's affirmation of feminism within the ruling class of the *Republic* is the strongest ever made by anyone in the classical period, I have no choice but to defend that claim in detail, letting the other three come in for their due as I proceed.

I begin by listing rights systematically denied to women in Plato's Athens which we have reason to believe would not be denied or abridged within the guardian class of his *Republic:*

1. Right to Education. In Athens schools, gymnasia and palaestrae were a male monopoly. In Plato's *Republic* access to them by members of the guardian class would be the same for women as for men in all respects, down to that last detail which has drawn so many prurient smirks: exercising in the nude with men. As we know from Herodotus and Thucydides, the Greeks thought total nudity in athletics a salient

feature of their Hellenic culture. Plato would not dream of rescinding it for males. To deny it to females would have been discriminatory.

2. Right to Vocational Opportunity. No secular gainful employment was open to all women in Athens, except prostitution of varying degrees of elegance or squalor. Within the lowest social strata there were other options outside the home: working-class women could be midwives, wet nurses, vegetable sellers, chaplet makers, and so forth. Aristotle apologizes for this exception to the rule, explaining it as a product of dire economic necessity: "How could you stop the women of the indigent from going outside the house?" (*Politics* 1300a6). In Plato's *Republic* career for highest talent is as open to women as to men. Both sexes qualify on equal terms for admission to guardianship and therewith to all those professional occupations bundled up in that nominally single job: military to begin with and, thereafter, all political offices—executive, legislative, and judicial—and all of the assorted tasks that would come along with these: economic planning, population management, critique and censorship of literature and the arts, direction of schools and sports, supervision of the military and religious establishment—all these along with research and teaching in the sciences and philosophy.

3. Right to Unimpeded Social Intercourse. Mingling with free men other than close relatives is denied in principle to all Athenian women except priestesses, hetaerae, prostitutes, and tradeswomen. Such segregation is wiped out in Plato's guardian class, where men and women "live in the same house, eat in common dining halls" (458c), and exercise in the same gymnasia.

4. Legal Capacity. In Athens only men have it. Women are wards of their nearest male relative, their *kurios.* They cannot sue or be sued, and even their right to give testimony in court is marginal. Among Plato's guardians such differences could not exist. Whatever legal capacity male guardians have, female ones have also.

5. Right to Sexual Choice. In Athens women have little say as to whom or when they will marry. The marriage contract is negotiated between their nearest male relative and the bridegroom. To what extent, if any, this gentleman was required to take the wishes of his female ward into account is unclear. Heterosexual intercourse outside of marriage is forbidden to women with the utmost severity. The ferocity of the interdict may be gauged from this: an Athenian virgin in breach of the rule may be sold into slavery by her *kurios.* This is the only case in which the law recognizes penal enslavement for an Athenian. In the case of a

married woman caught in adultery "anyone whatsoever may do to her at will anything short of death." On men there was no counterpart constraint. They could have any sexual relations they pleased with women other than Athenian virgins or spouses without incurring any legal disability, or even any moral censure so long as they did not do it for money and did not overdo it. Among Plato's guardians the interdict on sexual intercourse outside of the eugenic unions during the childbearing age is the same for men as it is for women. The liberty after that age is also the same for both. The double standard of sexual morality is wiped out.

6. Right to Own and Dispose of Property. Under Athenian law only men have it. Among Plato's guardians private property is denied equally to men and to women, public support is assured equally to both.

7. Political Rights. None for women in Athens. The same for women as for men among Plato's guardians.

Given this array of equalities of rights for women guardians in Book V of the *Republic*, can it be doubted that Plato's program for them is rigorously feminist in the sense defined?

To appraise its rigor we should compare it not only with Athenian practice, but also with Athenian fantasy in Aristophanes' *Ecclesiazousae*. The two dreams of gender equality have often been compared and the question of who cribbed what from whom has been debated. But I have yet to see it noticed that the philosopher's argument is bolder than the poet's whimsy. When Praxagora's conspiratorial women capture the state and turn their wishes into law, it never occurs to them to break up the segregated public rituals and private work-roles which had always been the lot of women. When a state banquet is laid on, only the men sit down to it: the ladies do not invite themselves to dine with the gentlemen. When Blepyros, on being informed that all of his work will now be done by slaves, asks where his clothes will be coming from, Praxagora replies, "When you wear out the ones you have, we will weave you new ones" (651–54): the women are still behind the loom where they have been since Homer.

The most radical innovation in Plato's vision of a new society is not the extension of legal and political rights to women. That had been thought of already, though it had taken the comic genius of Aristophanes to think of it. Nor is it the liquidation of the nuclear family; for this there had been earlier models in Herodotus's album of anthropological oddities. It is the reasoned rejection of the age-old dogma, never previously questioned in Greek prose or verse, that difference of sex must determine difference of work-allocation.

Is there any reasonable ground on which the feminist intent, so thoroughgoing on the face of it, of Plato's program for the ruling class of his utopia might still be doubted? Sarah Pomeroy has argued that there is, finding it in that curious language in which Plato speaks of the breeding unions: he refers to the women and the children as belonging in common to the men, with never a balancing allusion to the fact that the men, as also, of course, the children, belong in common to the women. Here are the suspect expressions: "community (*koinonia*) of children and wives for the Guardians" (450c); "possession (*ktesis*) and use (*chreia*) of children and of wives" (451c). From this asymmetry of references to who-belongs-to-whom Pomeroy infers that the female guardians are to be the property of the male ones. The inference is unwarranted. The conclusion is not entailed by the evidence, and it is inconsistent with the following data: in any given marriage-group every woman belongs to all the men in the peculiar, but precise, sense that, so far as she knows and so far as they know, the eugenic "lottery" might make any one of them the father of her child. Mutatis mutandis every man belongs to every woman in his group in exactly the same sense. And there is no other relevant sense of "belonging." So the relation cannot be ownership. It would make no sense to say that x is y's property when y is also x's property.

Why then should Plato have used that kind of language? One could reply that this is the way group-marriages are talked about: they are always viewed from the man's point of view. Thus Herodotus writes that the Agathyrsoi "have in common intercourse with the women" (4.104) and that the Namasonians "believe in having many wives and in having intercourse with them in common" (4.172.2). Aristophanes makes even Praxagora, the liberator, talk in the same arsenocentric way. Though the licensed promiscuity is perfectly symmetrical, she speaks of it as "making the young women common bedmates for the men to produce children for any man who wants it" (614). Should we be surprised that Plato should have used similar language? Verbal habits could outlast the prejudices which created them. But can we be sure that Plato has outgrown the prejudices? Some of them he must have, else he could not have written Book V of the *Republic.* But there are others he has not. The evidence has been surveyed brilliantly by Dorothea Wender. Here is part of it: that Plato's estimate of the common run of female intelligence is very low slips out even within Book V of the *Republic*. Remarking that people who desecrate enemy corpses must be acting on the stupid belief that your enemy's body is your real enemy, he says that to give credence to this notion would be "the mark of a womanish and small intellect" (469d). To distinguish the higher from the lower appetites he says earlier on (431b–c) that the former are those "you would find among the few, those with the best nature and the best education," while their opposites "one would find chiefly in children and in women and in slaves and, among so-called freemen, in the base multitude." So too in his critique of music and of poetry. The great complaint here is that in their present form those arts weaken the controls on strong emotion which decent persons ought to keep and women typically don't: "We pride ourselves on bearing up quietly in affliction, for this is the part of a man, while the other is the part of a woman" (605d–e). He refers to scenes in Homer and tragedy where heroes and other great men abandon themselves to outbursts of grief whose pathos, softies that we are at heart, we enjoy sharing vicariously, though we would feel disgraced if we had so behaved ourselves.

"The element common to all that was said of women by the Greeks," writes Kenneth Dover, "is the woman's inability to resist fear, desire, or impulse. . . . A woman, in fact, was thought to have a 'butterfly mind,' equally incapable of intelligent, far-sighted, deliberation and of foregoing the emotional reaction of the moment in pursuit of distant and impersonal aims." We may note that he is not saying that this is how individual women are always portrayed. He knows well this is not so. He says that this is how they are generalized about on the stage and in oratory, and not only by men: women too are made to say such things about themselves. From women's lips we hear in Euripides and Aristophanes that their sex is weak, weepy, impulsive, irresolute, perfidious, garrulous, gluttonous, bibulous, lascivious. What I have just quoted from Plato fits this stereotype.

And now one last item to the same effect from the venomous caricature of Athenian democracy in Book VIII of the *Republic*. Plato pictures its mania for liberty as condoning the collapse of all deference due to authority: citizens no longer obey the magistrates, nor do sons their parents, nor pupils their teachers, nor slaves their owners, and "even the horses and donkeys have the habit of promenading on the street with all the rights and privileges of freemen." Just before the promenading quadrupeds at the climax of the satire (563b), comes the following: "I nearly forgot to mention how great *isonomia* and liberty has entered the mutual relations of men and women." *Isonomia* is a very strong word. It stands not just for equality before the law, but for equality by means of law—for substantively equal civic rights established and maintained by law. Now if progress toward sexual equality were being currently made in Athens, the last person in the world we might expect to damn his city for it would be the author of Book V of the *Republic*. What then should we make of his conduct in the present passage? Must we reckon it a great man's lapse into peevishness, his hatred of democracy blinding him at this point, making him forget the feminist line he had taken just three books earlier in the *Republic*? We can make better sense of it if we connect it with the image of Athenian womanhood he must have carried in his head, judging from those chance remarks in which "womanish" stands for persons with diminutive intellects, obsessive appetites, and ungovernable emotions. If this is how Plato thought of the common run of women, he might well believe that in the present state of society continued subjection would be better for them than any degree of emancipation. Keeping them down, under their nearest male relative's thumb, he could hardly think an ideal solution, considering how benighted most of those males were on his own reckoning. But it might still strike him as the lesser of two evils: *isonomia* for creatures who cannot reason and keep their baser impulses under control would be worse.

This is the streak in Plato's thinking I had in view when putting forward the last of the four theses above. Whatever improvements had occurred within his lifetime must have been so minuscule as to leave no discernible record in Athens's legal history and provide no known relief from those massive inequalities I have detailed. That Plato should have seized on those minute changes, magnifying them in hostile fantasy, blowing them up into *isonomia*, should suffice to show that on the emancipation of women within the framework of his own society Plato's position would be not only conservative but reactionary.

But could he retain this attitude side by side with the feminism of Book V? On the face of it, it looks as though only schizophrenia could have enabled him to do this. I want to argue that this appearance is false. Prisoner of the sexist stereotype though Plato was in his reactions to the contemporary scene, he could still take, without formal inconsistency, a radically opposite view of the place women were to have in the highest stratum of his ideal society. He could do so because the "womanish" traits he denigrates are those of the great mass of women, not of those brilliant exceptions from whom the guardians would be recruited; and, moreover, they are the traits common to women *now*, under conditions now prevailing which do not foster the development of energetic minds and resolute characters. In the most damning of the disparaging remarks cited it is clear that he is speaking of women as they are under present, nonideal, conditions: those motley appetites predominant in women, along with children, slaves, and men of the vulgar mass, are those, he says, "which one would find" (431c) in these creatures. What one "would find" is what is already there. And he is not saying that it is there as the permanently fixed, invariant, character of the female of the species, its nature: there is no reference to women's *phusis* in this passage or any of the others I have cited from the *Republic*, as there would have been if his point had been that those bad "womanish" traits were inherent in femaleness as such. In the absence of any such indications the right way to read those passages is as reflections on what Plato thinks women are now, formed and shaped, deformed and misshaped, by the society which has reared them.

We should recall here his vivid sense of the power of a corrupt society to pervert the heart and conversely of the power of education to improve moral character. Putting into that context those woman-denigrating remarks, we can understand them as voicing what Plato thinks most Athenian women grow up to be in their present habitat, the domestic ghetto, which stunts them intellectually and warps them morally, robbing them of what they might have been had they enjoyed that marvellous *paideia* which both sexes are to have in the ideal polis.

Moreover the butts of those nasty remarks differ in still another way from the women for whom Plato reserves the feminist program of Book V. They are females of the common run, while those who will be guardians are as exceptional within their own sex as the male guardians are to be in theirs: in each case Plato is counting on paragons of intellect and character. And if you ask: why should he expect the female half of the population to produce such superlative specimens? the answer is: why not, when he expects this of its male half? If there are to be stars in the population why should they be only male? Why should Plato have assumed that being female would decrease one's chances of turning out to be a superperson instead of a mass-person?

The Greek poetic vision of humanity would give no quarter to that prejudice. Homer and tragedy present a gallery of distinguished women who rise as high above ordinary females as do its heroic males above the mass of men. Consider Penelope. In cunning, in farsighted purpose, in composure under nagging harassment, in unrelenting steadfastness of resolve, she dwarfs the people, male or female, who crowd her world. Compared to her the suitors are pygmies and Telemachus a likeable mediocrity. Only the great Odysseus is her match. In tragedy we have Clytemnestra, the counterpart in Aeschylus's masterpiece of Lady Macbeth in Shakespeare's. That both are evil is beside the point, which is that each is as far as human flesh and blood could be from Dover's "butterfly mind." Each has the qualities which, differently used, could have produced heroic goodness. The same is true of Medea. And if we are looking for high stature in a woman who stays completely within the conventional social role, instead of breaking out of it, like Antigone, in her defiance of an unjust decree, consider Alcestis in Euripides. Of perfect outward self-possession while suffering inner agony there is no better example in Greek literature than Alcestis as she moves toward her death. Dressed and adorned as for a festive occasion, she makes the round of the altars in the palace "without a tear, without a groan, without a change of colour on her lovely face" (173). So long as she remains on public view even skin color is under control.

But there is no need to give the poets sole, or even major, credit for freeing Plato from the prejudice that an intellectual and moral elite could only be recruited from male stock. We know of two other liberating influences: the theory of moral virtue he learned from Socrates and the metaphysical theory he invented himself.

One could scarcely overstress the shattering effect in Plato's mind of Socrates' rejection of the age-old axiom that excellence of character was class-bound and gender-bound. The Socratic doctrine that virtue is the same in women as in men may seem a commonplace to us. But it flouts the certainties of his people and it outrages Aristotle, who takes their parochial intuitions for universal moral truths. Nothing shows up so well the novelty of the Socratic view as do Aristotle's remarks in Book III of the *Politics* (1277b20–23). To prove that virtue *is* different in women Aristotle argues that if a man were no braver than a brave woman he would be a coward, and if a woman were as talkative as a decent (*kosmios*) man, she would be a chatterbox; female excellence, he assumes, could be no better than male mediocrity. If Plato had shared that premise he could not have composed Book V of the *Republic,* even if he had written everything else in that work. He did not share it because he derived from

Socrates the conviction that human excellence, intellectual and moral, is unisex. So when he designed a state where that kind of excellence would be the passport to dictatorial authority, he had to make the tenure of political power also unisex.

To his Socratic heritage Plato adds his own metaphysical theory without which the absolute powers entrusted to his philosopher-kings would be incomprehensible. Assured of access to the world of Forms, they will come to know the Form of the Good and be themselves transformed by that knowledge. Their initiation into that eternal world Plato calls a "turnabout of the soul from a day that is like night to the true day" (521c). The change is so profound that not only the mind, but the whole psyche, down to the libido, is transformed. It is a translation into a world of the mind whose magnificence beggars the prizes of the world of sense. *Sub specie aeternitatis* sensual attractions pale: Plato's imagery makes them fugitive, flat, unsubstantial—shadows on a wall. This in the last analysis is what he expects will keep his philosophers from misusing their vast unchecked authority. Their power will not corrupt them because to denizens of eternity the bribes and lures of power are trash.

Now obviously there is nothing about maleness that fits one to experience this rebirth. What one needs is, first of all, the capacity to go through its preparatory *paideia* in one's teens—a capacity Plato must think unrestricted by sex since he prescribes that *paideia* for both sexes—and thereafter the intellectual talent and the moral fiber to survive the grueling fifteen-year course of graduate studies in mathematics and dialectic. There is a cutoff point here that will separate the men and women who are to rule from those they are to rule. Plato has no way of specifying that point. But it is clear that he is thinking of a threshold that can be crossed by persons who, though vastly superior to the great mass, may still differ considerably in ability among themselves. He believes that when the male population, taken as a whole, is compared with the female population, taken as a whole, the incidence of ability is on the average higher among males than among females. Does he then believe that in the small subgroup which passes the tests for admission to the higher studies the same differential obtains? He may, though he nowhere says so. If so, he would believe that within the guardian class men are on the average abler than women in each of the tasks to be performed. It would then follow that on the average there would be more men than women in the higher offices. It would not follow that there would be no women in the highest ones.

That women are expected to share in the topmost offices becomes explicitly clear at the close of Book VII. Here Socrates speaks of those "who have survived the tests and have excelled in all things in action and in knowledge," have beheld the Form of the Good, taken their part in governing, and at their death received quasi-divine honors. Glaucon is moved to exclaim: "Like a statuary, you have made your men-rulers matchless in beauty." Socrates retorts: "Yes, the women-rulers too, Glaucon, for you must not suppose that my description applies to men any more than it does to all the women who arise among them with the requisite natural endowment."

If the foregoing argument has been sound, the feminist program for the ruling elite in Book V of the *Republic* becomes perfectly understandable as a consistent application of Plato's theory of social justice. According to that theory the rights and duties justly allocated to citizens of the polis would be all and only those which would enable each of them to make the greatest personal contribution to the happiness and excellence of the whole polis, their own included. This is the criterion by which the abolition of private property for the guardians is justified: guardians must own no property because they would be "best craftsmen at their own work" (421c) without rather than with private property. The same criterion would dictate full equality of rights within the guardian class in all of the categories I detailed at the start. Nothing less will explain the rationality of Plato's extraordinary program, so unprecedented in Greek experience, philosophy, or even fantasy. In particular, it cannot be explained as a mere by-product of the decision earlier on in the *Republic* to deprive guardians of private property, thereby abolishing in their case the traditional pattern of Greek marriage whose base *was* private property. The claim that this is the correct explanation has been made repeatedly in the scholarly literature. The conclusive objection is that Plato could have abolished the private family along with private property in the guardian class, could have followed to the letter the formula "common possession of goods and wives," *without* granting equality of status to those wives. He could have made them collective consorts, nurses for the children, factotums for the men, but not guardians, rulers of the state, sharing supreme political authority and civic dignity.

That the theory of social justice propounded in the *Republic* is the decisive reason for the feminism of Book V gets added support from what happens when Plato turns away from that theory in his last work, the *Laws*. That move marks a retreat along a broad front from his stand in the *Republic*. The retreat is not a rout. The equal right to education and to unimpeded social intercourse women retain in the *Laws*, and here all citizen women will have it, regardless of class. But they lose equality in vocational opportunity, in legal capacity, in the right to own property, and in choice of marriage partner. I would argue that both changes—in the theory of social justice and in the conception of the status of women—are due to the more conservative philosophical and political outlook which comes over Plato with increasing age. So if we are looking for feminism in Plato there is only one place where we do not need to invent it: in the legislation for the guardians in the *Republic*. Among all of Plato's writings and among all the writings which have survived from the classical age of Greece, that work alone projects a vision of society in whose dominant segment the equal rights of human beings are not denied or abridged on account of sex.

This innovation owed nothing to a belief in what we have now come to call "human rights"—rights which belong to persons as their human birthright, without regard to their membership in any ethnic, political, economic, or religious grouping, rights pertaining to each of them individually as human beings for no reason other than their humanity. It should go without saying that Plato had no such belief. His ideal society has no place for the freedoms enumerated in the Bill of Rights: freedom of religion, of speech, of assembly, of the press. It never occurs to him that without these any attempt to apply his pattern for that society in the real world would result in the opposite of his dream of it—corruption in the rulers, oppression of the ruled. Who, man or women, should want equality on those terms? So to think of Plato as an advocate of women's liberation would be perverse. Liberation Plato advocates for no one, man or woman. Excellence, not liberty, is his goal, and he rejects liberty as the enemy of excellence. Still less could we think of him as a champion of affirmative action. Nowhere in the presentation of his program does one catch a gleam of a desire to right wrongs sexist oppression had done to women in the past. Of compassion there seems to be all too little in Plato even for me, so how could there be for women, given those sour views of them he voices in the *Republic*?

I would not call him a misogynist on that account. Certainly those derogatory remarks of his would have warmed the heart of a real woman-hater. But they hardly warrant classifying him as such himself. If they did, then by the same token we would have to classify as woman-haters the women in Euripides and Aristophanes who say equally bitter things about their sex. And while it is not unknown for members of an oppressed group to internalize masochistically the sentiments of their oppressor, it would still be misleading to say that those women hate their sex. Anyhow, "hatred" would just misdescribe the feelings Plato harbors for the women in his world: a certain dislike perhaps, condescension tinged with disdain, though more striking is the fact that he so largely ignores them in his reflections on the state, in his analyses of moral concepts and, what may be more significant, in his references to human beauty. (In the great erotic passages in the *Symposium* [210–12] and the *Phaedrus* [245–57] human beauty is desired by men desiring boys; to females desired for their beauty by men or desiring it in one another and in men there is no allusion.) When he does encounter them on the human landscape he seems to view them with an abstract gaze, as he would stare at members of a curious species, distantly related to his own. (In all other passages where Plato's Socrates expresses or simulates sexual longing the object is male; only in Xenophon [*Mem.* 3.11.3] do we ever see Socrates sexually excited at the sight of a beautiful female). This is perhaps all that could be expected of a one-track pedophile deficient in that instinctual attraction which women would have had for him if he had been one of those regular Athenians for whom Aristophanes cracked his bisexual jokes.

But whatever may be the right account of his personal feeling for living women, we can be sure it was not sentiment that moved him to legislate for the ruling class of his utopia rights for women equal to those of men. If he had followed sentiment he would have gone the other way. His achievement is all the more remarkable on that account. In a triumph of imaginative impartiality he separated the character his inherited prejudices imputed to the mass of women in his own society from the character which, he reasoned, a few exceptional women could develop under ideal conditions of equal nurture, awarding to them what his own theory of social justice required: status commensurate with the greatest contribution each of them could make personally to their own society and *therefore* equal in all respects to that of men. Few philosophers have achieved such transcendence of personal inclination in response to the dictates of impersonal moral theory.

2

Plato, Irony, and Equality*

Janet Farrell Smith

Introduction

"Sex equality," as we understand the contemporary term, is not the focus of Plato's arguments in Book V of the *Republic.* Plato did, however, advance the thesis that the differences which did exist between the sexes were not sufficient to bar women of guardian caliber from equal training with men, so that the best talent could be selected for philosophic leadership. In *Republic* V Plato gives at least three arguments on the nature of sex differences in social context. When reconstructed, these arguments can be seen to be closely related to contemporary scientific interpretations of the data on sex differences. These interpretations challenge inferences to a generalized sex difference in human nature,

*For support during the research and writing of this essay I am grateful to the Smith College Mellon Project on Women and Social Change. My thanks to Dr. Carla Golden (Psychology, Smith College), who gave technical advice and to the referees of *Hypatia* for helpful suggestions.

where these inferences are based on statistical differences in performance between the sexes.

Plato's irony signals his awareness of the ridicule and discomfort likely to be elicited by his proposals. Because Plato was well aware of the radical nature of his proposals about women, he couched his arguments in an ironic frame, utilizing a style which has caused continuing misinterpretation. I discuss sources of these misunderstandings and attempt to clarify them in part I of this essay. Part II reconstructs what can be called Plato's "burden of proof" argument in favor of equal education for women. Part III analyses the crucial "argument from individual variation," which is related to current psychology in part IV. Part V shows how Plato, in an ironic turn, argues, contrary to the popular assumption of the time that it is "unnatural" to educate women equally with men, that it is rather "unnatural" to fail to do so.

I

Several factors have continued to obscure Plato's intent in presenting the claim for equal training for guardian women. The first is the tendency to read Plato with the cultural assumptions and terminology of a later historical period. The second is Plato's genuine ambivalence about women. The third is Plato's ironic and literary style in presenting his philosophical views.

Was Plato a Feminist?

If we ask the question "Was Plato a feminist?" or "Was Plato in favor of sex equality?" we are sure to find evidence in the Platonic corpus to justify both positive and negative answers to these questions. This is partly because Plato's issues concerned neither the questions of contemporary feminism nor the liberal ideal of equality between the sexes. Sex equality in the fullest sense today includes the eradication of sex discrimination both in economic and educational opportunity and also in attitudes which are derogatory or devaluing of women and men. On most current definitions feminism asserts that women are objectified or made into "the other," in Simone de Beauvoir's phrase. Feminism involves self-consciously adopting the viewpoints and interests of women to overcome objectification and subordination of women. Plato did not focus on the elimination of sex discrimination throughout his ideal state. Nor did he himself escape the objectifying of women. It is doubtful that he even conceived of either criterion for sex equality or feminism.

On the other hand, Plato was concerned with justice in an organic and functionalist sense. In elaborating the psychic and social structure of justice in the ideal state of the Republic, he explicitly argues against sex discrimination in education for guardian women. He also argues for giving qualified persons full opportunity for guardian training regardless of whether they are male or female. It must be noted that these arguments do not stand alone, but are made in the service of Plato's larger aim, which is to arrange hierarchy, social power, and control, so that "the best" rules over the worst, with reason, according to nature. These hierarchic, aristocratic premises are inconsistent with most of the ideals which motivate sex equality or feminism in the post-Enlightenment era. Plato disdained democratic egalitarianism and accepted the principle that the greatest (moral) talent should correlate with the highest social status. Plato did not use terms such as "equality," "fairness," "equality of opportunity," and of course, "feminism." As long as we frame his questions in these terms the debate over his position on women will be confused and unending.

Despite these cultural and political differences, Plato was the first Western philosopher to work out a philosophical thesis which takes a central place in many contemporary investigations in feminist theory. He recognized that cultural, social, and political relations play a major role in forming what is commonly regarded as "natural" in sex roles and familial behavior. Although contemporary theorists may not agree with Plato's purpose and conclusions, they may find some reasoning in his arguments which anticipates current scientific inquiry. For Plato did scrutinize the question of what is "natural" in sex-related and familial structure more carefully than Aristotle, who simply took female subordination as a fact of nature.[1] Plato's scrutiny amounted to more than utopian tinkering with family structure. He saw the family and woman's role as intimately connected with property relations within the economic form of justice.

"Except for the Fact that Women Are Weaker"

Plato was genuinely ambivalent about women. He makes seriously misogynistic and derogatory comments about women within the same dialogue in which he argues that (some) women should be educated "the same" as men. These attitudes have been extensively documented.[2] While these attitudes may indicate that Plato's views on women are "an enigma" (Okin, 1979, 14) or "inconsistent,"[3] they are perhaps no more so than the presence of attitudinal sexism in those who argue for equality between the sexes, or of anti-Semitism or racism in those who argue against minority or racial discrimination. This observation does not, of course, justify holding such attitudinal prejudice.

Another curious factor in Plato's arguments concerning equal training for women guardians is his insistent qualification of every positive thesis: "Except for the fact that women are weaker." If "weaker" is taken to mean "generally inferior" including inferior intellectual ability, then the thesis that women should be equally educated falls prey to a series of *reductios.* Some commentators have indeed taken Plato in this manner. Strauss and Bloom regard Book V as a comedy, with the consequence that Plato's arguments on human nature there are neither serious investigations nor serious proposals for women's entry into philosophic rulership. Whether the comedic interpretation shows an insistence on logical consistency or a predilection to take an interpretation least sympathetic to women, there remains a problem for a consistent portrayal of Plato as a serious advocate of equal training for women.[4]

There is, however, a way out of this dilemma. Rather than regarding the qualification as undermining all Plato's arguments, on the one hand, or indicating his merely playful toying with the notion of women's education, on the other, we could take the "weaker" qualification as merely implying that women should be excused from certain activities. But these activities, primarily concerning warfare, do not affect their ability to participate fully in political leadership. For example, in gymnastics, women might not be expected to perform at the same level as men did. In physical combat, or "guarding," women might not be called to the same duties as men might: "So women must share in war and in all the guarding of the city, and that shall be their only work. But in these same things lighter parts will be given to women than men because of the weakness of their sex" (*Republic* 457a). Reference to the "lighter parts" of guarding may indicate lighter physical exertion in keeping with certain physical differences between the sexes. But these physical differences and their implied differential military functions do not disturb Plato's basic thesis—namely, that women should be trained equally with men, and that women and men alike should on the basis of individual talent rise to the position of leadership to which they are best suited.

Plato's insistence that "women are weaker" must be seen in the context of his time and culture, that is, a society called to defend itself against invasion. In addition, on the Athenian model of strength and physical excellence, handed down in the Western tradition of Olympic sport, women's capacities did indicate a lesser degree of performance and achievement. But this fact does not imply that certain women, for example, Olympic Javelin champion Kathy Schmidt, cannot excel beyond the capacities of the average man. Indeed, Plato himself makes this observation for other activities. So, given Plato's own arguments, it might initially seem odd that he should repeat the qualification where it might not be relevant. Yet, keeping in mind that Plato and his fellow Athenians had little opportunity to observe the women's athletic achievement, his qualification may indicate only relative ignorance within the cultural realities of his time. On other models of excellence of physical strength, for example, in sports or activities featuring stamina, endurance, agility, and coordination, in which women are "strong" rather than "weak," women should achieve as well as or better than men. But Plato might not have adequately incorporated even his own observation that Spartan and Sarmation women had aggressive and warlike natures.[5]

Irony, Laughter, and Truth

Plato's "three waves," leading to the establishment of the ideal state, are the equal training of guardian women, the abolition of the private family and its property, and finally, the institution of philosophic wisdom as "king" or ruler of the state. If we regard the *Republic* as an integrated dramatic presentation, then Plato's heightened awareness of the ridicule each "wave" might bring leads him to present it in a specialized manner. It is helpful to keep in mind that Book VI, following the radical proposals on women and the family, presents the even more radical views on the nature of the good.

Plato is a master stylist. He wields his powers of dramatic expression, wit, and, most of all, irony for a strategic purpose, when he presents material which he fears may be taken lightly or misunderstood. He often gives radical or dangerous material an ironic frame, a mode of presentation which both emphasizes and mitigates his point to those enveloped in shadows. While writing simultaneously on levels which may be only dimly grasped by someone who catches only part of his point, he recognizes that what he says may be taken as a joke, provoking laughter. Yet his ironic recognition of this signifies that he is well aware of the difference between presenting a joke and presenting something which may be taken as a joke. At the beginning of his discussion of equal training for guardian women he remarks: "He is a vain fool who thinks anything ridiculous but what is evil" (452d).[6] Bloom (1968, 382) takes the discussion of nakedness to imply the impossibility of training women and men equally (because, presumably, of licentiousness).[7] However, Plato is not talking about physical stripping alone, but using the Athenian custom of exercising naked as an ironic metaphor for stripping to reveal the truth: "It was better to strip than to hide all such things; and soon the seemingly funny to the eyes melted away before that which was revealed in the light of reason to be the best" (*Republic* 452d; Rouse translation).

Plato also uses the occasion to remark that at one time the Greeks also thought it "ridiculous" and "comedic" to exercise naked when the Cretans originated the custom. Plato is also well aware of the fact that what seems "natural" depends on what is "customary," as John Stuart Mill remarked in his *Subjection of Women.*[8] He is also well aware of the ridicule that might follow his implicit thesis in Book V, that "female nature is in fact what different societies have made of it" (Okin, 1979, 69). He completes his ironic frame around the discussion of the "first wave" with the warning on ignorance and ridicule: "And the man who laughs at naked women, exercising for the greatest good, plucks an unripe fruit of wisdom from his laughter. He apparently does not know what he laughs at or what he is doing. For . . . the useful is beautiful and the harmful is ugly" (*Republic* 457b).

II

The "Burden of Proof" Argument

Starting with the premise that "each single person must do his own business according to nature," (*Republic* 454a), Socrates takes up Glaucon's challenge of self-contradiction. If there is a putative difference between the natures of the sexes, then how can we say that men and women should do the same work? "We agreed, you know, that a different nature ought to practice a different work, and that man and woman have different natures; now we say that these different natures must do the same work. Is that the accusation against us?" The problem has to do with the oversimplification on "same" and "different" natures which have led into "eristic wrangling." Socrates' response further refines Plato's views on the nature of a person. If we inquire into the nature of the same versus different we find that (1) the nature of a thing is not absolute but qualified relevant to its calling or function. ["We were thinking of only that kind of sameness or difference which had to do with their actual callings." (454c).] (2) Only differences relevant to actual callings are properly used to assign social functions to persons' natures. (3) Procreative differences between the sexes alone are not relevant to the actual callings (Cf. civic responsibility) under consideration.[9] (4) Hence, if procreative differences in function are the only differences between male and female, these are not sufficient to deny equal training to women of guardian potential.

Now, the last point concludes with the conditional proposition that *if* the only differences between male and female consist in procreative function, then these differences are not relevant. Does Plato concede a prima facie plausibility to the supposition that they are the only differences when he next casts the burden of proof on he who would "say the opposite to tell us just which art or practice for which the nature of woman and man is not the same but different?" (455a).

I do not think that Plato does concede prima facie plausibility to a supposition of minimal procreative differences between the sexes. Rather, he takes a position in which a neutral or open scientific question on the differences between the sexes yields to a social and moral imperative. The evidence on sex differences is not all in. If there is a lack of definitive evidence, why suppose unequal status or training is preferable to equal training? Give the benefit of the open question to those who might excel under the more generous proposal of equal education. The burden of proof lies with those who would deny equal status.

In Plato's terms the reason why this argument stands is left implicit and unstated. It is that the basis (education) for the selection process for "the best" philosophical rulers should be cast as widely as possible. The moral and social imperative is aristocratic, hierarchical, and elitist. Plato wants the society structured so that it is more likely than not that the most talented and naturally gifted be prepared to rule. Hence, he claims that the burden of proof is on those who would deny equal training.

The argument as interpreted here states that the basis of sex differences relevant to civic leadership is an open question, emphasizing the fact that there is no evidence that sex differences do affect civic practice. Yet it infers on separate grounds that the practice which extends the more generous social policy is preferable to one which does not. A similar type of argument arises for racial differences. In the absence of definitive evidence on innate racial differences, the burden of proof lies with those who would deny equal education. It should be noted, however, that most contemporary advocates of racial equality and sex equality argue that even if biological differences do exist, these differences are not grounds for denying social equality in a democratic state.

Contemporary social psychology of sex characteristics does in fact consider most sex differences an open question. In their definitive *Psychology of Sex Differences,* Maccoby and Jacklin (1974) cite such characteristics as women's fear, timidity, competitiveness, dominance and activity level, nurturance and "material" behavior, as "Open questions: too little evidence or findings ambiguous." Even their summary of "Sex differences that are fairly well-established"—for example, girls excel in verbal ability, boys in visual-spatial ability—faces challenge both from competing interpretations and new data (Maccoby and Jacklin, 1974, 352).

Given a lack of definitive evidence for sex differences relevant to education, what is the basis for social policy concerning it? Plato's case is instructive, for he, facing this lack of definitive evidence, appeals to a set of normative (moral and political) assumptions. In Plato's case, these assumptions amount to a principle for selecting the "best" for a moral aristocracy, which would lead in the social hierarchy. Plato's basic premise, however, that in the absence of scientific evidence, social and moral assumptions account for political structuring of sex roles, can be extrapolated to contemporary democratic and egalitarian arguments.[10] Plato would not have agreed with the democratic aim of many of these arguments. Nor do many contemporaries committed to democratic aims agree with his political assumptions. Yet his philosophical moves illustrate similar transitions—in his case, openly stated and justified—in the face of open or disputed questions on sex differences.

III

The Argument from Individual Variation

In the previous argument Plato throws the burden of proof on those who would deny equal training to women *if* sex differences amount merely to procreative differences in function. In the next stage of his presentation he himself takes up the question, what, relevant to the practice of civic leadership, is the "nature" of differences between the sexes? He argues for a conclusion which anticipates the findings of contemporary psychology, that there exists greater variation *among* individuals within one sex group than *between* the two sex groupings, male versus female.

Plato begins with the general query: what civic practice is there "for which the nature of woman and the nature of man is not the same but different?" A subsidiary purpose is to show the dubious interlocutor "that there is no practice peculiar to women in the management of a city." The argument is premised on the thesis that those who have the same nature should perform the same functions and those who have different natures should perform different functions.

Plato's argument requires a distinction which would resolve an ambiguity on the "nature" of a person. Plato failed to draw this distinction as sharply as he could, causing confusion. It is doubtful whether his arguments are valid without it. The "nature" of a person could be interpreted as (a) what a person *actually* does, or (b) what a person is *capable* of doing (or has a natural gift to do). This distinction, between performance and capability in the "nature" of persons, turns out to be critical in interpreting what I call Plato's "argument from individual variation." In the following reconstruction, I first give an interpretation of each step of Plato's argument. The relevant passage from the text follows.

(1) First, Plato defines by example what it means to have a "natural gift" to do something. He seems to mean what we might call "individual aptitude" or "individual innate talent," e.g. for rapid or inventive learning, or ability to coordinate mental-physical functioning. In illustrating "natural gift," he refers to capacity (in sense [b] above), not performance (though, of course, the former could be made evident by the latter). "[We mean by] having or not having a natural gift for anything—that one learned easily, the other with difficulty? One after

short learning was very inventive in what he learnt, the other after long learning and practice could not even recall what he had learnt?" (455b).

(2) In the second step of the argument Plato moves to what can only be interpreted as performance on the part of groups, not innate natural talents of individuals. He must be talking about what could be called today mean or average performance, (appealing to sense [a] above). The claim is: in average (mean) performance the male sex group excels the female sex group in all activities in the above respects.

> Do you know anything at all practiced among mankind in which all these respects the male sex is not far better than the female? Or should we make a long story of it—take weaving, tending of cakes and boiling pots, in which women think themselves somebody and would be most laughed at if beaten? You are right, he said, That one sex is much better than the other in almost everything.

The third step asserts:

(3) However, despite the differential in group performance, many individual women excel many individual men in many things. Glaucon says: "Many women, it is true, are better than many men in many things, but generally it is as you say" (455d).

Next, Socrates draws the pivotal and crucial inference on which the argument turns.

(4) The "natures" or individual talents and aptitudes are distributed in individuals in both sex groupings.

(5) Hence, from (4), woman can participate in all practices according to her "nature."

(6) Therefore, no civic practice is justifiably assigned to woman (or man) on the basis of membership in a sex group.

"Natures" in steps (4) and (5) draws on sense (b) above as what a person is capable of doing. The text states: "Therefore, my friend, there is no practice of a city's governors which belongs to woman because she is woman, or to a man because he is man; but the natures are scattered alike among both sexes; and woman participates according to nature in all practices, and man in all, but in all of them woman is weaker than man" (455e). In the remainder of the argument Plato elaborates the character of individual variation, reinforcing (4) and (5) above, and moves to his positive conclusion.

(7) Among women, individual variation in aptitude and talent ranges across all activities relevant to social roles in the ideal society, for example, from medical, athletic, fighting, to philosophical talent:

> We shall say that one woman is athletic or warlike, and another is unwarlike and unathletic?
> Indeed.
> Shall we not say the same of philosophy and misosophy, that one loves wisdom and one hates it? One has high spirit and one has no spirit?
> That is so also.
> Then there may be a woman fit to be a guardian, although another is not; for such was the nature we chose for our guardian men also?
> Yes it was.

(8) Individuals of the "same nature" ((b) above) appropriate for civic leadership (guardian status) are found in both sex groupings, male and female: "Then both woman and man have the same nature fit for guarding the city, only one is weaker and one is stronger."

The final conclusion:

(9) Civic leadership and social functions (social roles relevant to occupations) must therefore be assigned to [individual members of] both sexes, appropriate to the aptitudes ("natures" in the sense [b] above) of each. Those "akin by nature" who have the same aptitudes should associate and receive the same training and education.

> Such women, then must be chosen for such men, to live with them and to guard with them, since they are fit for it and akin to them by nature.
> Certainly.
> Practice and calling must be assigned to both the same for the same natures.

Some comments on the soundness of the above argument: First, Plato could be accused of equivocation on "same nature" between step (2) and step (3), if we did not take him as making the distinction between performance and capacity (see [a] and [b] above). In addition, if "natural gift or capacity" is defined only in terms of what an individual actually does (and hence "can" do), Plato can also be accused of circularity. But since he makes explicit (*Republic* II, 369d) an assumption of individual innate talent he cannot be accused of circularity here.[11] That is, of course, a separate question from the empirical validity of his assumption of innate individual capacities or his claim in step (3), that individual women excel individual men in many things. The claim in step (3) can be demonstrated empirically in contemporary psychological data. But it is questionable whether there can be solid "proof" of innate capacities.

It is reasonable to extend to Plato the distinction between "nature" as innate capacity or educable talent and "nature" as group performance. For he began the discussion with a determination to unravel the semantic tangle of "same" versus "different" natures. The "ideal" state of the Republic is founded on a faith that innate human capacities can be socialized to higher moral ends, by joining "intellectual wisdom with political power" (*Republic* 473d).[12]

Finally, the qualification repeatedly inserted on the "weaker" capabilities of females is relatively harmless if taken to mean "physically weaker with respect to combat." If this is not the likely interpretation and Plato means to assert a general inferiority of women in all physical—mental capacities, then he has indeed produced a series of reductio ad absurdam arguments. But this is unlikely. His seriousness in eliciting "the best" from the population overrides prejudice on sex or class differentials. Although definitive textual evidence cannot be given for the "physically weaker" interpretation, the additional point of joining women and men of the "same nature" supports the abolition of private families and private property in the guardian class. This latter purpose is tied in explicitly with his eagerness to avoid oligarchy and class interest over inherited property. (See Book VIII.)[13]

Julia Annas in her article "Plato's Republic and Feminism," interprets Plato's argument here somewhat differently. She takes as Plato's leading query: "Is there no practice peculiar to women in the management of a city?" and interprets Plato's point that "men can do better than women" as "men would do better than women" (Annas, 1976, 309).[14] Then, she concludes, "Now it is hardly a feminist argument to claim that women do not have a special sphere because men can outdo them at everything" (309). In contrast to Annas's interpretation, I take the claim that men "can do better than women" as dealing with group averages. It implies neither that "men *would* do better" under different conditions nor that individual women are not capable of doing better than individual men.

Annas's point that Plato is not making a feminist argument is well taken. But Plato would also argue that men ("just because they are men") do not have a special sphere or social role. Neither sex has a special sphere, practice or calling because individual variability exceeds any differential in average (sex) group performance.

IV

Findings in Contemporary Psychology

Plato's argument from individual variation finds support in the data of contemporary psychology, particularly in the critical step (3) asserting that individual women excel individual men in many things. This claim (3), combined with claim (7) on the wide variability of female aptitude and achievement (which ranges from musical talent to aggression in fighting), asserts that individual variability among one sex (women) is of greater magnitude than the differences in observed "natures" between the sexes. Let us make this claim more precise: "The difference between the means of male versus female groups on behavior *x* is less than the range of variation existing within one group for that behavior *x*." This claim has been found to hold for the differences between verbal and spatial ability, which might be taken to be the least susceptible to cultural and social variation. The difference between the highest and the lowest scoring female, for example, has been found to be greater than the differences between the average female and the average male scorer. When psychologists, in other words, speak of one sex outperforming the other, they are speaking of averages, not individuals (Maccoby and Jacklin, 1974, chap. 1).

Furthermore, even given statistically significant differences between the sexes on, say, verbal or spatial ability, these differences are never more than 0.25–0.50 standard deviation. It is questionable whether these differences constitute a practically significant difference. In her *Sex-Related Cognitive Differences* Julia Sherman remarks: "Besides the *statistical* significance of a finding one may be concerned with its *practical* significance. Many apparently demonstrated sex-related differences are so small that they are of essentially no practical importance" (1978, 23).

Concerning data which show that girls exceed boys in verbal ability, Sherman remarks, "the demonstrated differences are so small as to be trivial" (1978, 38). "While females scored significantly higher than males, the amount of the variance accounted for by sex (omega squared) did not even reach 1 per cent" (1978, 43).

Evidence in psychology is continually challenged by new data. The result is that the so-called well-established differences found today may be outdated tomorrow. In 1974, Maccoby and Jacklin's "fairly well established" results on verbal differences, though conceded to be small, were widely accepted. In 1978, Sherman considered these to be "challenged and questioned" by current data (1978: 38–44).

In addition, verbal ability, as well as spatial ability, may be class and culture-bound. Cultural and social variation inhibit generalizations about sex-differences. For example, "Greater variability occurs across social class in maternal behavior with daughters [than with sons]. Upper middle class mothers have greater faith in their ability to affect their daughter's destinies, and spend more time talking to and entertaining them" (Williams, 1977, 129).[15] On the superior male performance on spatial ability, cultural factors are possible, but highly disputed. For example, this is said about Eskimos: "The lack of sex-difference in Eskimos has been variously attributed to the permissiveness of Eskimo childrearing, the relative emancipation of Eskimo women, the unique visual features of the Arctical environment, and/or an isolated gene pool among Eskimos" (Lambert, 1978, 112).[16]

Another factor in tests showing sex differences may have to do, not with the specific aptitudes, but with the connection between certain testing conditions and performance. Boys and girls, for example, were tested for spatial ability under usual conditions and under "empathy condition," (empathy is a stereotypically female trait). "Males did better than females under the usual conditions and females did better than males under the empathy condition" (Sherman, 1978, 144).[17]

These tests indicate that social conditions and background of performance may have a greater role than has been realized. Conclusions about "well-established" sex differences, founded unwittingly on cultural background factors rather than intrinsic differences, must be reexamined.

These considerations show, not that the data themselves are intrinsically unreliable, but that it is questionable what they mean. What may be interpreted as "innate" or intrinsic biological differences between the sexes may, on another model of interpretation, be taken as indicating differences in social and cultural factors in male-female socialization in a given society. But Helen Lambert claims that it may be an "unrealistic goal," especially in the case of higher mental functions, to expect a precise separation of "the biological bases . . . which are intrinsic in origin and those which are not" (1978, 105).

The few attempts to correlate cross-cultural sex differences with social factors, such as food accumulation and stratification, have not been consistent. Lambert remarks: "Even if they had, this would not prove that intrinsic factors do not affect spatial ability, but only that the sum of the interaction between intrinsic and extrinsic factors varies with culture and geography" (1978, 113).

Thus, questioning of the magnitude and relevance of observable sex difference as opposed to individual performance and capacity is typical of contemporary science, as it is of Plato's arguments on the "nature" of sex differences. The within-sex variability of maternal behavior toward daughters indicates still a further factor which is ultimately Plato's concern: education and training (socialization). In Plato's most elite class grouping, the guardian children's training does not take the sex of the child into account, (except for the "weaker" qualification). This point suggests Plato's theoretical position on psychic capacities in relation to social structure.

Plato's philosophical psychology is based within a functionalist framework. The individual's characteristics are those which make him or her best suited for a certain practice, that is, a function in society. Correspondingly, the appropriate function for an individual in society is that which he or she is, by nature (individual innate aptitude), best suited to do. This position is not, as it may sound, circular. Rather, Plato's position is that what a person is, is constituted, in part by social processes.

Although he did not make the following distinctions in precisely the same way, we can clarify Plato's intent by separating:

(a) Individual innate talents or capacities
(b) Psychic traits
(c) Behaviors
(d) Social roles

In (a) individual talent ("nature" in the sense of capacity), is a given, presumably from birth. Plato does not take a definitive position on whether it is inheritable or not, though he argues for social mobility on the basis that a "gold" child could be born to "brass" parents. He has argued, on the present interpretation, that because of (a), individual characteristics are subject to a broad *principle of individual variation.* Such variation is greater than any group of differences between the sexes in observed traits (b), or behaviors (c). Hence, Plato argues, social roles (what he would think of as functions) are not justifiably assigned on the basis of membership in a sex group, because individual natures (a) could lead to traits (b) and behaviors (c) which are appropriate to certain social roles (d) *if training and education appropriate* to (d) are given

Plato's point can be put as follows: Traits and behaviors are educable. They can be shaped by socialization processes which take individual talents into account. They are not simply "givens" apart from social processes. Hence, there is a centrality of education in the *Republic* as a whole. It is a mistake to attribute entrance into Plato's aristocracy to "merit" and "qualification." For these, as he emphasizes repeatedly, are results of a process of training individuals' capacities. Yet Plato's individual is not totally malleable. He assumes a "nature" from birth, perhaps somewhat like the "readiness to learn" hypothesis in contemporary psychology.

Plato's arrangements for family structure and childrearing must be mentioned as supporting factors for his thesis on equal training for women guardians. The entire community is "the family." "Marriages" in the form of ritualized matings appear to be spontaneous but are actually arranged by a "lawgiver" who selects partners who are "as nearly as possible of the same nature" (*Republic* 458d). Part of the purpose appears to be to avoid the disorder of ill-matched unions (458e). The important aim is to mate the "best" men with the "best" women so as to produce a sterling "herd" of guardians. If Plato's eugenic intentions are taken seriously, then, presumably, there would eventually be effects in the aptitudes of individual children produced. It is difficult to estimate these effects. From the standpoint of contemporary values concerning freedom of choice, Plato's eugenic program appears coercive and especially objectifying of women who were supposed to be freely available to the "best" warriors.

Communal childrearing, carried out by male and female caretakers (*Republic* 460b), makes an "easy job" of motherhood for the female guardians. "Sleepless nights and other troubles will be left for nurses" and the guardian women will be left free for civic activities. It is worth pointing out here that Plato's sex-blind specialization of function in professional childrearing might affect the formation of traits and behaviors associated with the child's female or male character structure. In societies where women mother, according to Nancy Chodorow in *Reproduction of Mothering,* female character structure is passed down from mothers (or other female caretakers) to daughters by a complex set of psychological and social relations. Chodorow claims that character structure would develop differently in female and male children if women and men were equally involved in caretaking of infants and young children. Plato did not explicitly anticipate such a situation. But his rearrangement of the social function of parenting does imply at least an absence of certain developmental factors such as maternal influence, which play a strong role in socialization of young children.

If certain "predisposing factors" (Lambert, 1978, 113), factors such as verbal precocity in infant girls "bend the twig" in a certain direction, then it is sociocultural factors which shape the extent and the direction of the growth (Sherman, 1978, 174).[18] In Alexander Pope's words:

> Tis education forms the common mind;
> Just as the twig is bent, the tree's inclined.

In this analogy, if cultural factors were to change, then the growth might alter and the twig might bend the branch in a different direction.

Sherman points out that in certain cultures biological factors might lead to the development of male versus female differences which for other cultures would no longer be "maximally functional." For example, the attraction of animal attacks by menstruating women perhaps bars women from hunting in primitive societies. But what is functional in one society may be nonfunctional or even deleterious in another societal structure. What these cultures regard as "natural" may vary with their needs, constraints and customs regarding the functions of individuals versus the functions of sex groupings. Something like this point is concluded by Plato in his third argument on what is "natural" versus "unnatural" in the education of males and females in his *Republic.* I turn now to his final argument on the nature of sex differences in education.

V

The Argument on What is "Natural" versus "Unnatural"

What is "natural," in Plato's terms, is "according to nature" (*kata physin*). What is "unnatural" is "contrary to nature" (*para physin*). What is most interesting about all these points in favor of educating women to guardian status is that Plato wants to conclude ultimately that it is "natural," whereas the previous and traditional practice of not so educating women is "unnatural." Hence, discrimination against women gifted enough for guardianship is "unnatural."

> Practice and calling must be assigned to both sexes, the same for the same natures?
>
> Just the same.
>
> So we have come round to where we began, and we agree that is not against nature to assign music and gymnastic to the wives of the guardians.
>
> By all means.
>
> Then our law was not impossible, not only like a pious dream; the law we laid down was natural.
>
> But rather, it seems, what happens now, the other way of doing things, is unnatural. (*Republic* 456c)

The reasoning appears to draw on the previous argument on the "nature" of individual talent and the principle that persons ought to do what they are "best suited" to do by nature. If each person and part of society (and each part of the soul) performs the function they are best suited for by nature, then we have a balanced and harmonious society (and person). Plato's conclusion, that education regardless of sex is "natural," fits with and is partially derived from his definition of justice in Book IV, which immediately precedes his discussion of women and family structure in Book V.

> To make health is to settle the parts of the body so as to rule or to be ruled together, *according to nature;* To make disease is to settle that this part rules and that is ruled by another contrary to nature.

> It is.
>
> On the other hand, . . . to implant justice is to settle the parts of the soul so as to rule and be ruled together *according to nature;* to implant injustice is to settle things so that one part rules and one part is ruled by another *contrary to nature.* (*Republic* 445a, my emphasis)

Also, the guardians require a special "nature" and training:

> It needs more leisure than all the others, and more practice and further more skill and care.
>
> Does it also need a *nature* fitted for this pursuit?
>
> Of course. (*Republic* 374e)

From this definition of justice and the claim that the guardians possess a certain "nature" which is found in women as well as men, it follows that exclusion of women from guardian education is both *unjust and unnatural.* Inclusion of women is therefore both *just and natural.*

In this last argument Plato politicizes what is "natural." Against the Aristotelian claim that it is "natural" that women be ruled by men, Plato puts the more radical claim that it is "unnatural" that power be distributed in a way that prohibits women from attaining the social function (role) or leadership for which they may be suited. In Aristotle's view, the relation between the male and female is a union "not of deliberate purpose," but a union of "natural ruler and subject," (*Politics* 1252a30). In Plato's view, "natural leadership" must not slip by unexamined.

Plato, however, does not implicitly state that his proposals for women are just. Nor does he state that lack of equal education for women is unjust. So the above inference, that exclusion of gifted women from guardian education is unjust, needs further support.

We may distinguish three senses of "natural" in the above argument. (1) A person's work in society is "natural" in that it is suited to his or her individual nature; (2) when X is arranged "according to nature," X functions well; (3) a law or practice arranged "according to nature," is one that functions well. The best-functioning society is one which is arranged according to nature so that the best rules. (3) is the social application of the more general (2) (which may apply to the soul or to society). It follows that when a society has laws or practices which bar persons from functions for which their nature (1) best suits them, such practices are "unnatural" in sense (3). They fail to be arranged "according to nature." Plato develops the connection between (1) and (2)–(3) in the definition of justice: the best functioning society—that is, the *just* society—is one which is arranged on a principle of specialization in accordance with individual natures, so that each part does its own function, namely, that for which it is best suited (*Republic* 433a).

Perhaps what is required here is a principle of maximal functioning to supplement Plato's principle of specialization of functioning. Justice requires not only that each part do its *own* work, but that *all* parts function according to their proper natures, and not lie dormant and unawakened. If the force of "each" is taken to include "all," then the criterion is met. At *Republic* 433a justice is defined: "Every single person ought to engage in that social function [literally: that function which concerns the polis] for which their own nature is best fitted"(Vlastos, 1971, 73).[19] On the other hand, the active prohibition of some thing or person from functioning according to its nature runs counter to the requirement that the ideal society be structured along lines beneficial to the state. What fails stands in the way of such benefit, falls short of justice and in that sense is unjust. Plato explicitly concludes that education of women is both "possible" and "the best way" (*Republic* 456a). Then, because there is "nothing better for the state than the generation of the best leaders out of the best men and women" (*Republic* 457a), education of women is both possible and beneficial.

Given the close connections between Plato's arguments on the "nature" of persons in Book V and his preceding definitions of justice, it seems misleading to claim that the "sole ground" for his proposals is "their usefulness to the state" (Annas, 1976, 312–13). Rather, the implication is that practices such as education of women fit into a conception of justice which is worthy for its own sake, in which one part rules according to nature. The value of justice, under this conception, is that it is a good in itself (Irwin, 1977, 213). But this does not preclude that it could have beneficial consequences in addition, as Plato points out.

Plato can be criticized for (1) objectifying women from a masculine viewpoint, for example, in his frequent references to guardian women as "wives of guardians"; (2) failing to take account of the sex of guardian children, for example, of the fact that incoming female children might already have certain traits which would make the results of equal education be unequal for boys and girls (Martin, 1982); (3) imposing a masculine education on female guardians to such an extent that women lose their sense of identity as women (Elshtain, 1981, 37–38).

In response, Plato deserves criticisms on (1). But on (2) one wonders whether "the same" education could be overinterpreted. Granted, socialized females and males, already possessed of a gender identity, will respond differently to the same curriculum. Yet "the same" curriculum need not imply identical programs and methods, as Plato has already indicated in his (physically) "weaker" qualification for the exercises for guardians. He remarks, in Book VII, that children should be taught, not by compulsory methods, but "by a kind of a game, and then you will be able to see more clearly the natural bent of each" (*Republic* 537b). Such methods could allow for developmental sex differences, for example, that girls mature faster verbally and physically (contrary to Plato) than boys. Although misogyny and objectification remain in Plato's account, his educational program gives some principles for removing them. Plato's censors could be updated so that they would extract submissive wives from children's tales and feature strong women-gods. In (3), Plato's war-readiness training appears masculinized. Yet a careful reading of Plato shows that he considers the training in music and poetry equally important, to a degree that might make some contemporary men balk at being feminized. There is no evidence that gender identity would disappear in the *Republic*, although there is indication that the concept of gender and its specific form of gender might be modified for the guardians. It is precisely this aspect of Plato's ideal state which illustrates how radical it actually is.

In concluding, I would like to emphasize the connection between what I have taken to be Plato's analytic probing of the "nature" of sex differences and his radical assertion that, ideally, society would be arranged to elicit the best from individuals regardless of gender. He claims that the latter is "natural," whereas societal arrangements which preserve traditional gender-roles and division of labor are "unnatural" if they fail to allow women civic leadership. As mentioned in the introduction, this last claim has more than a touch of irony. Plato surely recognizes that shifts in gender structure are deviations and commonly held to be "unnatural." Yet, when subjected to analytic scrutiny, the traditional sex-role divisions of labor are not based on the "nature" of actual individuals but on another set of social and political imperatives.

Plato, it might be said, draws out the best *of* women (as individuals), rather than the best *from* women (as a group). This is a defect of his "equality" of education. It is only "equal" for a select set of guardian women. While there is strong basis for this criticism if Plato's discussion of his aristocracy is taken solely as a proposal for a social structure, I wish to suggest an alternate, less literal reading of Plato. In his dialogue *The Republic,* Plato continually shifts between and intertwines moral and social levels. The "ideal state" presents the analogue to the soul, "writ large" on the scale of society. In the ideal state, moral ends always inform social organization. What Plato says about the guardians is a metaphor for "the best" in society as well as the soul. It is in the true interests of all that women contribute the best they have to offer, because whatever is beneficial to the ideal state is beneficial to all within it. In Book VII Plato follows his discussion of the cave with a description of the final stages of education in dialectic. In an indication of Plato's seriousness, Socrates admonishes Glaucon: "And do not forget the women, Glaucon. They may be rulers too. Do not suppose that what I have said [on education into dialectic] was meant only for men; women too, as are born among us with natures sufficiently capable" (*Republic* 540c). Plato's reminder may be taken as an affirmation that women as well as men can live the philosophic life—in Plato's political analogy, become guardians. Such a life, which Plato has described in Book VII, is one of contemplation and practical action in pursuit of wisdom.

Notes

1. Aristotle simply assumes in the *Politics* (1252a30) that the social dominance of male over female is a "natural" dominance or rulership, like that of master over slave, father over child. I take Plato as questioning the connection between "natural" and social dominance. For treatment of Aristotle on this question see Okin (1979, chap. 4). For a detailed examination of Aristotle's arguments on how these are assimilated to the "natural" relations within the soul, see Spelman (1983).

2. See, e.g. Okin (1979, chap. 1), Annas (1976, 307–21) stresses Plato's patronizing treatment of women. Spelman, in her *Inessential Woman,* chap. 1, ties Plato's misogyny to his dualistic metaphysics.

3. For an analysis of their positions see Allen (1975, 131). Also Lange (1979).

4. Pierce (1973, 1–11). Also see Okin (1979, appendix to chap. 2). Both present counterarguments and textual evidence against the Bloom–Strauss interpretation.

5. See Okin (p. 69) [Laws, 806b]. Annas, in her *Philosophy* (p. 309) article, takes the passage at 455b in the *Republic* as evidence that Plato considers women both mentally and physically inferior to men. I think this is a misinterpretation. Plato merely distinguishes here what he means by a "natural gift," e.g. rapid and inventive learning. It is not until the next

speech at 455c7–8 that he introduces differential performance of the sexes. See section below on "Argument from individual variation."

6. All translations, unless otherwise noted, are from Rouse (1956).

7. Bloom (1968, 382). See Okin's discussion, p. 306.

8. See Mill and Taylor (1970, 153).

9. By "procreative differences" Plato appears to refer simply to the minimal reproductive function: "The male begets and the female bears" (454e). In other words he is not referring to what we understand as "biological factors," which include genetic, hormonal, genital and secondary sex differences, but merely to differences in biological reproductive activity.

10. While the political assumptions are quite different, and he is dealing with an IQ question, not sex differences, Green makes a related point in his criticism of the objectivity of studies by Jensen and Hernstein: "The distribution of IQ scores, and their alleged and partial correlation with occupational rank, is no guide at all to the amount of underlying intellectual talent that is potentially available to us" (Green, 1976, 142).

11. We are not born all exactly alike but different in nature, for all sorts of different jobs" (*Republic* II, 369d).

12. This is the "greatest wave," the third and final of the "three waves" which will bring about the ideal society. It is "certainly not small or easy, but it is possible," as, presumably, the other waves are.

13. See also Lange (1979) who supports this view with her analysis that "Plato has attempted to remove the contradiction between public and private life for the guardians by raising familial impulses from the private to the public sphere, where their effect is to promote unity in the state, rather than disunity" (11).

14. The illicit transition depends on an inference from Plato's descriptive and declarative claim that (as a group) "man is better than woman" or "man can [in sense (a) above] do better" to the prescriptive and counterfactual claim that "men would do better than women [in cake baking]." The latter is nowhere said or implied at *Republic* 457a.

15. Williams (1977, 129). The study is Rothbart (1971, 113–20).

16. Cited by Lambert. The studies are Berry (1966); Kagan and Kogan (1970).

17. The study is Naditch (1976).

18. Sherman refers to the "trivial and fragile nature of sex related differences in cognition and the flimsy quality of the theories of biological influence" (172) in her conclusion to her detailed review of the evidence. Further,

> The bent twig hypothesis suggests that verbal skill may be sex preferred for more females than males. . . . Visual spatial skills have been sex-typed male; they have been part of the historic male role which has commonly involved tasks ranging far from home. As such, visual spatial skills have been thought to be "*naturally*" acquired. However, these skills are probably maximally acquired only by males participating in relevant activities sex-typed male (and by those females who in one way or another manage to acquire the relevant experiences). Thus, without awareness, and because of the historic, cultural reasons based in biology, the male subculture has included activities which develop spatial skill (e.g. construction toys). (173)

19. Vlastos (1971, 73) points out that the principle—to do one's own—rests on an assumption of human interdependence.

References

Allen, Christine. 1975. "Plato on Women." *Feminist Studies* 11 (2–3): 131–38.
Annas, Julia. 1976. "Plato's Republic and Feminism." *Philosophy* 51: 307–21.

Berry, J. W. 1966. "Temne and Eskimo Perceptual Skills." *International Journal of Psychology* 1: 207–29.

Bloom, Allan. 1968. "Interpretive Essay." In *The Republic of Plato.* New York: Basic Books.

Chodorow, Nancy. 1978. *The Reproduction of Mothering.* Berkeley and Los Angeles: University of California Press.

Elshtain, Jean B. 1981. *Public Man, Private Woman.* Princeton: Princeton University Press.

Green, Philip. 1976. "IQ and the Future of Equality." *Dissent*: 409–24.

Irwin, Terence. 1977. *Plato's Moral Theory.* Oxford: Clarendon Press.

Kagan, J., and N. Kogan. 1970. "Individual Variation in Cognitive Processes." In *Carmichael's Manual of Child Psychology*, edited by P. H. Mussen. New York: John Wiley.

Lambert, Helen. 1978. "Biology and Equality: A Perspective on Sex Differences." *Signs* 4(1): 97–117.

Lange, Lynda. 1979. "The Function of Equal Education in Plato's *Republic* and *Laws.*" In *The Sexism of Social and Political Theory*, edited by L. Clark and L. Lange. Toronto: University of Toronto Press.

Maccoby, E., and C. Jacklin. 1974. *The Psychology of Sex Differences.* Stanford: Stanford University Press.

Martin, Jane. 1982. "Sex Equality and Education in Plato's Just State: A Case Study." In *"Femininity," "Masculinity," and "Androgeny": A Modern Philosophical Discussion*, edited by Mary Vetterling-Braggin. Totowa, N.J.: Littlefield, Adams.

Mill, J. S., and Harriet Taylor. 1970. *Essays on Sex Equality.* Edited by Alice Rossi. Chicago: University of Chicago Press.

Naditch, S. F. 1976. *Sex Differences in Field Dependence.* Washington, D.C.: American Psychological Association.

Okin, Susan. 1979. *Women in Western Political Thought.* Princeton: Princeton University Press.

Pierce, Christine. 1973. "Equality: *Republic* V." *Monist* 57: 1–11.

Rossi, Alice, ed. 1970. *Essays on Sex Equality.* By J. S. Mill and Harriet Taylor. Chicago: University of Chicago Press.

Rothbart, M. K. 1971. "Birth order and Mother-Child Interaction in an Achievement Situation." *Journal of Personality and Social Psychology* 17: 113–20.

Rouse, W. H. D. 1956. *Great Dialogues of Plato.* New York: New American Library.

Sherman, Julia. 1978. *Sex-Related Cognitive Differences.* Springfield, Ill.: Charles Thomas.

Spelman, Elizabeth V. 1983. "Aristotle and the Politicalization of the Soul." In *Discovering Reality*, edited by S. Harding and Merill Hintikka. Dordrecht, Holland: D. Reidel.

———. 1988. *Inessential Woman: Problems of Exclusion in Feminist Thought.* Boston: Beacon Press.

Vlastos, Gregory. 1971. "Justice and Happiness in the *Republic*." In *Plato II*, edited by Gregory Vlastos. Notre Dame: University of Notre Dame Press.

Williams, J. H. 1977. *Psychology of Women: Behavior in a Bisocial Context.* New York: Norton.

3

The Politics of Women's Bodies: Reflections on Plato

Monique Canto

Translated by Arthur Goldhammer

As I have already said . . . such tactics will not deter us from insisting on our principle that there must be the completest association of the female sex with the male in education as in everything else. . . . If women are not to take their part along with men in all the business of life, we are bound, are we not, to propose some different scheme for them? . . .

Should they perform menial offices, exactly like slaves? Should they stay at home and take care of the belongings of their men? Or should they be granted dispensation from the meanest labor and encouraged to cultivate their minds and bodies, to make for themselves a life that is far from unworthy or frivolous, occupied with the concerns of the household and the education of the children but taking no part in preparations for war, that is, in politics in the broad sense, in debate over public issues.

I can only speak as I think. A legislator should be thorough, not halfhearted; he must not, after making regulations for the male sex, leave the other to the enjoyment of an existence of

> uncontrolled luxury and expense, and so endow his society with a mere half of a thoroughly felicitous life in place of the whole.

The foregoing passage (part of it directly quoted, part of it my own summary) is a feminist political manifesto. It is important to be clear about the meaning of the term. Feminist politics is politics that could not exist without women. And since politics requires that we know who we are, who are our friends and who our enemies, women must constantly apprise themselves of their strength, and exercise it. Above all, they must know how to fight, and they must be sure that everyone knows that they know. Everything depends, therefore, on presence. Feminist politics is real only if women, together with their bodies, their works, their labor, and their voice, are present in a place where everyone can see them—let us say, in the marketplace. Finally, it may be worth mentioning in passing what the political woman's modern utopia would look like: it would consist of women in control of certain *media,* that is, certain objects and forms of communication, or again, of women in control of an ideology that would make it impossible for woman's image to usurp the place of woman's reality. What the manifesto demands is nothing less than the presence of women on the political scene.

But it contains something more as well. For women, necessary as they are to life in the city, define two possibilities without which political life would be inconceivable. One of these has to do with existence, with life understood in temporal terms. Procreation is woman's work, but if women are included in the city it may be a political idea as well. The second possibility has to do with desire, the primary datum of human life and the general form of all life. Now, every city must come to terms with pleasure and pain, with the whole realm of the emotions; for pleasure and pain are the vital principle of the city itself, yet their inevitable excesses threaten the city's very existence. The city's only recourse is to politicize the emotions, but it cannot discharge this function unless women are granted a fully legitimate political role. Thus the politics of women's bodies has far-reaching implications. The two most important questions about the city are How can it maintain its present form? and How can it ensure that its citizens' desires are satisfied by what it is? To both these questions woman-as-political-animal provides an answer. With woman, a place can be found in political theory for both procreation and the representation of desire—and hence also the satisfaction of desire. Procreation and representation are related questions, moreover; taken together, they indicate the difficulty of conceptualizing, within a given political framework, the possibility of reproduction: reproduction of the real in order to satisfy desire, and reproduction of human life so that the city may endure. In both cases, reproduction is possible only if a difference exists, for without difference the idea of the same and the idea of the other make no sense. In both cases, woman is necessary in order for this difference to be present. But this difference is above all an insistence upon the political. The whole question is where this difference resides: inside or outside the city. The answer to this question will determine the strategy that women must adopt. Women must know how to fight, because no human politics has ever been conducted in the realm of the same. So much is stated in the manifesto. A politics of women's bodies gives rise to a politics of the real, precisely because only such a feminist politics can make reproduction—a major gamble in which a city can easily lose its model and its norm—one of the principles of the political.

Thus far we have spoken of cities, pleasures, pains and procreation. As terms of political discourse these may appear outmoded. It is true that the political manifesto cited above was composed by an ancient, but his thinking in regard to women and the conditions of political life is not so old-fashioned as it may seem. In fact, the question he raises is rarely asked, and it has never been answered quite so candidly since (the answer is: the female body politic). And when he speaks of women's bodies, he means the real thing: naked women, pregnant women, women armed like warriors and, above all, women who have to be looked at. But enough. The time has come to identify the source of these ideas.

The text with which this essay begins is a passage from Book VII of *Laws*, the long dialogue that Plato wrote toward the end of his life.[1] It is clearly a testament, not only because of the ideas it contains but even more because of the manner in which they are set forth. The dialogue unfolds serenely, without conflict. Three old men discuss, while walking, the best laws for a city to adopt and the nature of a perfect constitution. There are no serious disagreements among them, and no real objections are raised. Thoughts are expressed in a straightforward way, without subterfuge or irony. Such tranquillity of thought is not frequently encountered in Plato's dialogues, where the idea being presented often has to be defended against the laughter, sarcasm, or violence of one interlocutor or another. This is particularly true where women are involved. Plato discussed women frequently, even in the *Laws*. The protagonist of *Laws,* the Athenian, prior to stating as clearly as he does that the presence of women in the city requires that they know the art of war, just as men do, and that no genuine political life is possible without them, repeatedly raises the question of women's bodies, as if this question had a special bearing on the very definition of political reality. We know what conclusion he draws: that women are at the heart of the city, hence they are also at the heart of war; furthermore, if they keep solely to slavery, the household, or private culture, there is no political life.

The line of argument that leads to this conclusion is surprising: it involves a detailed consideration of the place of women's bodies in the city. But before we can comprehend this detail, which is what makes Plato's thought on this subject interesting, we must answer another question: Is it possible for women to occupy this kind of political position? Plato deals with this in another dialogue, the *Republic,* the tone of which is quite different from that of the *Laws.* The *Republic* is a kind of inspired outline, in which answers to questions are sketched out but not developed with precision. Hence some of those answers are extreme, provocative, or utopian (*Republic* V, 449a–465d). Yet they pave the way for the minute precision of the *Laws,* in which the question of women and politics is always inextricably bound up with that of political reality. Yet even this minute precision does not exhaust the question. For Plato also considers the woman issue in a mythological context. Woman's necessity comes from elsewhere, from an archaic time, from another, and completely self-absorbed, meaning of the feminine. The myth recounted by Aristophanes in the *Symposium* gives the basic idea (189d–193c).

The *Laws,* with its scrupulous, detailed, and precise history, must be set alongside two narrative treatments of the same theme. The first of these is found in the *Republic:* this is the mise en scène, what Plato calls the *drama,* of the feminine in the city. It is an abstract scheme for conceptualizing a community composed of men and women. The second occurs in the *Symposium,* where it is asserted that political life and the female body have a common origin. This idea is also somewhat extreme, and we should bear in mind that Aristophanes, the author of the myth, is gifted with the art of the comic poet. Hence we have a history, a drama, and a comic fable, all asserting the political necessity of the female body. The question must be a very difficult one to have called forth so many different answers, and if we wish to know exactly what

Plato thought about it, and how his thoughts have influenced one way of thinking about women's bodies, then doubtless we must patiently follow the development of his thinking from the beginning. Let us begin, then, with the drama of the *Republic*, the first certain entry of women's bodies into the city.

The question of women, says Socrates in the *Republic*, is the initial move in a discussion devoted to the nature of the best city. Indeed, if the condition of public happiness is that the good of the citizen should coincide with the good of the state; if citizens must share all pleasures and pains in common; and if nothing apart from their own bodies belongs to them; then "the possessions of friends will be in common" and there will be no exclusive possession of women and children (V, 449a–d and 451b–c). Now, the condition of such a community of women and children is that men and women hold all political functions in common. To prove this, however, Socrates dismisses the question of the real: don't ask me to prove that what I'm describing is realizable, he says, just let me show that, if such a community were to be achieved, it would procure the greatest of benefits for the city. The question of the real is deferred to the *Laws*. In the *Republic*, Socrates deals with the possible (V, 457d–458b). Women, he says, have the same aptitudes as men. Hence there are no functions reserved for men alone, from which women are excluded. On the contrary, women should receive the same education as men in music, gymnastics, the art of war, and horsemanship. They must exercise "unclad in the palaestra together with the men, not only the young, but even the older" (V, 452b). With this training they will have access to responsibilities identical to those of men: medicine, philosophy, government. No doubt their physical resources are inferior to those of men, but even here we must beware of hasty generalization. At bottom, there is only one enduring difference between the two sexes according to Socrates: the male "begets" whereas the female "bears" (V, 454e and 458c–d).

Thus the difference between man and woman lies in the complementarity of their roles in procreation. But since the meaning of the community of men and women is in the first place political, only a political idea of procreation would be capable of neutralizing the effects of this difference. That procreation should be the city's first concern is actually what Socrates is proposing when he calls for child-rearing in common. Men and women, attracted to one another by "erotic necessity," are married according to their excellence and obliged to see and meet one another frequently, so as to multiply opportunities for procreation. Children are turned over to nurses at birth to live in a special quarter of the city. Mothers will come to suckle offspring only so long as their breasts are full of milk, and children are to be presented to them in such a way that no mother will recognize her own. Hence there is nothing to distinguish the mother from the father of a child. A man "will call all male offspring born in the tenth and the seventh month after he became a bridegroom his sons, and all female, daughters, and they will call him father." Similarly, every possible step is to be taken to prevent a woman from calling a child her own (V, 460b–461e). The living all belong to the city, and the first resolutions adopted by the state are designed to emphasize the fact that birth is a matter of deliberate policy: both public policy, which establishes the laws governing marriage and celebrates the institution (punishing men and women who copulate without proper regard to selection or without any intention to procreate), and secret policy, which determines who shall mate with whom and prevents union between partners whose coupling would, for one reason or another, be undesirable (459e).

The possibility of making procreation the first political act is thus the condition that necessitates, and also legitimizes, the identity of the civic functions of men and women. "Civic functions" comprise duties pertaining to both internal government, or law and order within the city, and defense of the constitution against all enemies, domestic and foreign (V, 464a–465c). Now, the idea of a politics for which procreation is the primary issue, which, as we have seen, is the basis of the community of male and female functions is domestic government as well as in the conduct of war, is inconceivable unless both men and women, men's bodies and women's bodies, are equally present in the center of the city. This is the other meaning of community: community is the space within which men and women circulate, meet, and enter into union with one another, the place where they can see and be seen. Women, in this city whose political life they make possible, show themselves and look about them, openly and without reserve. Their body is a political body.

Thus the *gynaeceum,* the place of women, no longer harbors either the secret or the private. Nor is there any longer a place reserved to women alone, because men and women now live together throughout the city. The public space is necessarily held in common. Together men and women in fact constitute and delineate this space, and keep it under surveillance in order that it shall remain what it is, always identical to itself, absolutely excluding any real presence of the other. Socrates suggests that it may be necessary to tell the men and women of the city "a sort of Phoenician tale," a myth of foundation, according to which all citizens believe that they are brothers (414c–417b)—even the women, because, as political bodies, they are the same as men, and because, like the men, they work to drive otherness to the periphery of politics. This shows that within the city woman is in no sense the representative of otherness. It also shows that the civic space is apparently unable to tolerate the presence of any kind of otherness, not even to the extent of affirming the difference between men and women. But the city in which men and women have, so to speak, the same political body is a city that subsists outside history. It is also a city without images or desire.

"In this city we do not wish it to be possible that a being can be said to be manifold." Socrates dismisses the poet and condemns imitation. Imitation can not only reproduce multiple examples of any being, but can also alter that being, introduce multiplicity into what was unique, and engender an infinity of further replicas that are both alike and different. Imitation generally takes the form of images (*Republic* X passim, especially 595c–607a). The city will, therefore, be deprived of those images that Socrates shows to be the obvious objects of human desire. Not that images are the only such objects. Desire for the good or for absolutely real being are surely more essential. But only the desire for images allows us to grasp the faculty of desiring as a specific, autonomous faculty that cannot be reduced to either reason or feeling (*Republic* IV, 439b–441d). Furthermore, desire is the point of reference for the reality of pleasure and pain, so that, when pleasure and pain are wholly political, it is desire that makes citizens happy about whatever is good for the city and unhappy about whatever is bad. Fundamentally, the requirements that there exist no private pleasure or pain, that whatever is susceptible of gratifying or frustrating desire should not be the property of any isolated individual, and that no citizen may say of an object or person sought by desire that "this is mine, this satisfies my desire"—all these conditions are basic to the most human reality of the community present in the city (*Republic* V, 464c–465c).

But since the city must be protected against both temporality and otherness, all desires are educated so that they direct themselves to a single object, itself identical with those who feel desire: the city itself is the object of its own desire. This common desire, so easily identified when it is desire for images, wants nothing other than an image of what the city is, that is, a reality formed in identity, at the edge of history and at the limit of representations (*Republic* III passim, especially 398a–403c). What is more, this desire is maintained distinct from any evolution in its own formula, from any modification in the objects that satisfy it. No innovation is allowed, says Socrates, because for the city, the slightest change would be fatal (*Republic* II, *Laws* II; III; VII, 799a–c). In the city composed of men and women, politically mingled, unions are celebrated and representations sacralized outside of real time; they are the expression of a desire for the same, which, so long as man and woman exist, is already impotent to articulate amorous desire. In the city of the *Republic,* the political body of women is not really desired. Nor does it desire. Desire requires a real relation to temporality and density of representations that yield pleasure only because they are representations of otherness. Now, in order to legitimate the public presence of woman in the city, both of these conditions would have had to be eliminated. The body of women protects the city against time and images. It is dedicated to the same. Women's politics creates the ascesis of desire.

The object of politics receives a quite different treatment in the *Laws.* No doubt the idea is the same, but the basis upon which it stands is different. The three old men engaged in conversation are representatives of three real cities, Athens, Sparta, and Crete, to which they constantly refer in the course of their discussions. All three are trying to describe political reality in a way that takes account of time and history on the one hand, and pleasure, pain, and the emotions that determine the orientation of human desire on the other; these are the conditions of existence of any real city. Thus, the primary data of political discussion in the *Laws* are the real effect of time, which causes people to age, change, and deteriorate; and the need for pleasure, for which a political definition must be sought in a public manner as soon as a city is established (for example, *Laws* III, 673a–b). Hence the first propositions in *Laws* are intended to explain the essential connection between politics and temporality as well as to discover the representations with which desire can exert its intrinsic force and overcome whatever threatens to alter it or to alienate it from the city's ends. The three old men accordingly discuss cities that live in time, and their first concern is to examine the political effects of public intoxication, poetic representations, and civic choirs (*Laws* II, 652–654c). The presence of history and the power of images are there to bring politics back to reality. What remains, then, of the astonishing idea put forward in the *Republic?* The idea that women and men are in the same position, that the female body is one reason why politics exists, and that it must be present in the center of the city as well as in war; the idea that the female body is a body politic that reproduces itself under the strict control of the law, in procreation and representation, and in such a way as to stretch identity to its limit and to exhaust the reality of desire. Is the body politic so absolutely separated from desire? Let us turn now to the text of *Laws* to find out.

"A state should be like a well-compounded bowl," in which the masculine and the feminine, politically associated, can mix to form "a healthful and modest draught." Hence men and women who are citizens of the city must assemble, meet, and marry (*Laws* VI, 773c–d). Mixing is the first condition of politics, and this condition cannot be satisfied without the presence of women. But the civic "compound" of the *Laws* is different in composition from the "political identity" of the *Republic.* The main difference is that the former compound makes sense only thanks to the persistence of "otherness" within it, rather like "a web or other piece of woven work (in which) woof and warp cannot be fashioned of the same threads" (*Laws* V, 734e–735a). The meaning of marriage depends on the difference between the men and women who enter into it. The reproduction that is necessary to political life will therefore play itself out in relation to otherness. The "well-compounded bowl" is Plato's most general image for political reality, which he seems to have conceptualized as requiring a mixture in which otherness must be present and its effects dealt with one way or another. A truly political law is also a mixture, combining declaration and exhortation; or perhaps I should say that a law is the mise en scène of a declaration, which makes it persuasive in the city and which combines the general disposition with the concrete conditions under which that disposition is to be put into effect (*Laws* IV, 722c–724e). This dual nature of law is expressed by the distinction, made by the Athenian, between the law proper and its "preamble," which is understood to be not just an introductory text but a fundamental summary of the historical development of the law and the forces that threaten its integrity; thus the preamble invests the law with its full political reality. It is something rather similar to this, a condition constitutive of political reality, that makes it possible to establish the presence of women at the center of the city.

Women, therefore, participate in politics by constituting the reality of the city's life out of a mixture of time and the other. But how can one express in these terms, which are already political, a constitution that would incorporate the presence of women as a necessary condition? This was no doubt the difficulty that the political construction set forth in the *Republic* sought to avoid, by saying nothing about how such a constitution would allow for "difference" and "historical change" (*devenir*). Women were of necessity included in the city, but in return a "limit-reality" was ascribed to time and desire. In *Laws* the political presence of women is harder to express and at times leads to incredible statements. But what the Athenian is trying to conceptualize with such obstinacy and at times in such strange ways is the possibility of a political reality that is able to come to terms with difference and images, with the force of time and the force of desire. For this, women are absolutely necessary.

Thus the city constitutes itself by coming to terms with the place of women. But we must be careful about what this means. It does not mean a numerically real presence but rather a condition of activity: the feminine must be there in order to reproduce and represent. And in the city itself, the origin of politics is assignable only through the presence of women: theirs is a dual mode of presence, a model of dissociation that makes it possible to articulate the transition to the political condition. The status of women in the city is dual, as is that of tragic representation and poetic imagery. All three seem capable of movement, circulation, and encounter, capable of being the one and the other, of facing in two different directions; it is upon these resources that the city must draw to sustain its own political functioning, but it must also control the real destructive power they contain (*Laws* III, 700a–701b; IV, 719a–e). The first concern of politics is to gain control over the profusion of images, to prevent them from being misused and misappropriated. The poet is the first person to be received into the city, and his poetry is real insofar as it satisfies the political desire for representations (*Laws* II, 667b–673d). Women are allowed in the city, but without dowry or artifice—in order to guard against luxury, rivalry, and the passion for money that is linked to the conquest and seduction of women (*Laws* V, 742a–744, 774d). This of course means that neither women nor images are commodity values and, more generally, that no object has value apart from the political reality of which women are the condition. Values are, as it were, constituted by women, who are the foundation of the political order. A real women's politics is what makes possible the transition from nature to the city.

Now, this politics is what orders the representations that are also, along with women, the condition of political life. Furthermore, the first law of any city that proceeds according to nature is, according to the Athenian, a law regulating *genesis,* not only human procreation but also the genesis of the political (*Laws* IV, 721a–d). It is against this same apparent circularity that the political presence of women stands out. Women are otherness, indeed the very condition of otherness, the basis of political life. This accounts for their dual function. Women in the city are also at war—not in the sense of being in combat, but rather in the sense that they bear the stamp of an otherness that they themselves must render political. The women of the *Republic* relegated difference to a place outside the city—and first of all the difference between themselves and men; but it is with this difference that the women of *Laws* constitute the political. This is a highly singular way of reckoning the same and the other, of somehow waging war within the city. Being in the city, women negotiate what their functions will be in terms of the same and the other, and it is once again the idea of their political bodies that permits this dual presence to be secured (*Laws* VI, 771a–776e). Real time and desire are the two true actors that figure, along with women, in this second act of the *gunaikon drama.* In *Laws* the need for a political presence of women, first set forth in the *Republic,* is assumed as a basis for conceptualizing the possibility of a representation and a desire of the political body of women.

First, time: everything in the discussion in *Laws* serves to make it real. The men who are talking are old, and they talk at great length, often repeating what they said an hour or two before or much earlier in the morning (*Laws* I, 625a–b). They know the force of time in history: initially, the state of the world was perfect, says the Athenian, and the effect of time suggests that the god has been slowly but inexorably withdrawing from his work. But no politics is conceivable outside man's temporal condition, which the succession of generations obliges us to measure. When the gods governed man under the reign of Kronos, there was no time, there were no generations, and there was no politics. The historical condition is not necessarily fatal to the city, however; it does entail change and decadence, but it also makes possible renewal and progress. And then, too, the human race has neither beginning nor end. It has a genuine affinity with temporality and hence cannot escape desiring its own reproduction. Births must therefore be controlled, and women are once again the primary object and the first principle of political regulation (*Laws* VI, 771b–774c). This is where the two fundamental dimensions of political reality come together. Time is the element in which human desire is elaborated. The elaboration of desire feeds on representations and images that constitute the reality of pleasures and pains. Finally, the political presence of women makes it possible to articulate the necessity and efficacy of this elaboration. It is again a function of the female body politic to negotiate the reality of a desire for the city.

The desire of the citizens, essentially linked to temporality, thus depends for its expression on images and representations of otherness. Apparently, this is the price to be paid for the constitution of political affect; it explains why the Athenian at first recommends that public intoxication be required periodically (*Laws* II, 671a–672e). What makes this a political measure, however, is essentially that it represents an ordeal: citizens must submit to the power of the wine and allow their souls to be assaulted by their most extreme desires before the eyes of their fellows. Such public revels are thus a form of mock combat in which each person must publicly overcome and vanquish his or her desires, that is, in which each person must come to terms with otherness. All citizens' acts, as well as all acts of the rulers, derive their political meaning from this constant war with the other. The issue is always one of maintaining and preserving otherness—and thus of delineating its place—or, to put it another way, it is to exert oneself, to involve oneself in negotiations with the other, so as to determine oneself in relation to it. This is why public banquets are necessary and why free movement at home and abroad to trade and converse is an important political issue: it is necessary to accept otherness and try to shape it to one's purpose (*Laws* VI, 760a–761d, 762c–765b). All marriage laws, which express the obligation to achieve a desired civic composition and which are so crucial to political life, can be translated back into terms of transfer, installation, and movement. The Athenian does not shrink from giving a general statement of the problem of sexual union: legislation concerning marriage must be laid down, he says, simultaneously with the architecture of the city itself. Both are indeed at the very root of the political, whose first principle they express: the need for composition, the joining of the one with the other.

Women therefore make politics possible to the extent that their presence in the city gives evidence and assurance to the forms of temporality and otherness that are the principle of all political life. Women also represent the necessity of the following challenge, which every city must meet despite the enormous risk involved: to make sure that time and desire, which threaten the political order, become its surest foundations. To make procreation, pleasure, and pain political would make politics the fundamental dimension of all forms of existence, that to which all behavior, all discourse, and all life would owe their legitimacy. This latter possibility no doubt plays upon the whole question of the relations between public and private. If it were conceivable that all private acts could be given a political interpretation, then nothing could challenge the existence of the city (*Laws* VI, 780a–c). The private part of existence is in fact an important form of otherness, which the terms of politics must allow for and at the same time try to shape. Within the city space the portion allotted to private life is first made concrete in the reality of a private place: in an emblematic sense, the gynaeceum is that place apart in which all that is not political is gathered together. But it is not merely an emblem: the gynaeceum is the most commonly cited example of the persistence of private space within the city.

But the gynaeceum is women's space, hence an impediment to the political constitution. In another sense, however, the political constitution seems to rest entirely on the women's portion. On the one hand women seem to prevent the city from achieving a true political organization, while on the other they represent the only means of impressing the form of political reality upon the city. How are these two aspects of the status of women to be reconciled? This question is most difficult to answer, because it bears upon the reality of a desire which, in this women's politics, would be transferred to the body represented by the city.

When one builds the city, says the Athenian in *Laws,* one is both spectator and spectacle (*Laws* VI, 779d). This is especially true of women, whose presence in the city, as I said earlier, is to a remarkable degree torn in two directions: on the one hand it stands for what is not yet political but must become so, and on the other hand it stands for that which makes the political real. Women certainly occupy a dual role, because they represent the existence of the private sphere and the need to make the private wholly public in order to establish the political realm. In other words, the reality of time and emotion are given a political formulation. The *Republic* tried to show how this might be done, but there the point was to demonstrate the need for a total community of function and status among men and women in order that politics be possible. The ensuing conditions are utopian in the sense that they do not take the reality of history and desire into account. But the *Laws* follows up this analysis by attempting to define just how women are present in the city and hence to represent the transition to politics, not in a chronological sense, but by designating the political institutions upon which the transition from private to public depends.

It stands to reason that these institutions will have something to do with women—women negotiating on their own behalf with the otherness which in part they represent. This may take the form of engaging in gymnastic exercises, in common forms of apprenticeship, and in an education identical to that of men, in order to show that men and women present in the city must be treated in the same way (*Laws* VI, 757a–e; VII, passim; VIII). It may also take the form of marriage laws, which politicize the desire that impels the man who wishes to reproduce himself to enter into union with an other. No man in the city may willfully deprive himself of a woman, says the Athenian, nor of images nor even of what brings gratification through pleasure (*Laws* V, 721a–e). The political condition necessarily includes such gratification; indeed, gratification is instrumental in its definition. But it is up to women to determine the conditions of their presence in the city and the associated imagery. One institution is crucial above all others, the Athenian continues; in this institution there is enacted a scene in which women are the only actors and whose sole purpose is to represent the transition from the private to the public. This scene also figures in real time: women represent themselves and are themselves desired as images. It hardly needs to be said that this scene, in which the transition from the private to the public is shown in a clear political light, when left to the initiative of women who make use of every means of representation available, is a scene of seduction, which shows seduction as the first political act, an act of public mastery over a private weakness. What is this scene, an institution? In fact it is a warrior's custom that inscribes the power of war as one of the forces of the city. It is also an incredible act: nothing less than a women's banquet in the center of the city.

The women's symposium then, is the touchstone of the city. Ordinarily women live apart, withdrawn from public life and confined to their own private world, as a result of which it is easy to accuse them of secrecy and cunning; now, however, they must come to the center of the city to eat, drink, and speak, together and in the view of all. Fundamentally, it is the same with women as with representations: both are deceitful so long as they remain private, but become legitimate as soon as they become public and produce a political effect. That the banquet scene is possible attests to the reality of a desire directed to the body of women, which confirms the force of the representation, of political reproduction. In a sense it is a celebration of the primordial political act. It belongs to women, who act here as in war. This is what allows the transition from a half city, which is not a city at all, to a double city, which is the only city of political reality. As the Athenian says, this custom is the expression of the only true foundation of politics (*Laws* VI, 780d–781e).

Body, desire, women as the foundation of politics—it is also a tale of war, which brings together the same and the other. Desire and time must both account for their objects: the same or the other. Politics no doubt depends on woman, for the feminine directs desire toward love's first destinations. The need for women is spelled out in a myth, taken from another banquet, the *Symposium,* where it is recounted by Aristophanes. There are two conditions of love. One is narcissistic: the person loves only himself, he is the offspring of the sun, the earth, and the moon, and one may call him, accordingly, man, woman or hermaphrodite. But these terms are not really appropriate, for they only make sense in relation to a difference of which the narcissist takes no notice. The other condition of love is adulterous: love is addressed to another person, another person divided in two as a result of the terrible punishment inflicted by the gods on those who loved only themselves (*Symposium,* 190a–b).

The reality of time and of otherness is linked to the adulterous condition of love and hence to the existence of a sexual world. The three kinds of beings who live in the prior condition of narcissistic love do not yet form three sexes. For they are three complete beings, who cannot love any but themselves and who bear toward themselves a love that the subsequent tradition would call divine love, to be understood reflexively, as the love that God directs toward his own perfection. Now, God cannot abide any challenge to his privilege of love. His punishment is therefore to cut each of these original beings in two. The main effect of this is to put an end to the narcissistic state in which these creatures have lived. From that point on, desire is separate from its object, and it becomes necessary to seek the former object (the self in a sense, but located within another) outside the self. The possibility of male and female, the very idea of difference (understood in the first instance as sexual difference) begins with this separation. The reality of human love and of time and desire are absolute consequences of this division. And the feminine itself may be thought of as one way of defining the separation of desire and its object. In this sense, any search for another, even if that other is represented as having the same sex as oneself, attests to the presence of otherness and time. For the necessity of the other and the reality of becoming are preconditions for conceiving the human world, the sexual and political world, the world of men and women, of cities and images, the world, finally, that is forced to become more fully conscious of the conditions of its own existence because of woman's political share and presence in this world.

Women are necessary, then, to conceptualize the status of eros and to involve humankind in politics. In the mythology of the *Symposium* Plato even goes so far as to attempt a sort of amorous ontology from which the need for women's political presence might be deduced. Above all, if love, subject as it is to time and desire, always seems to be directed toward the other, as the *Symposium* shows, the only way for love to discover its reality and truth is for the one and the other to be united, as in the union of both sexes in the city, for example, without which there is no true politics. Yet in this union otherness must remain present as a condition of thought: this is what the fact that men and women must remain warriors teaches us. Women especially must celebrate, in a banquet and by the act of their political and combative body, the reality of desire and time. Women must prove through war the reality of the other whom they represent. Apart from such a war, women's politics and women's liberation are inconceivable.

And this is precisely the message of the feminist manifesto that was no doubt Plato's last word on the question—in any case it concludes his remarks on women in the *Laws.* Yet to make women the equals of men and to envision the political possibilities raised by such equality—to give women the education and capabilities they need to govern with perfect confidence both the public and private spheres, the household and the state—is not possible unless they are also given access to all the resources of war. Only on that condition do they enter into the political, as a force of otherness.

To say this openly will no doubt provoke laughter in certain quarters.

Socrates in the *Republic* and the Athenian in the *Laws* expect nothing else by way of response, not even criticism or refutation. Laughter, sarcasm, or silence is all they look forward to as soon as they speak of political women, of women's bodies in the city, and above all of women of war (*Republic* VI, 452b–e; *Laws* VI, 780c–d). Socrates and the Athenian have nothing more to say: they simply repeat what they have already said. People are going to laugh at the idea of women in the city and at war, but in fact it will be politics that they laugh at, and also at the human condition, which bears the stamps of time, desire, fear, and the search for the other. And perhaps anyone who can laugh at the human condition is not yet a man.

Note

1. *Laws* VII, 805d–807c. All English citations from the works of Plato are taken from *The Collected Dialogues of Plato,* ed. Edith Hamilton and Huntington Cairns (New York: Pantheon-Bollingen, 1963). The translators are as follows: *Republic,* Paul Shorey; *Symposium,* Michael Joyce; *Laws,* A. E. Taylor (translator's note).

4

The Philosopher and the Female in the Political Thought of Plato

Arlene W. Saxonhouse

At the beginning of the fifth book of Plato's *Republic* Socrates offers his radical proposals for the inclusion of women in the guardian class of his just city. The women are to train and exercise with the men as they prepare to become warriors to protect the city. They are to eat and live communally with the men, and when the philosopher-rulers are introduced women are allowed to enter their exalted rank. Though some have accepted the sincerity of Plato's attempts to rescue the female from her low status and sheltered life during the fourth century B.C. in Athens,[1] there are enough questions raised within Book V itself and elsewhere in the dialogue to make us doubt the seriousness of these proposals. While Socrates allows women to enter the ruling class, he affirms that they will always be weaker than men (455e; 456a; 457a).[2] While he argues that they are not by nature necessarily different from men, he calls the plundering of a corpse the work of a small and "womanish" mind (469d). As the discussion proceeds, the presence of

Author's Note: I am indebted to the thoughtful insights offered by Martha Meier Dean on the topic of women and Plato.

women in the guardian class is sometimes forgotten (460a–b; 465a–b; 467)[3] or Glaucon, hesitant to include them in the army (471d), must be reminded of the participation to which he had agreed earlier (540c). Elsewhere in the dialogue the critical remarks about women are more forthright: they succumb easily to grief while men remain strong (388a; 605e); they are like children in their enjoyment of the multifarious and the multicolored (431c; 557c); they bring about the degeneration of various political systems described in Book VIII. In Book V there is talk of equal participation in the governance of the city, common meals, and common education; yet in Book VIII it is equality and freedom between the sexes that characterize the city degenerating into anarchy and tyranny (563b). Socrates' famous proposals must be read with an awareness of these qualifications.

Since I cannot accept the view that Socrates wishes to emancipate the Athenian woman, I would like in this essay to raise the issue of how and why the female is introduced into Book V. As Socrates attempts to turn women into men by making them equal participants in the political community, he ignores the peculiar natures of each and thus undermines the perfection of the political society in the *Republic.* I shall be concerned with the appearance of women in the *Republic* as they go from courtesans in the early books to the de-sexed and unnatural females of Book V, and once again to the sexual female in Book VI—after eros has been reintroduced into the dialogue with the appearance of the philosopher. We can, I shall argue, gain from an understanding of this development an insight into the Platonic perception of the relationship between politics and philosophy, and how each, like the male and female, is to be allowed to preserve its independent nature. The opposition between women and men becomes a model for the opposition between philosophy and politics; the attempt to equalize both sets of opposites destroys all.

Republic V: The Female De-Sexed

The women who enter the rank of the guardian class in Book V of the *Republic* are almost without body and, more important, free from eros. They are neither the desired nor the desiring. It is these women whom I shall call the "de-sexed" females. Before they make their appearance in Book V, however, there is much to prepare us and Socrates' companions for their arrival. The abstraction from the biological body is part of a continuing theme from the beginning of Book I. There the old Cephalus, in whose house the dialogue takes place, talks for a short while with Socrates. During the discussion women first appear; though Cephalus found them desirable once, his body now is weak and he no longer needs or responds to them. He describes his current condition with a quote from Sophocles who, when asked how at ninety he was faring with regard to the sexual passion, replied: "Most happily I escaped it, as if fleeing a raging and wild master" (329c). Cephalus thus signifies the death of sexual eros and the deadening of the bodily desires that had been so strong in his youth. Though the old man leaves the scene, he has bequeathed his abstraction from the physical body to the remaining group, who in turn must go through a whole evening of discourse without the dinner that was promised.

The training which is given to the warrior class of the just city reinforces this abstraction. The warrior class emerges because Glaucon has been dissatisfied with the true city, or the city of pigs as he calls it (372d). He wants relishes (among which are women who had not appeared in the earlier city). However, to protect these relishes and acquire more, a warrior class must be established, a class that itself must be purged of all the desires for delights. Their education is first presented as "gymnastics for the body and *mousike* for the soul" (376e). The former, though, is entirely forgotten except for a short passage buried in Book III in which the details of the gymnastic education are left to the well-trained mind (403d). Rather, *mousike* that dominates the warrior's education works to eliminate all concern with the body and to purge the young men of any strong physical desires for food, drink, or sex. The discussion of gymnastics is replaced with admonitions against all forms of excessive bodily passions. Even doctors who tend to the needs of the body are expelled from the city and the sick are left to die (405a–410a).

Prior to Book V, the women who do appear are the ones who excite men's erotic passions and are therefore in opposition to the process of abstraction from body that characterizes the founding of the just city. Cephalus focuses specifically on the sexual desire for women in his discussion of old age. When Glaucon gives his speech extolling the benefits of injustice, he refers to the queen of Lydia who is seduced by Gyges during his rise to power (360b).[4] In Glaucon's fevered city, women appear as courtesans right in the midst of an enumeration of delights including seasonings, perfumes, incense, and cakes (373a), as needing womanly dress or ornaments (373b), or as wet nurses (373c). In Book III, as the educational program for the warriors is developed, Syracusan tables (that is, feasts), Sicilian relishes, and Corinthian maidens who serve as mistresses must be removed from the experiences of the youth (404c–d). And it is noted later that members of the warrior class, having been deprived of all personal wealth, will be unable to make gifts to their mistresses (420a). Women, far from participating in the political structure in the early books,[5] are presented as the provokers of the sexual eros, which must be restrained among the guardians as well as among the founders of the just city. The one reference to the female as a member of this city before Book V has to do with "the [common] possession of women, marriages and the procreation of children" (423e), not with their participation in the affairs of the city, much less equal participation.

Thus, it is with much hesitation, as one who might "be an unwilling murderer of someone" (451a), that Socrates suddenly introduces the female as the equal of the male among all species, canine or human. In order to establish this equation Socrates must disregard his earlier portrait; he must de-sex the female, make her void of any special erotic attraction or function. In so doing he must disregard the principle that had guided his original search for justice, namely the principle of nature or *phusis* that dominated the founding of the first city and the subsequent definition of justice. Socrates' use of the concept of *phusis* is different from his Sophistic contemporaries who focused on the distinction between nature (*phusis*) and convention (*nomos*) and the inhibitions which the *nomoi* imposed on the pursuit of power and pleasure.[6] The Socratic definition of *phusis* has nothing to do with power or pleasure; it has to do with virtue (*arete*). *Arete* is the excellence of a thing—a shoe or a man. *Arete,* in Plato, is no longer the exclusive property of the courageous warrior who fights nobly before the Trojan walls. Rather, one's excellence or potential for *arete* is defined by one's *phusis,* one's natural capabilities. A person's *phusis* is what that person does well or better than anyone else. The man naturally (*phusei*) fit to build houses is the man who builds the best houses most efficiently. If he builds them well according to his abilities he possesses *arete.* This interpretation of *phusis* and *arete* leads directly to a theory of specialization, to the performance by each person or thing of that for which he/she/it is most suited.

The definition of justice which Socrates discovers in Book IV is based on this ideal of specialization as each part of the polis (or the soul) performs that function for which it is most suited. The first city in Book II had originated through a process of specialization as each member performed the function for which he was suited by nature. "Each one of us grows (*phuetai*) not entirely similar to another, but differing in nature (*kata phusin*), each one fitted for a separate task" (370a–b). As the city grows out of an agrarian community into a commercial society with expansion of trades and occupations, it does not turn into a city of convention such as we with our modern notions of a "return to nature" might imagine; as long as the specialization of function according to ability continues, this city is according to nature.

When Socrates begins to discuss the role of woman as potentially man's equal in his best city, he indicates the apparent contradiction that his earlier use of *phusis* based on specialization presents for his proposals. He puts the argument in the words of a fictitious opponent:

> Is it the case then that a woman does not differ very much from a man with regard to their nature (*phusis*)?
>
> How does she not differ?
>
> Then is it not fitting to assign a different task according to his/her nature? (453b–c)

Socrates makes his apology by suggesting that men and women differ only as much as bald men differ from those with long hair, that is, superficially and not with regard to their natures. Disregarding the sexual qualities of the female, he concentrates only on physical strength and notes that since women are weaker than men they will be given lighter tasks. However, while Socrates does give women this opportunity to participate in the protection of the city with men and recognizes only insignificant differences, he goes on to argue that there is no area except such ridiculous ones as weaving or cooking in which the male is not superior to the female (455c–d). This is patently absurd, for Socrates, ignoring the sexual female, also ignores the peculiar biological qualities that women, and women alone, have. Clearly the female is superior to the male of any species in her ability to bear children; even those women least skillful in this task do it better than any man—except perhaps for Zeus. If one's *phusis* is defined by that which one does better than anyone else, then Socrates has disregarded the *phusis* of the female.

Socrates does acknowledge that "the female bears, while the male covers" (454d–e), but rather than consider the implications of this distinction he chooses to undermine it. Motherhood after birth is reduced to the bare minimum of nursing some child at appointed times. As Glaucon refers to it: "You describe an exceedingly easy child bearing for women guardians" (460d). This minimizing of the female's reproductive role is what makes women in Socrates' city not only weaker but ultimately also inferior to men. "There is no pursuit," he says to Glaucon, "concerning the governance of the city which belongs particularly to a woman" (455b). Her natural role in the preservation of the city through the procreation of the next generation is left unconsidered. By forcing her to participate in the activities of the male warriors and later philosopher rulers, Socrates removes from woman her individual *phusis*—that particular specialty in which she excels. Woman's sexual, bodily nature is forgotten and she becomes almost irrelevant in Socrates' best city.

Body or biological attributes apparently do not determine the *phusis* of the guardians; rather, it is the skill or *techne* which they have. "We said that the souls of a man and a woman who are skilled in medicine have the same nature" (454d). On the other hand, a doctor, male or female, has a nature different from a carpenter, male or female. This argument is surrounded by laughter (452a–d) and must be seen as comic in intent. One's ability to be proficient in any craft is dependent upon the use of one's body, with the notable exception of philosophy.[7] What craft one executes well cannot be dissociated from one's bodily abilities. As the first city grows in Book II, the artisans perform those tasks for which they are suited, but all of the tasks described require the full use of their bodies—housebuilding, weaving, sailing, farming, and so on. The men engaged in the lowly profession of trade (which cannot be called a craft) are those who are "weakest in body and useless for doing any other work" (371c). The female body as the bearer of children cannot be dissociated from her *phusis* by Socrates. Likewise, the body cannot be removed from the particular *techne* under discussion in Book V: warfare.

The importance of the body for warfare appears when the participation of women in the warrior class is discussed, particularly in terms of gymnastics. In the earlier books when the training of the warriors was under consideration and there was an attempt to abstract from body, gymnastics was left to the well-trained mind. Suddenly, in Book V in the sexually integrated group, the training of warriors focuses not on *mousike,* which one might expect would have greater appeal to the feminine, but on the exercise of the body. Once it has been purged of its pertinent biological characteristics and once its needs have been severely circumscribed, the body may be readmitted to the city. It is a body that is to be primed for war, not a body that responds to stimuli—whether food or sex. Women and men exercise in the palaestra, naked next to each other; this causes neither laughter nor shame since both sexes are insensitive to the erotic qualities of their bodies and the desire for procreation.

After Socrates has purged the sexual desire so effectively in his equalizing of the male and female, he is confronted with the problem of reinstituting it in order to preserve his city through procreation. Women cannot bear children without attention to the biological aspects of their bodies and without yielding to the sexual eros. Socrates admits that men and women who are together all the time and in all circumstances

> will be drawn by an inner natural necessity to mixing with one another. Or do I seem to you to talk of needs?
>
> Not geometrical, he [Glaucon] said, but erotic needs, which may happen to be the sharpest of those for convincing and drawing the mass of common men. (458d)

The discussion in Book V prior to this point had been carried on as if there were only such "geometrical" needs, and indeed continues in this fashion; for Socrates disregards the bulk of the population and treats breeding among his warriors as if they were dogs or show birds. In fact, it is precisely an error in the mathematics of the breeding process that leads to the downfall of the best city (546b–d). The erotic necessities are to be circumscribed by what is most beneficial (for appearance's sake translated into what is most sacred, 458e). There is to be no mixing in a "disorderly manner" (*ataktos*) (458d). The image is that of a disorganized army; procreation is to be practiced with the same precision that warfare demands.

Socrates relies on a certain residual drive to surface only at precisely defined moments. These opportunities for intercourse may come as the result of a "sacred marriage" or as a prize for valor in war (460b). The sharing of a woman's bed as a reward for bravery does not mean that the warriors of Book V are driven during battle by a sexual eros. The laurel leaf was not of value in and of itself. The opportunity to sleep with a woman would represent such an honor and therefore be desirable for men who are driven on by spirit (*thumos*); the female prize, though, has social benefits in terms of reproducing the best warriors, which the laurel leaf does not. The sexual passion then reenters the city under the guise of the sacred and the honorable, but only to the extent that it serves the needs of the city.

The question must now arise as to why Socrates (or Plato) suddenly introduced women, de-sexed them, and put them on the same level as men. Why discuss them at all? Why not leave them as mistresses forsaken by the well-trained warrior class? Allan Bloom in his interpretive essay on the *Republic* argues first that men need women and that unless the women are also properly trained they will destroy the men whom the city has so carefully educated.[8] Second, he suggests that the male qualities developed in the education for battle must be tempered by female gentleness, that "humanity is a discreet mixture of masculinity and femininity."[9] Bloom then argues that feminine qualities cannot be forgotten as we are about to leave the warrior guardians, with their particularly male attributes, and encounter the philosopher-guardians. The philosopher needs the gentleness of a woman, and must, like the woman of Socrates' city, strip himself bare of all conventions before he can function.[10] In this analysis, however, Bloom is overlooking the distortion which is perpetrated on the female in order to bring her into the political community and the significance that this distortion may have.

The sudden introduction of the de-sexed female must be studied within the context of Book V, the book in which the philosopher-ruler makes his or her first appearance. However, we must note that the female is introduced into political life—which is historically, at least, alien to her—only through a perversion of her *phusis* or nature. In order to become political, she must sacrifice her role as the female of the species. When Aristophanes introduced women into the political arena in both the *Lysistrata* and the *Ecclesiazusae*, he did not remove from them their femininity or their sexuality. It is precisely their sexuality that is the motive cause in both plays, and it is their love of family life that gives the *Lysistrata* its central theme.[11] As far as we know, other literature of the time did not cast women into a political role. Rather, as Thucydides writes in Pericles' funeral oration, women were to bear children as a security to the state and, while doing this, to be unseen and unheard.[12] Socrates rejects this portrayal of women in Book V and goes even further to reject his own definition of nature. The female does not engage in politics in order to satisfy the female eros and *phusis* as Lysistrata and Praxagora do. Rather, she is destroyed as woman in order to participate. This is only preparatory to Socrates' perversion of philosophy. For just as woman is "de-natured," treated without regard for that in which she can excel, in order to be made part of the political world, so too is philosophy. To Socrates, try as he might to create the natural city where each individual performs according to his or her natural capabilities (whether it be the bearing of children or the making of shoes), politics can only be a perversion of what is natural; for it turns some men and all women away not from the pleasure and power of the Sophists but from the pursuit of excellence.

The relationship of philosophy to politics parallels that of women to politics. Neither one naturally participates in politics, and in both cases the needs of politics distort the needs of the individual. While the female is brought into politics through a disregard for her body, the philosopher enters politics through a disregard for his soul. The absurdity of a naked old woman practicing gymnastics is matched by the absurdity of a philosopher ruling over a city. Socrates recognizes this as he dreads the tidal wave of laughter that threatens him just before he offers his famous proposals (473c). Glaucon's reaction is filled with warnings of the indignation that men "who are not foolish" will feel (474a). As the imagery of the cave is developed in Book VII, it becomes clear that it is not only the city that does not want philosophy but also the philosopher who does not want to be involved in the affairs of the city. The compulsion that fills this section of the dialogue is necessary because the philosopher does not by nature move to the world of politics. The philosopher hates the lie (485c–d; 490b–c), and yet as political leader he must lie (414c; 459c). Socrates in founding his just city is unjust to philosophers, whose souls are oriented away from the political world of opinion and toward the world of being.

In order to create the best city, Socrates must do the worst to philosophers; he must make them live worse lives, *cheiron zein* (519d). The injustice which Socrates does to the female at the beginning of Book V is a forewarning of the injustice that politics imposes on the philosopher himself. In other Platonic dialogues, women usually appear as an inferior form of human being (*Phaedo* 60a; *Timaeus* 90e). Socrates tells us in the *Republic* that as the political community may by its demands destroy even the lowest human natures (women), so too it may destroy the highest natures. For Socrates the human animal does not find fulfillment of his *phusis* through politics. Women and philosophers fit awkwardly into the political world, even the one which aims to be most just. Their *phuseis* are opposed to it, and it in turn makes unjust demands upon them.

Republic VI: The Sexual Female

The equation between the female and the philosopher, which occurs in Book V of the *Republic,* is carried on to Book VI. Here, however, Socrates is attempting to develop the characteristics of philosophy without the encumbrances that political life imposes. Consequently neither woman nor philosophy is perverted by her/its relationship to politics, and both regain their true *phuseis.* While the philosopher is allowed to pursue reality freed from the demands of the political community, the female regains her body, her reproductive capabilities, and her sexuality. In so doing she becomes a symbol of the vital pursuit of wisdom. Up through Book V, eros had been persistently eliminated from the discussion. Immediately after the introduction of the philosopher in Book V, words having to do with eros and desire begin to predominate. The philosopher is first compared to a lover of young boys, an erotic man who loves young men whether they have snubnoses or long ones, and then to wine-lovers, to lovers of honor, and to lovers of food (474d–475c). With the emergence of the philosopher, the erotic and bodily passions are introduced into the purged city.

The eroticism of the philosopher is most fully developed in the sixth book, the book devoted to the discovery of the nature of the philosopher. It is here that the object of philosophy and the process of philosophy itself are described in feminine terms. The pedophile of the previous book is left behind; consummation there leads to no birth. As the male erotically desires the female, the true lover of learning is similarly portrayed at one point as desiring what is (*to on*):

> He naturally struggles to obtain what is, and not tarrying by the many particulars which are thought to be, but he goes and is not dulled nor does he cease from his love until he has laid hold of

> the nature of each thing itself which is with the part of the soul that is suitable to seize hold of such a thing. It is suitable for that which is akin to it. Being near to it and joining together with what really is, having begotten mind and truth, he both knows and lives truly and is nourished and thus ceases from the pangs of labor, but not before. (409a–b)

The language in this passage is explicitly sexual (*migeis, gennesas,* and *odinos*) and bears a close relationship to language and imagery found in the *Theatetus.* In that dialogue Socrates frequently portrays himself as a midwife to philosophical ideas (for example, 150b–151c; 157c; 161e; 210c). This analogy gives Socrates frequent cause to describe the philosophical process in terms of labor and birth, images which constantly call to mind the biological function of women (156a; 160e; 210b). Though most of the fetuses which Socrates brings forth turn out to be wind eggs, the relationship between the intellectual and bodily process of labor and birth ties Socrates and his activities to biological woman.

While the philosophic process is portrayed as resembling the sexual experience of woman from being desired to giving birth, philosophy itself in the *Republic* is also portrayed as a woman with the erotic qualities of the sexual female. At one point, philosophy is the deserted female, left unfulfilled by those who live neither appropriate nor true lives: "Others, unworthy, come to her, as one bereft of relatives, and defile her" (495c). Or philosophy is compared to the daughter of a lowly craftsman about to be married to the unworthy but recently wealthy employee of her father (495e). Socrates is concerned with the quality of the offspring of such a poor match: "What sort of things are such men likely to engender? Will they not be bastards and undistinguished?" (496a). They parallel the offspring of those men who are incapable of philosophy and yet attach themselves to her. "Whenever those who have been inappropriately educated come to her and consort with her not according to what is appropriate, what sort of thoughts and opinions shall we say they engender?" (496a)—again the language is of birth. Though the female may be deserted or married to someone who does not deserve her, she nevertheless preserves her feminine function and is defined explicitly by her biological attributes. Philosophy, too, is allowed to be itself and is not, at least in Book VI, forced into the service to the political community. Once this freedom is achieved, Socrates can begin the ascent to the good. Meanwhile, women submit to marriages arranged by their money-conscious fathers and bear children.

In Book VII the philosopher is once gain perverted and forced to engage in politics. This brings on a new round of laughter (516e; 517d; 518a–b), reminding us of the beginning of Book V. Then it was the naked women in the palaestras; now it is the philosopher returning to the world of the cave who is subjected to ridicule. The situation is the same; in each case the natural is perverted, and an injustice is done to the individual. Laughter arises at the sight of the absurd or fantastical—birds founding a city, women stopping a war, or a philosopher entering the world of politics. In Book VI there is little laughter;[13] *phusis* is permitted to fulfill itself, as both the philosopher and the female do that for which they are most suited. Eros has returned.

Philosophy and the Female

Once the equation between the philosopher and the female has been suggested, the question arises as to why Socrates (Plato) introduces it and what he means to tell us about the philosophic pursuit through it. Bloom is again one of the few commentators to deal with this particular question. Considering the dramatic structure of the dialogue, he argues that the sexual metaphors will appeal particularly to Glaucon, the erotic young interlocutor,[14] though the sexual imagery that appeals to him is mostly concerned with pederasty (474d–e; 485c). Bloom argues further that the male, the *aner,* with his qualities of courage and strength, represents only half of humanity. Philosophy needs the feminine qualities like gentleness as well.[15] I believe that the significance of this analogy can be carried somewhat further.

Philosophers in the Platonic corpus and women in the Greek tradition are private individuals. They belong to the world of the *idios,* not to the community or the *koinon.* While women may stay in seclusion inside their homes, the philosopher must insulate himself not from the activity of the agora, but from the opinions of the city. He must remain independent of the demands that the city makes upon his intellect. To be a member of the city, a *polites,* one must sacrifice one's private knowledge and accept the views demanded by the city. This is something the philosopher cannot do. He must ask his questions without regard for the political consequences or the political needs of the community; women likewise perform their functions privately, irrespective of the political circumstances. Women bear children whether they live in Sparta, Thebes, or Troy. Their nature traditionally has removed them from politics. True philosophers pursue the good whether they live in Sparta or Thebes. But political man behaves quite differently wherever he may live. The female and the philosopher live apart from the political world. They both satisfy their erotic desires independently of the needs or demands of the city, though they both may need the security that the city offers.

The philosopher like Socrates may become dangerous, but more often, again like the woman, he is simply useless for the actual practice of politics. When Adeimantus specifically accuses the philosopher of being useless (487d), he recalls the words of Pericles who is made to say by Thucydides: "'We alone think of one who does not participate in [public] affairs not as a quiet man, but as a useless one" (II.40.2). The Greek political community had no place for the *idios.* Thus, the tensions that surround the introduction of the female into political life are the same as those that surround the introduction of the philosopher. Both naturally belong to the world of the private. Yet the aim of Book V in which both enter political society is to make public all that previously had been private—from sexual intercourse to a hurt finger (462c).[16] In the process of becoming politicized the female and the philosopher are removed from their natural environments.

Pericles' oration is spoken for those who died in battle for the city. For Pericles the fulfillment of one's role as a member of the city is achieved through death for the city—the ultimate expression of the unity of the self and the political community. Participation in public affairs is defined in terms of war with other cities. It is precisely during war that the skills of women and philosophers are irrelevant. Yet it is war that is the theme particular to Book V.[17] War was a highly masculine affair in Greece. The word commending bravery in battle specifically denotes its masculine orientation (*andreia* from *aner*). At no point, especially in fifth- and fourth-century Athens, could political activity be isolated from relations with other cities and the potential for war. Politics was inherently a masculine pursuit. Yet women guardians are obviously to be trained for war (452c; 453a; 457a). When Glaucon discusses their actual participation in a battle, qualifications to the original proposals for equality appear. After describing an army composed of "brothers, fathers, and sons," he adds the note: "And if the female part should join the campaign, stationed either in the line itself or behind in order to frighten off the enemies if ever there would be any necessity for aid, I know that with all these things they would be unbeatable" (471d). Glaucon still seems hesitant to accord women full equality in war. Even Socrates apparently undercuts his own arguments when he offers as a prize for valor in battle "more frequent opportunity to share the bed of women," as a means to increase the offspring of brave warriors (460b). The philosopher in battle does not appear in the *Republic,* but we do find him in Alcibiades' speech in the *Symposium.* Alcibiades reports Socrates' unshakable countenance during battle, but he also makes the philosopher appear ridiculous. He uses a quote from Aristophanes to describe Socrates' stride during the retreat from Delium. The language of the comic poet underlines the absurdity of a philosopher engaging in war.

Though both the philosopher and women are cast uncomfortably into a political community that concentrates on war, there is a sudden shift in the discussion in Book V to the manner in which the best city will carry on war. With absolutely no warning, we are jolted away from the question of the possibility of the best city to a discussion which seems completely alien to the topic at hand.

> Is it not now left, I said, to go through whether it is possible among men as among the other animals, that there come into being such a community and in what way it is possible?
>
> You were the first to mention, he [Glaucon] said, what I intended to raise.
>
> About the affairs during war, I think it is obvious, I said, in what manner they will carry on war. (466d–e)

With this we are launched into several pages of how and whom the warriors shall fight. I would suggest that this sudden change in topic intrudes at this point to highlight the position of both women and philosophers as poor citizens in a city which needs to do battle against its enemies.[18]

The analogy presented in the *Politicus* between the art of statesmanship and the art of weaving (279b) creates some difficulty in the parallel opposition of both female and philosopher to the masculine art of politics. Weaving is a woman's craft that is practiced privately at home. Penelope, our most famous weaver, used the craft as an excuse to escape from involvement in the politics of Ithaca. Weaving is one of the two crafts, specifically mentioned in the *Republic,* where women may have a superiority (455c). In the *Politicus,* though, the analogy is developed of the statesman who, like the weaver, oversees the handling of the wool before uniting the woof and warp into a strong cloak. However, the most important task of weaving together the courageous and temperate souls is ultimately achieved through control over matrimony—the proper breeding of disparate types. The task becomes a sexual one, one having specifically to do with reproduction, the arena for female activity. Politics in the *Politicus* is isolated from the masculine pursuit of war (305a) and is more nearly akin to philosophy (299b–c). The true statesman in the *Politicus* is the philosopher, only here he is not forced down into the world of politics, his *phusis* is not perverted. Instead of interfering with the nature of the philosopher, political communities in the *Politicus* are guided by depersonalized laws, a second-best but nevertheless practical solution. Thus, the feminine analogy may still be appropriate. In fact, we learn at the beginning of the dialogue that in this particular discussion it is possible for a private individual (*idiotes*) to be the true statesman (259a–b). This would hardly be possible in the highly communal life of the rulers of the *Republic.*

The role of women as private beings cloistered in the home is related to their role in the bearing and raising of children. The female is generative; she gives birth and represents the beginning, but not necessarily the completion, of a project. It is this generative role that purposefully is ignored in the fifth book of the *Republic.* By forcing woman into politics, Socrates turns her away from the generation of life to a concern with death—politics in the *Republic* being identified with war and consequently with death as well. From the first step of Socrates down into the Piraeus, politics is discussed within a framework of death. It is death in the thoughts of Cephalus that introduces us to the discussion of justice, and it is death that concludes the dialogue. Gyges, who is to change from a private shepherd into a king, begins his transformation into a political man through contact with a corpse on whose finger he finds his magic ring (359d). The warriors of the just state must be trained specifically not to fear death lest they refuse to participate in the activities of the political community, which, as Pericles so powerfully expresses it, demand death. Thus, all the poets at the beginning of Book III must be purged of references to death. The cave imagery further supports the equation of politics with death. The image of the deep, dark cavern into which the philosophers are forced to return recalls Hades in the Greek myths. In the beginning of Book III the passages which must be excised from the poets are those that describe the world of Hades as a cave with fluttering shadows (386d–387a).[19] When women enter the world of politics in Book V they must forget their life-generating functions, for politics in this dialogue is not a life-generating process. To involve the female in politics, she must be reoriented toward death.

In the Socratic dialogues the practice of philosophy is likewise generative and characterized not as the attainment of knowledge but as the pursuit of knowledge. In the *Theaetetus,* Socrates portrays himself as sterile, incapable of giving birth to any idea himself (150c–d), but skilled at assisting in the birth of ideas. In the development of the *Theaetetus* no successful birth actually occurs, but in the process of trying to discover what knowledge is, the generative process is frequently described in terms of birth, and this tells us more about the complexities of the notion of knowledge than any specific definition might. While the body of the dialogue is devoted to an inquiry that replicates this process of birth, the *Theaetetus* is introduced with a brief conversation between Eucleides and Terpsion in which death and politics are once again united. Eucleides reports that he has just been with Theatetus who was being carried away from battle, "living, but barely" (142b). The demands of politics force Theatetus into battle for Athens and his involvement there leads to his death. It is the masculine activities of war that lead to his death; the feminine activities in which he engaged earlier with Socrates, and which are recorded in Eucleides' book, are related to life, birth, and generation. The short introduction to the *Theaetetus,* which may at first appear almost irrelevant to the subsequent dialogue, actually presents again the important contrast between the masculine/political world of death and the feminine/philosophical world of life.

The presentation of philosophy not as the completion but as the pursuit of knowledge is developed most vividly in the myth of the birth of Eros told by Diotima in the *Symposium.* She intends to equate Eros and philosophy: both are described as the pursuit of the good (204b). It is the striving of both Eros and philosophy that is important, not the final attainment. Once the good is attained, philosophy and eros cease. "No one of the gods philosophizes nor desires to be wise—for he is—and if anyone else is wise, he does not philosophize" (204a). Hans Kelson in his psychoanalytical study of Plato's sexual orientation finds in the story of the birth of Eros evidence of the hostility which Plato felt toward women. Poros (Plenty) is the father of Eros; Penia (need), the mother. "The sex act," Kelso argues, "occurs only against the will of the man, everything good in its result come from the father, everything bad from the mother."[20] While this is true in conventional terms, Eros would not be the philosopher without Penia as his mother. It is the mother who bequeaths to Eros those characteristics that make him so similar to Socrates: his squalor, his bare feet, his lack of bed, his hanging around gates and doors, and the like (203d). He is like his father in his manliness (*andreios*) and his eagerness and even in his "philosophizing throughout his life" (203d). But without the feminine qualities of incompletion and generation, Eros would not strive for the good or parallel the philosopher. In all the speeches prior to Socrates' in the *Symposium* (except for a moment in Phaedrus's speech, 179b–c) heterosexual love is either forgotten or else mockingly scorned. Though later in Diotima's presentation, love of a female and the generation of a child puts one on the lower rungs of the ladder of love, Eros is born from such a heterosexual relationship—not a necessity among the gods—and it is only through those qualities inherited from Penia, from the necessity to create, that Eros and philosophy are united in their pursuit of the good.

If, then, we see philosophy as united with the female in its generative powers and in its privatism, a failure or refusal to participate in the public world of politics and war—the paradoxes suggested by the notion of a philosopher-ruler—becomes distressing. In the same way that masculinity is the opposite of femininity, so too is (masculine) politics the opposite of (feminine) philosophy—just as going up out of the cave is the opposite of going down into the cave. However, in both cases the opposites are in need of each other. Male needs female in order to preserve the species, or, in more particular terms, to give the city sons; female needs male in order to fulfill her nature as the bearer of children. The philosopher, as both the *Apology* and *Crito* so vividly demonstrate, needs the city, the organized political unit, for without the city the philosopher would have no place to practice. Though the relationship is more tenuous, the city needs the philosopher as well. In the *Apology*, Socrates likens the city to a noble horse, which "because of its size is sluggish and in need of being stirred on by a certain gadfly, so that, it seems to me, God has given me to the city, who sitting down everywhere and for the whole day does not cease stirring you up and persuading you and chiding you about everything" (30e).

The need which each opposite has for the other, though, emphasizes that they must not be equalized. The female with her particular characteristics must not be turned into a male. The philosopher similarly cannot be made into a politician. The attempts to do both of these things in Book V of the *Republic* leads to much laughter among the listeners and talkers, but more seriously it shows an attempt to destroy the natural or *phusis* in both categories. That Socrates must so pervert the natural in order to create the best political system must raise doubts about its value. The appearance of women in the *Republic* must not be seen as an instance of "anti-Platon chez Platon,"[21] nor as a remnant of a "real" Socrates who was close to being a feminist,[22] but rather as a means of casting an important and philosophically significant shadow over the whole enterprise of trying to create the perfect city. Perhaps the *Republic* tells us that politics is fundamentally imperfectable and must always be plagued by the conflicts between the public and the private, between opinion and wisdom, between warfare and weaving.

Notes

1. For example, James Adam, *The Republic of Plato,* with critical notes, commentary, and appendices (Cambridge: University Press, 1902), 1:280; Ernest Barker, *Greek Political Theory* (London and New York: University Paperbacks, 1960), 254; Benjamin Jowett, *The Dialogues of Plato,* trans. with analyses and intros. (New York: Scribner, 1871), 2:129–30; H. D. Rankin, *Plato and the Individual* (London: Methuen, 1964), 92–93; Dorothea Wender, "Plato: Misogynist, Paedophile, and Feminist," *Arethusa* 6, no. 1 (Spring 1973): 76.

2. Standard Stephanus pagination will be used for all citations from the *Republic* and other Platonic dialogues.

3. In the first two instances Socrates uses the word *aner,* a specifically masculine word, to refer to the members of the auxiliary and guardians class. In 467c he refers only to fathers.

4. In Herodotus's story the queen does not have a passive role nor does she excite erotic passions; rather, upon secretly being seen naked by Gyges at the request of her husband, she instigates the overthrow and murder of the king, with threats to Gyges if he should not comply (I, 10–11).

5. Other references to women in Books I-IV show women to be weak, weepy, and unworthy of imitation (387e; 395d–e; 396a; 398e; and 431c).

6. See Antiphon, "On Truth," in Barker, *Greek Political Theory,* 95–98; Callicles in Plato's *Gorgias;* and the Melian Dialogue in Thucydides, V, 85–112.

7. See Cephalus, 328d, and especially Theages, 496b–c, whose care of a sickly body kept him from politics. Leo Strauss argues that this abstraction is necessary in order to "understand

the city as an association of artisans or in order to effect as complete a coincidence as possible between the city and the arts" (*The City and Man* [Chicago: Rand McNally, 1964], 95).

8. Allan Bloom, *The Republic of Plato,* trans. with notes and an interpretive essay (New York and London: Basic Books, 1968), 383.

9. Ibid., 384.

10. Ibid., and 458 n. 11.

11. See Cedric H. Whitman, *Aristophanes and the Comic Hero* (Cambridge: Harvard University Press for Oberlin College, 1964), 205–11.

12. Thucydides, *History,* II, 45.2; see also Xenophon's *Oeconomicus,* VII, where the wife is active but exclusively inside the home, directing domestics, supervising weaving, and managing what is brought in from without.

13. References to laughter are infrequent in Book VI and appear in a concentrated form only in section 504d to 509c (four times) when Socrates is being forced to discuss that which he should not—the good.

14. Bloom, *The Republic of Plato,* 461 n. 1.

15. Ibid., 384.

16. Ibid., 380.

17. From the moment that the inhabitants of the fevered city "cut off land from their neighbors" (373d), the focus of the *Republic* is on war. Neighbors are assumed to be present, and the good city must be concerned with self-protection (422a–d). In contrast, in the *Laws,* where there is the assumption of relative isolation from all other political communities, the Legislators can concentrate on the inculcation of individual virtue.

18. Benjamin Jowett and Lewis Campbell (*Plato's Republic: The Greek Text* [Oxford: Clarendon Press, 1894], 2:Notes, p. 241) offer this explanation of the sudden change in topic: "The real motive of the digression is an artistic one. The great *peripeteia,* the on-rushing of the 'third wave,' is made more impressive by being delayed." This is hardly satisfactory.

19. The parallel between these two sections is further emphasized by the repetition of the quote of Achilles from the *Odyssey* (386c and 516d).

20. Hans Kelsen, "Platonic Love," *American Imago* 3, nos. 1–2 (April 1942): 15.

21. Wender, "Plato . . .," 85.

22. A. E. Taylor, *Plato: The Man and His Work* (Cleveland and New York: World Publishing, Meridan Books, 1956), 278.

5

Hairy Cobblers and Philosopher-Queens

Elizabeth V. Spelman

In Book V of Plato's *Republic*, Socrates proposes that women are potentially just as good guardians or philosopher-rulers of the state as men. The notion of the equality of men and women must have been startling to Plato's contemporaries, since it went so much against the grain of Athenian society and its history.[1] But it should also be startling to modern readers of Plato who know how deeply undemocratic and antiegalitarian his views in general are.

In this chapter, I will describe what made it possible for Plato to imagine women in roles quite other than those defined by their society, and I also hope to make clear how he must have perceived their equality to men in light of his otherwise inegalitarian politics. Plato's notion of the equality of the sexes is carefully sculpted so as not to be inconsistent with his thinking of one class of people as the superiors of other classes.[2] If we can understand why it is not inconsistent, then perhaps we can gain some insight into troubling features of contemporary feminist thought: that is, perhaps we can see how one can argue against sexism in a way that leaves other forms of oppression intact; how one can argue for views that support, or at least leave unexamined, the domination of some women over others. We will see the sad irony in the description of Plato as the first feminist philosopher.[3]

I

Let us turn to the *Republic* for Plato's views about women. This central dialogue of the Platonic corpus is an examination of the nature of justice, and it becomes perforce a prescription for the best society: we can come to understand what justice in the individual is, Socrates urges, if we look at justice "writ large" in the state. What is justice in a state or society? Plato assumes the following as general principles of construction of that society in which we can find justice: (1) different kinds of people have different natures, and (2) both individuals and the state are best served if people perform the functions for which their natures, complemented by the appropriate education, best suit them.[4] The ideal state is based on the recognition of the mutuality of need among people who do different things. People stand in need of each other because not everybody does everything well; indeed, no one does everything well; in fact, everyone does only one thing well. People will lead the best and most flourishing lives of which they are capable, and the state will be the best and the happiest possible state, if each person fulfills his or her "natural" role. Justice consists in the harmony that prevails under these conditions. Individuals will enjoy the harmony that is justice if their reason, aided by the spirited part of their souls, rules their appetites; the state will enjoy the harmony that is justice if those individuals in whom the power of reasoning is strongest rule, with the aid of high-spirited soldiers, over the multitudes. That is, justice will prevail to the extent that a guardian class of philosophers, aided by the class of "auxiliaries" whom they command, rules over the class of artisans or producers. (Plato appears to assume that in addition to these three classes there will be the underclass of slaves.)[5]

It follows from Plato's argument that if women and men have different natures, they ought not to have the same pursuits, they ought not to perform the same functions in the state. Indeed, given Plato's definition of justice, it would be unjust for them to be delegated the same functions and responsibilities.

In Book V of the *Republic* Socrates insists that there is no reason women ought not to be included among the philosopher-rulers. He manages to do so without giving up the principle that we ought to assign "different pursuits to different natures and the same to the same" (454b) and without giving up entirely the notion that men and women have different natures. He points out to Glaucon that if one is careful enough to "apply the proper divisions and distinctions to the subject under consideration" (454a) one will think not simply about whether two natures are different or the same but whether they are different or the same *with respect to a particular pursuit.* In this connection, Socrates insists that just as whether a person is bald or long-haired is irrelevant to whether he has the kind of nature that makes him a good cobbler, so whether a person is male or female is irrelevant to whether he or she is suited to a task—indeed, a male and a female physician are more alike than a male physician and a male carpenter (454d–e). The two cases suggest that a difference in bodily features is not necessarily a sign of a difference in nature; what is crucial is whether two people have the same mind or soul: "A man and a woman who have a physician's mind[6] have the same nature" (454d). Yes, male and female differ in that "the female bears and the male begets," but this does nothing to show that "the woman differs from the man for our purposes" (454e). While the body can be a hindrance to performing a task well (455c)—that is, in cases in which "bodily faculties" do not adequately serve the mind—whether the body is or is not a hindrance doesn't depend on whether it is male or female.

So not all men will do the same things because they are men; not all women will do the same things because they are women. Some men will be suited to being carpenters, others suited to being guardians; similarly, "one woman has the qualities of a guardian and another not. . . . The women and the men, then, have the same nature in respect to the guardianship of the state, save in so far as the one is weaker, the other stronger" (456a).

In short, Socrates says, people ought to engage in different pursuits only when their differences are relevant to the capacity to carry out the task. He does not challenge the idea that men and women are different in some respects—specifically, in terms of their role in reproduction—but says that there are other respects in which they are or might be the same. Similarly, he does not challenge the idea that two men may be alike in some respect, or that two women may be the same in some respect, but argues that there may be other respects in which they are different. What is visible about you does not tell the whole story, or maybe any of the story, of who you are. Plato wants us to see that it takes the skill of a real philosopher to see which differences and similarities are relevant to which pursuits. Part of what enables Socrates to imagine women engaged in the same pursuits as men is this capacity.

The importance of being able to know what differences make a difference appears in another dialogue in which the significance of apparent differences between men and women is discussed. When Socrates asks young Meno, in the dialogue of that name, if he knows what virtue is, he replies by telling Socrates about the virtue of men and the virtue of women: "The virtue of a man consists in managing the city's affairs capably . . . a woman's virtue . . . is easily described. She must be a good housewife, careful with her stores and obedient to her husband" (71e).

Socrates responds by getting Meno to acknowledge that bees don't differ from one another as bees, even though they differ in size and beauty; he then leads Meno into considering by analogy whether "even if [virtues] are many and various, . . . they all have some common character which makes them virtues" (72c). He wants Meno to see that virtue will not "differ, in its character as virtue, whether it be in a child or an old man, a woman or a man" (73a).

Thus a man's having virtue doesn't mean the virtue he has is manly—that it belongs to him by virtue of his being male—and a woman's having virtue doesn't mean that her virtue is womanly. Just as a bee qua bee is neither big nor small, beautiful nor ugly, so virtue qua virtue is neither manly nor womanly—it is just virtue. Virtue itself cannot be various, even though there may be a variety of virtues. Again, it is Socrates' capacity to note similarities and to know their significance that is presented as crucial to his ability to see beyond the physical differences that exist between people or things.

Finally, Socrates is able to argue that sexual identity is irrelevant to the capacities required for the philosopher-ruler because he thought of those capacities as being of the soul and distinct from the qualities of the body. Whether or not you have the capacity to rule is determined by your soul and not your body; no inferences can be drawn from the fact that someone has a particular kind of body about what kind of soul they have.

Someone might well agree with Socrates that we can't simply note physical differences between people and conclude that they must have different natures. As Socrates makes us see, it would be absurd to think that because the excellent cobbler one knows has a full head of hair, no bald man could be a good cobbler; the presence or absence of hair is irrelevant to whether or not one might be a cobbler "by nature." But how, Socrates' critic might ask, could sexual identity *not* make a difference to one's ability? Young Meno easily grants Socrates the point about bees all being essentially the same, and about health being the same, as health, in men and women; but about whether virtue can be the same in men and women he expresses some reservations: "I somehow feel that this is not on the same level as the other cases" (73a).

There are at least two ways Plato could silence such doubts. He could argue that *no* facts about a person's body entail facts about that person's nature, or soul.[7] Or he could maintain that while some bodily facts entail something about people's natures, their sexual identities aren't among such facts. There is much in Plato's treatment of the soul/body distinction that suggests that his holding the former view enabled him to "see beyond" a person's sex. But we need to remind ourselves of the way, or ways, in which Plato described the soul and the body and the relation between them.

II

Plato took soul and body to be distinctly different kinds of things. The distinction hums continuously throughout the dialogues. According to Plato, souls are invisible, not observable by the senses; they are subject neither to generation or decay. Bodies, to the contrary, are quite visible, apprehendable by the senses, and they are entirely subject to generation and decay. In the *Phaedo,* Socrates summarizes a discussion with Cebes about the distinction between soul and body: "[The soul is] most like that which is divine, immortal, intelligible, uniform, indissoluble, and ever self-consistent and invariable, whereas [the] body is most like that which is human, mortal, multiform, unintelligible, dissoluble, and never self-consistent" (80b).

Precisely because the soul is not visible and is unchanging, it can "see" the invisible and unchanging things the senses never can (*Republic* 510e, 527e, 532a). Soul and body each have a kind of beauty, health, pleasure, and good and evil distinct from the qualities of the other

(*Phaedo* 114e; *Gorgias* 464a, 477b–c, 501b; *Philebus* 33c). There are concerns peculiar to the soul and those specific to the body (*Republic* 535b; *Laws* 673a, 795d).

The soul not only is different in kind from the body; it can exist without it. At death, the invisible, indissoluble soul separates from the visible decaying body (*Phaedo* 64c, 67d; *Gorgias* 524b; *Laws* 828e, 927a). The soul thus *is* the person; immortality is the continued existence of the person, the soul, after the death of the body.[8] The connection to the body is so contingent as to allow the soul to inhabit an entirely different body: for example, a soul that was in a man's body in one lifetime might inhabit a woman's body in another (*Timaeus* 42b–c, 76e, 91a; *Laws* 944e; *Republic* 614–21).

Finally, those who really care about the state of their souls (that is, those who are or aspire to being philosophers) will do everything they can to keep the body from interfering with the proper work of the soul. In the *Apology,* this is portrayed as the central concern of Socrates' life: "[I have spent] all my time going about trying to persuade you, young and old, to make your first and chief concern not for your bodies nor for your possessions, but for the highest welfare of your souls" (30a–b).

It is only through the soul that a person can come to have any real knowledge, for it is only through the soul that one can "see" what is real—the invisible, eternal, unchanging Forms. The body, with its deceptive senses, keeps us from real knowledge, insofar as it rivets us in a world of material things far removed from the world of reality. We are mistaken if we think that what we can touch or see or otherwise sense are real: the beautiful things we can hold in our hands are not Beauty itself, which is "an everlasting loveliness which neither comes nor goes, which neither flowers nor fades, for such beauty is the same on every hand, the same then as now, here as there, this way as that way, the same to every worshipper as it is to every other" (*Symposium* 221a). Only the soul can know the Forms, those eternal and unchanging denizens of reality; our changing, decaying bodies can put us in touch only with changing, decaying pieces of the material world. The philosophers who will rule the ideal state "are those who are capable of apprehending that which is eternal and unchanging, while those who are incapable of this, but lose themselves and wander amid the multiplicities of multifarious things, are not philosophers" (*Republic* 484b).

Our bodies (or sometimes, the lower parts of the soul) also are the source of temptations that must be resisted if we are to lead lives of virtue. "Enjoyment of flesh by flesh" is "wanton shame," while desire of soul for soul is at the heart of a relationship that "reverences, aye, and worships, chastity and manhood, greatness and wisdom" (*Laws* 837c–d). At a less anxious moment in the dialogues, Plato isn't so worried about the enjoyment of flesh by flesh as long as the enjoyment doesn't get in the way of the spiritual development of both lovers.[9]

The body is not without use, however: for example, appreciation of the physical beauty of another can lead to an understanding of Beauty itself. One can begin to learn about Beauty in the contemplation of those who are beautiful, which leads to the realization that Beauty is something beyond any particular beautiful body or thing.[10] We also learn from the dialogues that one shouldn't neglect the body: an ill-tuned body can prevent the proper functioning of the soul; and one ought to understand as well that the well-tuned body can serve certain epistemological ends, albeit severely limited ones.

But in general the dialogues tell us that one has no hope of understanding Knowledge, Reality, Goodness, Love, or Beauty unless one recognizes the distinction between soul and body; and one has no hope of attaining or comprehending any of these essential Forms unless one works hard on freeing the soul from the lazy, vulgar, beguiling body. The person is not only distinct from the body but is much better off finally without it.

These lessons from the dialogues about the relation of soul and body enable us to see, then, why Plato could see beyond someone's sex: What difference can having a male or female body make to whether one can be a philosopher-ruler, if it is the state of one's soul that determines whether or not one is a philosopher, and if the soul not only is distinct from the body but can exist without it? What kind of inference about someone's soul could possibly be based on whether their body is male or female, if the same soul could be in either a male or female body, or in no body at all? While one's body can be an obstacle to the proper functioning of the soul of a philosopher, a woman who is a philosopher will by her nature avoid the ensnarements of her body; and her education, which is the same as that of her male equals, will strengthen her natural resolve. Thus whatever differences there are between men and women are irrelevant in terms of their eligibility for guardianship of the state.

III

This was for the most part a startling political position: not even the democrats of Athens were proposing that women ought to share in the governance of the polis. But the arguments Plato relied on were not so clearly political as they were logical and metaphysical: he was trying to get his companions to see that it is irrational to differentiate between people on the basis of sex if sex is irrelevant to the point at hand.

What is particularly important here is that he does not appeal to existing arguments or institutions about equality—for example, he didn't turn to the democrats and try to convince them that on their own grounds women ought to have the chance to shape the policies of the state.[11] Paradoxically, his case rests on a metaphysical argument that establishes *inequality* in two ways: (1) People have different natures and in light of that ought to be educated differently to play different roles in the polis (as opposed to being given the opportunity to do anything they want). (2) It takes a special skill to see which differences and similarities are relevant to which pursuits; only people with this skill should be leaders. That is, the very same arguments meant to establish the equality of some women to some men are also meant to establish or reflect the inequality of some groups of women and men to other groups of women and men.

Now we must look more closely at the relation between the equality Plato appears to posit between men and women who are philosopher-rulers and the inequality he posits between the class of philosopher-rulers and all the other members of the state.

Plato's inegalitarianism—his view that some people are by nature meant to rule, others to assist them, and still others to be ruled—requires that there are different natures, rooted in different kinds of souls. His egalitarianism—his view that some women are as fit to rule as some men are—requires that whatever else might differentiate souls, being male or female does not. His inegalitarianism and egalitarinism thus seem to go neatly together: while the natures of men and women as philosophers do not differ, the natures of philosophers and cobblers do. In other words, the claim that souls are distinct from bodies—which is crucial to the idea that it doesn't matter whether you have a male or female body—does not mean that there cannot be different kinds of souls. All it means is that we can't tell from the kind of body a person has, what kind of soul she or he has. Some souls are of the kind to rule, some are of the kind to be ruled—but the body does not reveal, simply on the basis of whether it is male or female, what kind of soul is inside it.

Now as we've just seen, Plato seems to say not only that being male or female is irrelevant to the kind of soul you have, but that no aspect of the physical self can tell us anything about the kind of soul someone has. If that is the case, then given that souls are not visible, how are we to decide where the ruling and where the ruled souls reside?

When we ask this question, we end up wondering whether Plato can after all sustain the grounds for both his arguments. For it begins to look as if those he uses to establish a kind of equality of men and women among the rulers will finally undermine his description of the inequality among philosopher-rulers, auxiliaries, and the "multitude." Any argument strong enough to show that sexual identity is irrelevant must undermine attempts to make crucial distinctions between any people or groups of people.

The dialogues provide us with at least two ways to get around the dilemma. First of all, among the special skills of the philosopher-kings and -queens is the ability to tell what kind of nature a person has. Their nature and their training enable them to "distinguish the baseborn from the trueborn" (*Republic* 536a), and the well-being of the state depends on this ability: "For when the knowledge necessary to make such discrimination is lacking in individual or state, they unawares employ at random for any of these purposes the crippled and baseborn natures, as their friends or rulers" (*Republic* 536a). The rulers' responsibility for "assign[ing] to each the status due to his nature" is described as one they must address with the greatest care.[12] In fact they must be prepared to "thrust [their own sons] out among the artisans or the farmers" in the unlikely but possible case that they do not inherit their parent's nature (*Republic* 415b–c).

Second, we find in the dialogues that while Plato is at pains to argue that we can't tell, simply from the fact of someone's having a female body, what kind of soul she has, he is very concerned about how one behaves, since what happens in or to the body has profound effects on what happens in and to the soul, and vice versa. Thus although one's nature is not revealed through the kind of body one has, it is revealed through the activities one engages in. Plato is concerned about how philosophers comport themselves and what kind of activities they engage in. He thinks it crucial that those with philosophers' souls behave in certain ways rather than others—this is why education is so important in the *Republic.* The living conditions of philosopher-rulers resembles what in our time Erving Goffmann has called a "total institution": every aspect of their lives is controlled, for every action, every gesture, Plato thinks, has an effect on the state of their souls.[13] For example, since philosophers ought not to give in to grief when afflicted in their own lives, they should not give in to it in the theater either (*Republic* 604a–b): there are no occasions on which what we do does not seriously affect the quality of our souls. Philosophers-in-training thus have to be tested again and again to see if their souls are up to par—for example, to see if rather than being overcome by fear or by pleasure they remain "immune to such witchcraft and preserve [their] composure throughout," thereby showing themselves to be "good guardian[s] of [themselves] and the culture [they have] received" (*Republic* 13e). All children will receive the same initial education (there is no sure way of telling at birth what kind of nature a person has, so all should be educated up to the point at which differences among them emerge), but only those who pass such tests can be established as philosopher-rulers (*Republic* 414a, 503a).

Although the life of philosopher-rulers requires a kind of constant vigilance, it also requires a particular leisure. As Socrates said to his judges in the *Apology* (36d), anyone whose appointed task is to care for people's souls must be free of the need to earn a living. Wage-earning is suitable only for those "servitors who in the things of the mind are not altogether worthy of our fellowship, but whose strength of body is sufficient for toil; so they, selling the use of this strength and calling the price wages, are designated, I believe, "wage earners," are they not?" (*Republic* 371e).

Indeed, some commentators have insisted that "the whole of Plato's political philosophy is grounded in the conviction that to earn a livelihood, and especially by means of manual labour, corrupts the soul and disqualifies a man for politics, making it not only justifiable but necessary for him to subject himself to the command of others."[14]

We see now why Plato's example of the carpenter (*Republic* 454d–e; see 89 above) is so telling: Socrates is trying to get Glaucon to understand that if we think carefully about who is fit to be a ruler of the state, what matters is not whether you are male or female but what kinds of pursuits you are suited for, what kinds of activities you can do well, and how you respond to challenges to self-control. What matters is not what kind of body you have, but what you do with it, and how well you can control it. If you have the kind of soul that a carpenter does, you don't have the kind of soul a ruler does; both rulers and ruled might be male or female. We can only tell that some women have the souls of philosopher-rulers if they do what philosopher-rulers do and not what carpenters, say, or male or female slaves do.[15]

IV

Our rendering of Plato's account of the significance of being male or female becomes more complicated if we move beyond the fifth book of the *Republic,* the *Meno,* and aspects of the *Laws.* For the dialogues are very liberally peppered with misogynistic remarks of the most casual and offhand kind. We realize that Plato's proposals in Book V of the *Republic* are surprising not only in light of the sexism of fifth-century Athens, and his inegalitarianism, but especially in light of the sexism otherwise rampant in his own work. So even if Plato's account of the potential equality of men and women is one we could heartily embrace (a point to which we shall return), we nevertheless must admit that his vision of equality is hardly the whole story about women to be found in the dialogues.

Plato routinely tosses off what might appear to be gratuitous remarks about the foibles of womanhood. But these comments almost always function to clarify or make vivid an important philosophical point. As we saw earlier, for the most part he wants to convince us that the soul is much more important than the body: it is to our peril that we let ourselves be beckoned by the rumblings of the body at the expense of the soul. Plato sets out to convince us of this by holding up for our inspection the silly and sordid lives of those who pay too much attention to their bodies and do not care enough for their souls; he wants to remind us of how unruly, how without direction, are the lives of those in whom the lower part of the soul holds sway over the higher part.

Because he can't point to an adulterated soul—they are invisible—he points instead to those embodied beings whose lives are in such disarray that we can be sure their souls are corrupted. And whose lives exemplify the proper soul/body relationship gone haywire? Well, says Plato, look at the lives of women.[16] It is women who get hysterical at the thought of death; obviously, their emotions have overpowered their reason, and they can't control themselves (*Phaedo* 60a, 112d; *Apology* 356). "A woman, young or old or wrangling with her husband, defying heaven, loudly boasting, fortunate in her own conceit, or involved in misfortune or possessed by grief and lamentation" is a dreadful model for a young man—still worse is "a woman that is sick, in love, or in labor" (*Republic* 395d–e). "When in our own lives some affliction comes to us you are aware that we plume ourselves . . . on our ability to remain calm and endure, in the belief that this is the conduct of a man, and [giving in to grief] that of a woman" (*Republic* 605c–d).

To have more concern for your body than your soul is to act just like a woman; hence, the most proper penalty for a soldier who surrenders to save his body, when he should be willing to die out of the courage of his soul, is for him to be turned into a woman (*Laws* 944c).[17] Plato sometimes expresses the belief that souls can go through many different embodied lifetimes. There will be certain indications, in one's life, of the kind of life one is leading; and unless a man lives righteously, he will as his next incarnation "pass into a woman," and if he doesn't live rightly then, he'll become a brute (*Timaeus* 42b–c, 76e, 91a).[18]

The message is that in matters of knowledge, reality, and beauty, don't follow the example of women. They can only be mistaken about those things. In matters of love, women's lives serve as negative examples also. Those men who are drawn by "vulgar" love, that is, love of body for body, "turn to women as the object of their love, and raise a family" (*Symposium* 208e); those men drawn by a more "heavenly" kind of love, that is, love of soul for soul, turn to other men. But there are strong sanctions against physical love between men: physical unions, especially between older and younger men, are "unmanly." The older man isn't strong enough to resist his lust (as in women, the irrational part of the soul has overtaken the rational part), and the younger man, "the impersonator of the female," is reproached for this "likeness to the model" (*Laws* 836e). The problem with physical love between men, then, is that men are acting like women.[19]

It is true that Socrates apparently held at least one woman in very high regard: Diotima.[20] In the *Symposium,* Socrates describes her as being "deeply versed in this [love] and many other fields of knowledge" (201d). But this praise occurs in the context of a discussion from which women have been excluded in order to keep matters on a serious note, in the inquiry in the *Symposium* in which the love of men for women has been referred to—by Diotima among others—without challenge as vulgar and unmanly.

Socrates' reference to Diotima is perhaps of a piece with what he says in Book V of the *Republic* about women who would be philosopher-rulers; it stands in stark contrast to the generous scattering of misogynistic remarks throughout the dialogues. Misogyny has always been compatible with having high regard for "exceptional" (and surely for imaginary) women.

V

It is clear that the contradictory sides of Plato's views about women are in part tied to the distinction he makes between soul and body and the somatophobic lessons he hopes to teach his readers about their relative value. When preaching about the overwhelming importance of the soul, he can't but regard the kind of body one has as of no final significance, so there is no way for him to assess differentially the lives of women and men. But when making gloomy pronouncements about the worth of the body, he points an accusing finger at a class of people with a certain kind of body—a female body—because he regards them as embodying the very traits he wishes no one to have. In this way, women constitute a deviant class in Plato's philosophy. They live the kinds of lives that no one, especially philosophers, ought to live. It is true that Plato chastises certain kinds of men: sophists, tyrants, and cowards, for example. But he frequently puts them in their place by comparing them to women. We've already seen some examples of this, such as the ridicule of homosexuals for their likeness to women. There is a highly polished moral gloss to the soul/body distinction in Plato. A device that brings this moral gloss to a high luster is his holding up, for our contempt and ridicule, the lives of women in order to demonstrate that it makes no small difference whether you lead a soul-directed or a body-directed life.

If one explanation of Plato's apparently contradictory remarks about women is linked to the sharp distinction he makes between soul and body and the ranks he assigns them, a second explanation, paradoxically, is connected to the fact that sometimes the distinction is not so sharp.

Earlier we focused on Plato's insistence that we can't infer anything about a person's soul from the kind of body she or he has. This insistence has to be qualified when we notice that Plato elsewhere treats the soul as having a much closer, indeed an essential, relation to the body, inasmuch as certain states of the soul can only be expressed, or can best be expressed, in particular kinds of bodies. For example, Plato sometimes speaks as if he thought it easily imaginable for a soul of a man to come to inhabit the body of a woman. However, this kind of transformation is regarded as the appropriate turn of events only for the coward or for the man who has not led a righteous life.[21]

Plato seems to be saying—at least in these comments about reincarnation—that there is a fittingness of one kind of soul to one kind of body: the kind of soul you have shows in the kind of body you have, and can't be shown in another kind of body.[22] Or perhaps he is saying that the kind of soul you have *ought* to show in the kind of body you have—souls in the bodies of male soldiers ought to be brave souls—and if there isn't a good fit in this life there will be in the next. What we must notice here is that being stuck in a woman's body can be described as appropriate for a cowardly soul only if Plato believes that courage cannot be expressed in a body of the female form. The bodily medium is crucial to the message about the soul.[23]

I think we are observing here the conjunction of the two criteria said to reveal one's nature, that is, the kind of body one has and the kind of behavior one displays. Plato is implying that if a body is male, we expect certain kinds of behavior from it, for example, brave behavior. Given his general view, this means that if the body is male we expect the soul connected to it to be able to control it in a particular way. If the behavior of a male body is not what we'd expect from a male body, then the soul is not appropriate to that body; it ought really to live in a female body. So while we can't simply deduce from the presence of a male body what kind of soul it has, we can deduce what kind of soul it ought to have, that is, how the body ought to be conducted. This means that at least in these passages from the *Laws* and *Timaeus,* even if not always so clearly elsewhere, Plato is treating souls as if they are gendered—that is, he argues that some kinds of souls are manly, some are womanly; manly souls belong in males, womanly ones in females.

In the *Republic,* Plato makes sure that the expression of courage in women will not be different from the expression of courage in men: he insists that men and women have to *behave* in the same way to show that they are relevantly the same. Every act you perform counts. Your bodily activity is not simply correlated with activity and states of your soul; your bodily activity is the necessary expression of the state of your soul.[24] Doing what a cobbler does cannot be the expression of a soul contemplating the eternal Forms; thus the soul of a philosopher cannot be expressed in the life of a male cobbler. And though it can be expressed in the life of a woman, this is only so long as she acts in particular ways and engages in particular pursuits.

VI

We have been trying to account for Plato's apparently contradictory remarks about women—that they can be counted among the philosopher-rulers; that they lead just the kinds of lives the philosopher-rulers ought to avoid. But there is an alternative hypothesis to the idea that Plato contradicts himself: he uses "woman" ambiguously.

Plato's thinking of people as made up of body and soul allows for at least three different configurations of "woman." The female philosopher-ruler has a female body, but she doesn't have a typically feminine soul—that is, the kind of soul found in the typical Athenian female, a soul unable to resist the temptations of the body, a soul that doesn't know and doesn't care about the difference between appearance and reality. The female philosopher-ruler has a manly soul: the kind of soul that true philosophers have. Similarly, cowardly male soldiers have feminine souls: that is why in their next life they will come back in female bodies. In the examples below, the soul/body configurations described in b, c, and d all represent "woman" in some sense:

a. manly soul/male body:	brave soldier; male philosopher-ruler
b. manly soul/female body:	female philosopher-ruler
c. womanly soul/male body:	cowardly male soldier
d. womanly soul/female body:	typical Athenian woman

We might be tempted to use configuration b to represent the reincarnation of the cowardly soldier: for isn't such a person someone who used to be a man but now is in a woman's body? But d is really the better way to represent the reembodied cowardly soldier: if the soul always really belonged in a female body, it is a feminine or womanly soul. Example c represents a bad fit. We might have hoped that since there was a male body there would be a manly soul, as in a; but if someone with a male body behaves in a cowardly way, this shows that "he" really has a womanly soul. The configuration in b should be reserved for the philosopher-queens, who have a manly soul in a female body.

Part of what is confusing in the idea that there has to be the right "fit" between soul and body is this: if we can tell that there is not a fit between body and soul, then presumably there doesn't have to be a fit in order for us to know what kind of soul a person has. If we can tell that the soldier has a woman's cowardly soul without his having a female body, why is a "fit" necessary? For Plato, we see that the right fit in these cases represents the appropriate punishment for the soldier's cowardice. But we are still left in an epistemological and metaphysical quandary: Despite the demand for a right "fit," there doesn't have to be a male body in order for a manly soul to be recognized, nor does there have to be female body for a womanly soul to be recognized.

This quandary appears in modern dress in Jan Morris's description of the complicated phenomenon of transsexualism. In *Conundrum* (New York: Signet, 1974), Morris insists that "she" had always had a woman's soul housed in a man's body. That she could think about herself in this way suggests that she thought her bodily identity to be neither indicative of nor necessary for her having a particular kind of soul: she "knew," even though she had a male body, that she had a womanly soul. On the other hand, she felt compelled to change her body in order to reveal the gender of her soul.

Morris seems to be saying that while gender identity is more important than sexual identity, a person's sex is the clue others take to his or her gender. Gender systems teach us to expect certain kinds of behavior from persons who have male bodies and other kinds from persons who have female bodies. If our expectations are met, the fit is supposed to be right; if they are not met, the fit is wrong. Though Morris can't be said to be a whole lot like Plato, her example may help us understand what makes Plato's ambiguous use of "woman" possible by reminding us that the existence of gender identities represents the likelihood that not all males will be masculine nor all females feminine.

Plato is indeed revolutionary in his imagining and his valuing the possibility that there are women who are not typically feminine. In contrast, his contempt for the feminine in both its male and female embodiments indicates the extent to which he accepted the sexist stereotypes of the time. The problem with the mass of women, according to Plato, is that they can't become the people male philosopher-rulers are; the problem with the mass of men is that they are too much like most women.

In criticizing men for being feminine, Plato opens up the logical space to think of women as masculine and to praise them for it. However, it is not clear that people must be either masculine or feminine. We have heard nothing about the third class of people in Plato's world, the artisans, farmers, and other producers, who may not be masculine in the way philosopher-rulers are but are not feminine in the way typical Athenian women or cowardly guardians are.

What, then, can we conclude from this about what Plato might have meant when talking about "women"? What he means by "woman" in the fifth book of the *Republic* is quite different from what he means by "woman" elsewhere. Though both kinds of women are females, one kind is a female with a manly soul, the other kind a female with a womanly soul. That is, the one is what could become of a female person if she has a certain nature and is trained in the way of the philosophers; the other is what happens to a female person who hasn't such a nature and does not receive such training.

VII

Plato's claim to being a feminist surely has to do with his holding (1) that a woman's biology ought not to settle the question of her destiny, and (2) that women's intelligence and reason ought to be called upon in the running of the state. He refuses to assume that since women have different bodies than men they must have capacities significantly different from, and inferior to, those of men. According to Plato, not all women are inferior to all men; some women are equal to the best of men, and in fact superior to other men. In the best and most wisely governed state, we can expect to find women as well as men among the ruling class.

As has often been pointed out, Plato is not here relying upon or defending the notion of women's "rights." While the positions to which women will have access along with men are ones that involve great power and authority, every aspect of their lives is shaped to enable them to see and carry out their duties. They are not "free" in a sense very common to modern ears—free to do what they want, free not to have their lives interfered with by the needs and demands of others. As Ernest Barker puts it: "Plato is not a teacher of woman's rights so much as of woman's duties."[25] Or as Julia Annas has remarked: Plato "sees women merely as a huge untapped pool of resources: here are half the citizens sitting at home wasting effort doing identical trivial jobs! . . . Benefit to the state is the sole, frequently repeated ground" for the proposals about women's role in the ideal state.[26] Guardians have a single function: to run the state. From infancy they are to be trained to make sure that they develop the self-control and knowledge necessary for such heavy responsibility. If they are educated as Plato imagines, then in a sense they will be free to do what they want, but only because their desires will be constructed in such a way that they'll want to do exactly what they are supposed to do.

Moreover, part of the shaping of desire among the guardians and auxiliaries is their not wanting to have or own something by themselves: they will have no private property, which means among other things that men will not have their own wives or their own children (*Republic* 464a–b). However, this does not mean that women—even guardian women—cease to be property, or are to be in a position to decide whether or not they wish to be with men or to have children.[27] Women are now common property. Indeed, "more frequent intercourse with the women" will be the honor and prize for young men "who excel in war and other pursuits" (*Republic* 460b).

Nevertheless, Plato's claims are useful for feminists to turn back to, especially when what is claimed to be the wisdom of the ages is thrown against feminist proposals for creating a world in which it would not be assumed that women are the political, social, moral, and intellectual inferiors of men. But we must keep in mind that Plato's argument for the equality of some women to some men was inextricably intertwined with an argument for the superiority of that group of men and women to all other people. He may have refused to assume that biology is destiny, but that does not mean that all ways of ranking people disappear. The equality Plato talks about is only between men and women who would be guardians and philosopher-rulers. He is not talking about equality between slave men and philosopher women, or between slave women and philosopher women. Surely, then, we ought to ask: what kind of feminism is it that would gladly argue for a kind of equality between men and women of a certain class and at the same time for radical inequality between some women and some men, some women and some other women, some men and some other men?

When we emphasize that according to Plato bodily features don't provide grounds for distinguishing between people, we may thereby obscure the fact that he hardly thought that all people were the same "underneath"—indeed, that he didn't think all women were the same "underneath." Plato arrogates to philosopher-rulers the capacity and authority to decide what differences between people matter and why. Anybody can know whether a person is male or female; only philosopher-kings and -queens can tell what a person's soul is really like. This is a very important authority to have—as we saw, some take the exercise of it to be the most crucial task of philosopher-rulers.

Is the kind of power and authority Plato ascribes to philosopher-rulers a kind of power and authority that feminists ought to embrace? Should feminists support the notion that some women ought to be in the business of deciding what kinds of "natures" different kinds of people have and therefore what their best interests are? In order to find out the extent to which some versions of feminism may have more of Plato in them than they might ever have imagined, we need to ask still more questions: Is the authority about the significance of differences among people something that feminists have assumed in analyses of differences among women? How do we know which differences among us are significant and which aren't? Are some women in a better position than others to answer this? If so, how does that authority come to inhere in them? Through some kind of special metaphysical insight such as Plato thought philosopher-rulers had? Through the political contests waged and adjudicated in all the usual places, including academic conferences, publishing houses, and the pages of book reviews?

Notes

1. There is evidence that Pythagoras treated women as the equals of men, but as Sarah Pomeroy argues, "this phenomenon was unique in the Greek world of the sixth and fifth centuries B.C." (*Women in Hellenistic Egypt* [New York: Schocken, 1984], 65). There is considerable debate about the meaning of the portrayal of women in classical literature. See, for example, Sarah B. Pomeroy, *Goddesses, Whores, Wives, and Slaves: Women in Classical Antiquity* (New York: Schocken, 1975); Eva Cantarella, *Pandora's Daughters: The Role and Status of Women in Greek and Roman Antiquity* (Baltimore: Johns Hopkins University Press, 1987); M. R. Lefkowitz, *The Lives of the Greek Poets* (Baltimore: Johns Hopkins University Press, 1981); Martha C. Nussbaum, *The Fragility of Goodness: Luck and Ethics in Greek Tragedy and Philosophy* (Cambridge: Cambridge University Press, 1986).

2. Plato thus inverts what appears to us as a paradoxical situation in the Athenian society of his time: Democratic reforms in Athens in some ways lowered the status of many women (on this, see Pomeroy, *Goddesses, Whores, Wives, and Slaves,* 57–58, and Ellen M. Wood and Neal Wood, *Class Ideology and Ancient Political Theory: Socrates, Plato, and Aristotle in Social Context* [New York: Oxford University Press, 1978], 49–50), but Plato in effect raises the status of some women in the process of constructing a very undemocratic society.

3. Plato has most recently been described as a feminist by Nussbaum in *The Fragility of Goodness,* 4n.

4. For a useful summary of the meaning of "nature" or *phusis,* see Okin, *Women in Western Political Thought,* 51 ff.

5. See G. Vlastos, "Does Slavery Exist in Plato's *Republic?*" *Classical Philology* 63 (1968): 291–95.

6. Plato uses *psuchē* here, which usually is translated as "soul."

7. Soul (*psuchē*) and nature (*phusis*) are different concepts, but as we saw earlier, in the context of the inquiry into whether men and women have different natures, having the same soul settles for Plato the question of whether people have the same nature. See *Republic* 454d.

8. Plato does sometimes speak of a mortal part of the soul; see, for example, *Timaeus* 61d.

9. See G. Vlastos, "The Individual as an Object of Love in Plato," in his *Platonic Studies,* 2d ed. (Princeton: Princeton University Press, 1981), 40: "Body-to-body endearment is one of [the] normal features [of Platonic love], though always subject to the constraint that terminal gratification will be denied."

10. As Nussbaum points out, this message from the *Symposium* (210b ff.) is in effect reassessed in the *Phaedrus* (*The Fragility of Goodness,* 220 ff.)

11. While it is true that sometimes he argues to the effect that it is wasteful not to make use of women's capacities—see, for example, Annas, "Plato's *Republic* and Feminism"—his argument presupposes his being able to see that women have such capacities.

12. See A.W.H. Adkins, *From the Many to the One* (Ithaca: Cornell University Press, 1970), 148: "The whole well-being of the *polis* depends on the ability of the rulers to distinguish these natural kinds."

13. See Erving Goffmann, *Asylums* (Garden City, N.Y.: Anchor Doubleday, 1961): "A basic social arrangement in modern society is that the individual tends to sleep, lay, and work in different places, with different co-participants, under different authorities, and without an over-all rational plan. The central feature of total institutions can be described as a breakdown of the barriers ordinarily separating these three spheres of life. First, all aspects of life are conducted in the same place and under the same single authority. Second, each phase of the member's daily activity is carried on in the immediate company of a large batch of others, all of whom are treated alike and required to do the same thing together. Third, all phases of the day's activities are tightly scheduled, with one activity leading at a prearranged time into the next, the whole sequence of activities being imposed from above by a system of explicit formal rulings and a body of officials. Finally, the various enforced activities are brought together into a single rational plan purportedly designed to fulfill the official aims of the institution" (6). Total institutions are incompatible with the family (11). When spheres of life are "desegregated," a person's conduct "in one scene of activity is thrown up to him . . . as a comment and check upon his conduct in another context" (37).

14. Wood and Wood, *Class Ideology,* 53–54. See also Ernest Barker, *The Political Thought of Plato and Aristotle* (New York: Dover, 1959), 139.

15. While the philosopher-rulers of the *Republic* have to be able to distinguish between the well- and ill-born, the philosophers of the *Theaetetus* wouldn't bother: "whether any fellow citizen is well- or ill-born or has inherited some defect from his ancestors on either side, the philosopher knows no more than how many pints of water there are in the sea" (173d). This

suggests some ways in which the life of a philosopher who is not a ruler is quite different from the life of one who is; we might say that philosopher-rulers have to be interested in the particular historical identity of people in a way that mere philosophers are not.

16. Although Plato objects to certain types of men—sophists, tyrants, and so forth—his disdain for women is always expressed as disdain for women in general and not for any subgroup of women. Moreover, one of the ways he shows his disdain for certain types of men is to compare them to women. Children, slaves, and brutes also sometimes reveal the malfunctioning of the appropriate soul/body relation.

17. In passages like this we see Plato assuming that a certain kind of body implies the presence of a certain kind of soul. This is at odds with his explicit view elsewhere that what is really important about someone is that the person has a soul, no matter what kind of body she has.

18. In the *Phaedo* (82a ff.), Socrates suggests that those who have led wantonly reckless and lawless lives are likely to come back as wolves, hawks, and kites, while those with the "ordinary goodness" of "self-control and integrity . . . will probably pass into some other kind of social and disciplined creature like bees, wasps, and ants, or even back into the human race again, becoming decent citizens."

19. For elaboration on the extent and significance of Plato's misogyny, see Spelman, "Woman as Body: Ancient and Contemporary Views," *Feminist Studies* 1 (1982): 109–31.

20. In the *Menexenus* Socrates also expresses admiration for Aspasia as "an excellent mistress in the art of rhetoric" (235e). But there is serious doubt about whether Plato is the author of this dialogue. Moreover, Diotima may be a fictitious person.

21. In the examples from the *Laws* (944e) and *Timaeus* (42b–c, 91a), there is the suggestion that people are sentenced by the gods; in the Myth of Er at the end of the *Republic,* it is implied that people choose their next lives.

22. As should be clear already, Plato refers to the significance of reincarnation in a number of places throughout the dialogues; he doesn't always include ending up in a female body in his lists. See, for example, *Phaedrus* 248d ff.

23. The point is made less forcefully in the *Laws* (655a), when the Athenian legislator and Clinias agree that "a manly soul struggling with distress and a cowardly soul in the same or equal straits" will not express themselves in similar "postures . . . utterances . . . complexions." Later the Athenian suggests that a soul's "successive conjunction first with one body and then with another" is due to the power and responsibility of a god or gods "to shift the character that is becoming better to a better place, and that which is growing worse to a worser, each according to its due, that each may meet with its proper doom" (903d–e). See also Adkins, *From the Many to the One,* 134.

24. Necessary as long as you are alive; Plato would seem to believe that you don't need it after your soul is separated from your body, in death.

25. Barker, *Political Thought,* 145.

26. Annas, *An Introduction to Plato's "Republic"* (Oxford: Oxford University Press, 1981), 183.

27. In connection with this, see Lynda Lange, "The Function of Equal Education in Plato's *Republic* and *Laws,*" in *The Sexism of Social and Political Theory,* ed. Clark and Lange, 3–15.

6

Why Women Cannot Rule: Sexism in Plato Scholarship

Natalie Harris Bluestone

I

In Plato's *Republic,* the most influential philosophical work ever written, Socrates proposed an ideal society in which superior men and women would rule together equally. The Athenian philosopher thus became, more than twenty-four hundred years ago, the first advocate in human history of a measure of sexual equality. The guardians of his society were to be true philosophers, passionately committed to reason and trained in its rigorous application. Believing that some women possessed the necessary capacity for reason and philosophy, he introduced the then startling proposal that identical leadership roles required identical education for the most capable members of both sexes.

From Aristotle onward, writers and scholars have explored all aspects of Plato's great dialogue on the nature of justice and the just society. Some commentators had even expressed vague enthusiasm for greater civic participation by women. But until recently only a very few bothered to discuss the advisability or feasibility of identical education from earliest infancy for gifted boys and girls. And not until the 1970s has there been a single commentator who wholeheartedly agreed with the Platonic suggestion of identical leadership roles for both genders. In fact, throughout the centuries, Plato's passage on sexual equality has suffered a singular fate; it has been largely dismissed, deplored, or ignored.

In earlier eras, the excision of Plato's discussion of women rulers was deliberate. Modern awareness of the *Republic* begins in the fifteenth century when Marsilio Ficino reintroduced Plato into the mainstream of Western thought by translating all the known dialogues into Latin. Before Ficino, Leonardo Bruni had translated several of the *Dialogues* and the *Letters*, but declined to translate the *Republic.* He feared that its radical ideas, particularly those on women, would upset his readers. This dedicated classicist at least did not underestimate the importance and subversive character of the Platonic suggestions. He found Plato too searching, unconventional, and disturbing. And at a time when very few in the West knew Greek, he made the decision in effect to suppress the *Republic* because he knew its suggestion of the "community of wives" as he put it, would be offensive to his Florentine audience.[1]

Later scholarship, starting with the renewal of serious interest in Plato in nineteenth-century Germany, dismissed the subject of women rulers in a different way. Scholars in the German tradition did not censor Plato where they found his ideas threatening. On the contrary, beginning with Friedrich Schleiermacher's careful early nineteenth-century translations scholars made a conscious commitment to strict objectivity. Philosophers and historians of philosophy returned to the actual Greek texts, seeking to distinguish the authentic views of Plato from those of earlier translators and interpreters. Widespread attempts were made to establish the definitive Greek text, to offer the best translations in many languages, to explicate difficult passages. The ostensible purpose of all these efforts was solely to make clear what Plato really meant.

But in the numerous translations, explications, and "companions" that have continued to appear down to our own day, hostility toward the Platonic suggestion of equality persisted. Unsubstantiated views of women's differences, unexamined assumptions about women's limitations occurred repeatedly. Further, despite their stated aim of complete objectivity in rendering Plato's thought, commentators frequently offered their own beliefs that men and women cannot or should not play the same leadership role in society. In short, on this highly charged issue, objectivity faltered and scholars dealt with Plato's radical proposal for equality with a bias they themselves did not recognize.

This bias, although sometimes glaring, was far more often subterranean and subtle. Most of the commentators whose work I have examined would vociferously deny any outright contempt for women or their abilities. Such disdain is well documented among the Greeks; traces of it appear in Plato himself.[2] But scholars of the last hundred years are far less likely to avow such feelings openly.

Nevertheless, a pervasive, unexamined resistance to the idea of female rule has characterized most nineteenth- and twentieth-century scholarship. Since virtually all scholars had been male, their attitudes no doubt reflected the age-old fact of male dominance in Western society. However, the assumption that it is right for males to rule, carried into philosophic thought, also helped to sustain and even shape the antifemale biases of scholars, educators, and politicians across the generations. The very students who were most likely to speculate freely on fundamental questions and criticize prevalent social practices received no encouragement from the Plato scholars to examine freshly what came to be known as the Woman Question. By downplaying or disregarding Plato's provocative proposals for women rulers, philosophers, whose task it is to question the dominant assumptions, instead reinforced the tendency of the "educated gentleman" to ignore the matter of sexual equality as an important element of justice.

With the advent after 1960 of a new feminist movement and the entry of more women into the field of philosophy, Plato's argument for women rulers has been revived. The commentators of the 1970s and 1980s have made a significant contribution by successfully focusing attention on the long-neglected passage calling for philosopher-queens.[3] They show that Plato's admirers failed to see the inconsistencies in his beliefs about women, and some even expressly desire to dethrone and discredit Plato.[4] Many also recognize the hostility of previous commentators to the suggested reforms. For generations of commentators have perpetuated attitudes, often despite protests to the contrary, which have kept women excluded from the realms of reason, philosophy, and civic authority.

The details of Plato's proposal to include women among the true philosophers appear in Book V of the *Republic* from 449c to 473e. There, Plato's teacher, Socrates, protagonist of the dialogue, presents his listeners with three paradoxical features of his proposed "city of speech." These he describes as the Three Waves of his argument in defense of the arrangements for an ideal polis. The First Wave which threatens to drown his listeners is his suggestion that just as male and female sheep dogs are equally responsible for guarding the flock, so female and male rulers will guard the city, protect it in war and rule it in peace. The fact that there are differences between males and females, that as Plato puts it, the "female bears and the male mounts," is not a difference relevant to the governing of the state.[5] Just as the bald and the long-haired are opposite in one respect, but that respect does not affect their ability as shoemakers, so the differences between men and women are not differences with respect to any art or practice connected to the organization of the city. For Plato, it is true that the class of men excels that of women in all practices; however, many individual women are better than many men in many things. Plato puts it: "There is no practice of a city's governors which belongs to woman because she's woman, or to man because he's man; but the natures are scattered alike among both animals; and woman participates according to nature in all practices, and man in all, but in all of them woman is weaker than man" (445e). Since women and men have the same natures in regard to ruling, they must follow the same practices in preparation for ruling. They must be equally trained in gymnastic and music; this would be what Plato calls "according to nature," whereas the Athenian practice of highly dissimilar education he considers "against nature." For Plato, to reach truly just practices we must understand what is natural as opposed to what is merely conventional, legal, or customary. Women's participation in the gymnastic training that will ensure the necessary physical strength and discipline requires that female guardians must exercise naked in the gymnasium as men do. Although initially this will seem laughable, if properly considered the practice can be seen to be beneficial. In fact, Plato assures his listeners that in the last analysis his entire proposal of equal opportunity for both sexes is both possible and advantageous for the society.

The Second Wave of the Platonic scheme is that male and female guardians are to live communally, eliminating private marriage arrangements and also abolishing what we would call the nuclear family. Children will be raised communally with parents and offspring unaware of the biological connections between them. Marriages are arranged by the state with periodic festivals where temporary unions are consummated. Subtle lots must be fabricated, one of Plato's "noble lies," to assure that citizens will blame chance rather than the rulers for each union. As the offspring are born the task of caring for them will be taken over by the male and female officers designated for this job. With the help of wet nurses and governesses the women will be spared the "wakeful watching" and other labors connected with infancy, making for what Glaucon, Socrates' interrogator, calls an "easy-going kind of childbearing" (460d) for the women guardians.

The offspring must be born of those in their prime, which is between 20–40 for women, 25–55 for men. When the women and men are beyond the age of procreation they are free to have intercourse with whomever they wish with certain exceptions. However, the partners in these unofficial pairings must be especially careful to avoid conceptions. And they must understand that should a fetus force its way into the light of day, "there's to be no rearing for such a child" (473d).

Plato believes that the abolition of private property and of the family will keep the usual causes of dissension, the fighting over money, children, and relatives, from disturbing the tranquillity of his ideal state. His arrangements will promote very strong ties among the rulers. And although they will live simply, they will be rewarded by seeing the preservation of the whole city as well as by the support, prizes, and honors given them by the public.

The Third Wave, the final paradox of Socrates' argument, is that these guardians, men and women alike, must be true philosophers, reaching knowledge of the good through reason and dialectic. Only the rule of such philosopher-guardians can guarantee the welfare of the State. Plato thus calls for the ideal polis to be ruled jointly by philosopher-kings and—if the terminology be properly extended, as it rarely is—philosopher-queens.

This proposal for women guardians has met with overwhelming antipathy throughout the centuries. In an extensive survey of commentaries written in many languages, including French, Spanish, Italian, Russian, Hebrew, German—and English composed in Hong Kong, Canada, England, and the United States—I find repeated rejection of the plan for sexual equality. One of the few works expressing wholehearted sympathy was written in Arabic by the great Islamic philosopher Averroës. We have only a Hebrew translation of his extensive three-part commentary on the *Republic;* but if it is a faithful rendering of the original, Averroës' support for sexual equality is truly astonishing. The Arab thinker, despite the fact that he was a committed Muslim, seems to have been far more open in the twelfth century to the idea of female guardians than some American university professors are in the late twentieth. And even if, as I believe, he was somewhat less consistent and less completely egalitarian in his acceptance of Plato's program than some assert, he was nevertheless remarkably open-minded.[6]

Averroës finds it deplorable that in his own states women who are not being fitted for any of the human virtues often resemble plants. He writes: "In these States the *ability of women is not known* because they are only taken for procreation"[7] (my emphasis). This stands out particularly when compared with the views of the scholars I shall discuss who are quite certain they do know what women's abilities are. Averroës's belief that for Plato "women are essentially on the same level with men in respect of civic activities in the same classes" makes his agreement with the Greek philosopher even more striking.[8] Since he seems mistakenly to have believed that Plato clearly intended that for *every* class men would have intercourse only with women like themselves who had training identical to their own, what the egalitarian Averroës approved was even more far-reaching than what Plato actually proposed. Such enthusiasm for the Platonic proposals is unmatched so far as I can discover in the Western tradition.

The tone of modern Western scholarship is set by Schleiermacher who forcefully expresses his distaste for Plato's abolition of conventional marriage and elevation of women to leadership roles. He writes: "Christian morality . . . introduced into the world the purest idea of marriage, and the most perfect form of domesticity. . . . Plato's view on the contrary misled him . . . to an utter destruction of both; and this is what every individual of sound mind . . . would gladly erase out of his work, even to the very last trace. . . . [H]ere is concentrated all that was mistaken in the development of the Hellenic mind."[9] And in modern commentary from Benjamin Jowett's first influential translations of the *Dialogues* in 1871 for one hundred years this tradition of disdain for the Hellenic "mistake" has persisted.

II

The hostility toward the idea of philosopher-queens can be divided into seven distinguishable categories. I shall concern myself here primarily with the last and most pervasive view, the assumption that because women are biologically different it would be unnatural and therefore wrong for them to rule. First, however, I shall briefly outline the other types of hostility. One group of commentators exhibit a complete neglect of what others in the same period have termed Plato's "radical, even revolutionary" proposals.[10] Writers who might be expected to take a particular interest in such an important social reform, like the Soviet logician who translated the *Republic* into Russian or the left-wing Israeli author of an annotated Hebrew translation, simply fail to comment on the idea of female guardians.[11] Even Karl Popper in formulating his assault on Plato as an enemy of democracy does not find it necessary to mention the Athenian's views on women. It would seem essential for Popper to explain away the prima facie egalitarianism of the proposal for gender equality. But rather than stressing the tokenism of, or contradictions in, the proposed reforms, he simply ignores them completely.[12]

A second group of writers suggest—to a man—that the proposals are undesirable, that women have better things to do. A third group insist that Plato himself didn't really mean what he wrote. They find the suggestions for gender equality unintentional on his part, or unwelcome; or like Leo Strauss or the contemporary translator-commentator Allan Bloom, they see the passages as amusing, Plato's attempt to write comedy.[13] Still other commentators use other methods to explain away Plato's proposals. In the 1930s the Fascist apologist Joachim Bannes actually claims that Hitler has already incorporated Plato's plans for women into the state he envisions in *Mein Kampf!*[14]

A fifth distinct category of commentators make no overt statements of their disapproval of Plato's views, but nevertheless reveal a marked unconscious bias. This bias is apparent in their choice of language to state what Plato said, or in questionable translations from the Greek, or in what seem unwitting misreadings. The well-intentioned Jowett, for example, exhibits a high comedy of Victorian euphemism in his rendering of the line, "then the wives of our guardians will have a fine easy time when they are in the family way."[15] Even when there is meant to be no family, Jowett still cannot bring himself to describe the women as "pregnant," but persists in using "in the family way." The Victorians are not alone in their failure to alter linguistic convention to express the radical nature of Plato's proposal for gender equality. Well into the twentieth century the majority of commentators continue to describe the guardians as a "very small group of carefully chosen men" and to characterize the philosopher-ruler as a "man of quick mind, . . . gentle and just in his dealings with men."[16]

There is a sixth category of interpreters, writing primarily in the first half of this century who specifically describe themselves as "feminists" but end by cautioning women not to "go too far" in their search for equality. In his book *Les idées de Platon sur la condition de la femme* Jean Ithurriague repeatedly expresses his sympathy with women's liberation. He worries, however, that unreasonable ambition might lead women outside their natural paths. A woman is entitled to her rights he says so long as she is not estranged "from the functions that nature and reason reserve for her."[17] Just as Plato did not hide from her "the boundaries that the weakness of her sex sets" the modern liberated woman must know "how to remain within the limits . . . how to remain a woman, mother, wife."[18]

This leads us to the seventh and final group of commentators who since they represent the most common reaction will be my main focus here. These writers contend that in fact the equality, which Plato claims is "according to nature," is on the contrary "unnatural." Critics offer a variety of reasons to support their position. The argument takes many forms, from the well-meaning paternalism of Jowett, to the blatant sexism of Allan Bloom. A few, like Ernest Barker, are aware of the pitfalls of trying to determine what is "natural." Barker admits that though his aim is to interpret Plato *sub specie aeternitatis,* despite the political crisis of the time in which he is writing, his efforts may be only *sub specie temporum suorum.*[19] That is, he is aware of the difficulties of eliminating cultural bias. Nevertheless, the learned Oxford scholar explains that although many may sympathize with the emancipation of women, the fundamental argument which underlies Plato's scheme raises doubts. If the basic difference between men and women is that one begets while the other bears children, it produces a number of other differences "which cut deep."

> The fact of her sex is not one isolated thing in a woman's nature . . . : it colors her whole being. She is by nature the centre of the life of the family. . . . She has by nature a specific function of her own, which she will always refuse to delegate to a crèche, and the long period of growth and the need of nurture of her children (which finds no parallel in the children of "the other animals") will always make the discharge of this function

> the work of a lifetime. The unmarried woman may enter into the open field of the world's activities; the married woman has her life's work ready to her hand.[20]

Thus, what is really natural to women is a lifetime of motherhood. He concludes that the state ought not to abolish maternity but rather to recognize it as a function and a contribution to the community. Through childrearing the woman will take "her station in the common life," and by doing the thing which pertains to her station she will attain to Justice.

In another work, Barker tells us that it is not possible as Plato proposes for men and women to come together merely for sexual intercourse.[21] Given the current divorce rate and the statistics on multiple partners for both sexes in today's America, we can only conclude that his view of what is possible needs alteration. Barker finds Aristotle's more sympathetic treatment of marriage preferable to that of Plato, who he says failed to appreciate "the real nature" of the marriage tie. Aristotle's view of marriage, it will be recalled, is based on the natural domination of the male, as in the master-slave relation. Aristotle considers the female by nature inferior, born to obey and without the ability to be virtuous in the same way as a man.[22] Barker does not, however, allude to this aspect of Aristotle's admittedly more enthusiastic support of private marriages.

Benjamin Jowett also finds Plato's view of what is natural mistaken and offers his own idea of the natural differences between men and women in character and capacity. Jowett's views are not always easy to ascertain since they are only hinted at in the periodic summaries and paraphrases in the margin of his translation of the *Republic.* They can also be inferred from the vagaries of his linguistic usage, as I shall discuss later. But in an interpretive note in his edition of the Greek text, he spells out his ideas about equal education for women and offers a theory about women's true nature.[23]

First, he details four aspects of Plato's proposal which are worthy of attention, that presumably should be considered sympathetically. He phrases them carefully so as to avoid offending his readers and to persuade them that although Plato's views differ from modern, that is, Victorian English ideas of education, they nevertheless have merit. The meritorious aspects he finds are: (1) the consideration of the subject independently of existing practice and with reference solely to sexual differences; (2) the implication that bodily health and strength and the training by which they are achieved are equally necessary for males and females; (3) the belief that both sexes have the same interests and duties and are capable of the same occupations in a degree greater than that allowed by social practice; and (4) the contention that false delicacy is a poor foundation for manners and morals.[24]

But despite the value of these considerations, Jowett decides that Plato has actually made a major error. The error "seems to arise" from the Athenian's failure to consider the other differences "to which the differences in sex give rise"; these are differences "in mind and feeling."[25] The problem is that Plato has forgotten a crucial fact. Jowett quotes with approval from an unidentified source that "women's best education is the training of their children."

Furthermore, Jowett finds that Plato has lost sight of the fact that education is relative to character, and the character of women is necessarily formed by the universal opinion of mankind. Evidently, Jowett loses sight of the fact that Plato considered character only in connection with capacity regardless of the opinion of the multitude. That is, one human being learns quickly, the other less so; one female has the capacity for medicine, another does not. This is the only sense of character relevant in Book V. And it is on the basis of such judgments of individual character that Plato believes the opinions of mankind *ought* to be formed. Exactly what Jowett himself means by the "universal opinion" which forms the character of women is not clear. Throughout history there have been a few who held the opinion that women have the capacity for an education identical to men's, and such opinions have increased markedly in recent years. Presumably then, Jowett would have to admit that as views of women's nature changed, so too would the resultant character itself change.

But Jowett does not seem to allow for this possibility. Difficult as it is to be sure of his precise position, one aspect is entirely clear. Jowett assumes that his view and that of "modern philosophy" is preferable to that of Plato. Women in fact have "equal powers of different qualities" rather than the unequal powers of the same quality that Plato ascribes to them. Woman is not "undeveloped man" as he interprets Plato to have said. Her nature is diverse from man's, and it is therefore natural that she be educated differently.[26]

Unlike Barker, Jowett does not specifically comment on the unnaturalness of the prescribed mating arrangements for the guardians; but he does point out that the prohibited unions would no longer rest on any natural or rational principle.[27] In the interpretations of both thinkers two distinguishable but related issues regarding what is natural arise. There is (1) the question of "woman's nature" and its necessary consequences, and (2) the question of whether the monogamous (or perhaps more accurately, moderately polygamous, or "double standard") family is "natural." On both issues, the view of the eminent classicist K. J. Dover, who has taken the issue of Greek homosexuality out of its Victorian closet, has much appeal. Dover declares himself unwilling to engage with any enthusiasm in debates about the naturalness or unnaturalness of human behavior. He observes that any community encourages behavior which it regards as possibly conducive to an eventual situation of a kind desired by that community. It discourages behavior which seems likely to hinder the development of such a situation.[28]

I agree with Dover that the absence of any clear correlation between "natural" and "desirable" is self-evident. Rape and homicide are species-typical in men and orangutangs; in the sense that they occur regularly, they might then be described as natural to these species, but not to other "lower" animals where such behavior never occurs. Few, however, would argue that rape and homicide are therefore desirable. Nor could Plato's commentators defend their use of "natural" as meaning descriptive of a statistical majority of known cases in man's history. The majority of male humans that have lived thus far have died before their seventieth year; this too cannot be seen as ipso facto desirable.

Despite obvious ambiguities of the term, commentators throughout the period under discussion have automatically assumed that their readers would understand what they meant by natural. They have repeatedly attempted to equate the natural with the desirable, or at the very least, by labeling a situation "unnatural" to convince us automatically of its impossibility or undesirability.

A typical example of this procedure occurs in the work of the well-known Victorian Platonist, Walter Pater, who opposes Plato's views on both issues, that of women's nature and of marriage. He forthrightly opposes the Platonic view of women's leadership role and informs us that such modifications of married life would "deprive mothers of that privacy of affection regarding which the wisdom of Solomon beamed forth."[29] On the one hand, he complains that Plato would be dealing with humans in the same manner as a breeder of birds or dogs. The plan is a "strange and forbidding experiment" or so it should seem to us from the vantage point of "laws now irrevocably fixed on these subjects by the judgment of the Christian church."[30] Pater does not even attempt to answer Plato's contention that despite the conventions of the day, the sharing of rule by men and women actually preserves the natural relations of the sexes. Instead, he merely states without argument that female equality and identity of role are "altogether out of harmony with the facts of man's nature."[31] (By "man's nature" he of course means "woman's nature," that is, man in the generic sense.)

A later English philosopher, Bernard Bosanquet, is more sympathetic in principle than Pater to the need for similar education for males and females. He writes that the fact that the Greek household was almost Oriental in its seclusion of women makes Plato's revolutionary demands for women understandable.[32] Bosanquet doesn't find it surprising that Plato wanted to put an end to the Greek family because it was, he says, "a wretched institution." But his final word on the subject is the familiar refrain. On the matter of the lack of difference between the sexes except for the fact that one is weaker, he writes with careful phrasing that "we may be disposed to think that in this he was blind to essential facts of human nature."[33]

A. E. Taylor agrees that Plato is unaware of the true nature and purpose of human sex differences. He explains Plato's blindness by suggesting that Socrates' treatment of sex in the *Republic,* like that of all non-Christian moralists, involves an underestimation of the significance of sex for the whole of the spiritual life. Taylor assumes that the impulses of sex and family affections are for humans intrinsically, that is, naturally, connected. Natural sexual impulses, Taylor concludes, are subjected to much severer restraints in Plato's state than in any which has ever been adopted by a Christian society.[34] The intolerable severity and self-denial are the chief reasons that Plato's scheme is unfeasible. (As a male Christian moralist, Taylor's interests, unlike those of the present writer, cause him to overlook entirely that Plato grants almost complete sexual freedom to women over forty.)

Taylor makes no attempt whatsoever to compare Plato's proposals with the actual sexual satisfactions of the upper-class Greek wife. Demosthenes' often noted view of fourth-century Greek women, even if it is only one possible account of their status, is relevant here: "We have hetairai for pleasure, concubines for our day-to-day physical well-being, and wives in order to beget legitimate children and have trustworthy guardians of our households."[35] This clearly does not present a picture of extensive physical and consequent spiritual satisfaction for wives to be contrasted with the self-denial of Plato's ideal society. It is true that what women thought or experienced at this time comes almost entirely from literature written by men. Therefore, it is difficult to make reliable comparisons between the sexual satisfactions open to women in classical Athens as compared to those offered by nineteenth-century Christianity. Nevertheless, we have little reason to believe that throughout the centuries the ideal of Christian marriage has guaranteed more sexual satisfaction, for women at any rate, than actual Greek practices or Plato's reforms.

Taylor is also sure that the view of differences between the sexes which causes Plato to extend the duties of warfare and statesmanship to women is erroneous. He says Plato is wrong about sexual distinctions affecting the individual only in respect to procreating—and what Taylor includes as Platonic—to rearing a new generation. Here, this careful scholar actually uncharacteristically misreads Plato. In the *Republic,* only the bearing is admitted as a relevant sexual distinction. The *trophe,* rearing, or upbringing of the children is alterable; and as Taylor surely knows, the raising of new generations will be communal in the ideal state. It seems to have been hard for him to accept that Plato did not automatically assume, as he himself does, that children's upbringing is by nature a female task. For Taylor reproduction and child care are both natural to women, and these distinctions profoundly affect the rest of their functioning. Women cannot be soldiers or political leaders because sexual distinction "goes deeper and modifies the whole spiritual life profoundly."[36]

It is striking that scholars whose interpretations make the Platonic text vital and comprehensible in many respects, are so much less careful when dealing with matters of female equality. It has been suggested that there is no topic in classical studies except that of homosexuality on which a scholar's normal ability to perceive differences and draw inferences is so easily impaired. Only on the subject of homosexuality is a writer "so likely to be thought to have said what he has not said or to be charged with omitting to say something which he has said several times."[37] But I contend that the subject of women's nature and role provides as great a tendency to misread, misquote, and suspend the usual standards of evidence.

Taylor, like most other commentators, feels no obligation to offer evidence for the way in which sexual differences necessarily alter women's consciousness or consciences. In general, none of the commentators find it necessary to offer biological, historical, or anthropological data to support their view that, in the modern vernacular, "anatomy is destiny." Even men writing in the 1960s and 1970s do not attempt to provide evidence. Nor do commentators entertain the possibility of suspending judgment on women's true nature until more information is available.[38] A scholar as intent on objectivity as Taylor proclaims himself to be in his preface, might in 1926 have called for more investigations on the actual connections between gender and psychic characteristics. He suggests that the historical Socrates was influenced in his views on female emancipation by the existence of women like Pericles' mistress Aspasia who was famous for her intellectual attainments. He, however, does not seem to have been influenced by the attainments of Queen Elizabeth. Nor do most of the other writers who disparage women's abilities for leadership find it necessary to account for modern female parliamentarians and even heads of state who somehow, contrary to female nature, manage to display equal aptitude for statesmanship.

One of the most blatant distortions of Plato's view of what is natural occurs in the comments of a Canadian rabbi, Solomon Frank, in his study of Plato's theory of education. Like Pater, he makes the unself-conscious assumption that what he approves will be generally accepted as both desirable and natural. Frank uses as his chief source for Plato's theories the *Laws,* which contain the modified views of Plato's later years. These views constitute advantageous regulations for an actual Greek state rather than a description of what would be best in an ideal state. Although even in this latter book Plato advances reforms which would provide for more equitable treatment and use of the resources of half of the human race, his radical plan for complete equality is not sustained. But even in discussing the arrangements in the *Laws,* Frank superimposes his own opinions without even a minimal attempt to guard against seeing Plato through the presuppositions of a twentieth-century conservative Canadian religious educator. In his paraphrase, he speaks of the stages of a girl's life as "maid, wife, mother, and matron" with no prototype for this division in Plato's texts at all.[39] The main emphasis of his discussion, which largely ignores the topic of education in the *Republic,* is on the contrast between expert and amateur in male and female training. Plato, he tells us, believes that women should learn some of the same things boys do, but always in an "amateurish spirit" in distinction from the boys' expertise in such matters, for example, military drill. I am not suggesting that there is absolutely no basis for this distinction in Plato's *Laws.* However, to write as if this were all

Plato had to contribute to the subject of women's education is to downplay the ideals of the *Republic* to such an extent as to distort Plato's total views.

It is worth quoting in its entirety the footnote in which Frank attempts to deal with what he admits might be considered contrary to his interpretation of Plato's sole view of the connection between women and warfare. This footnote is a striking illustration of the way in which prejudice can interfere with our reading of important philosophical texts, as well as with the disinterested consideration of what is best for society. Frank writes: "It is thus only women with a natural turn for warlike pursuits who are to be selected and educated for this function; and *at that,* they are allotted the less heavy duties of military life (457) and are 'never to violate, but always to preserve, the natural relation of the sexes.' " (466).[40]

Frank intends this final quote from Plato to convince us that the "natural relation" for the Athenian philosopher, as for Rabbi Frank, is that even if girls did participate in war, they must be protected, as nature dictates, by their superior, expert menfolk. The reference given is to line 466d in the *Republic.* In fact, in that line Plato says exactly the opposite of what Frank intends. Having based his entire argument on *physis,* what is genuinely natural, rather than *nomos,* the merely conventional, Plato in this passage (only part of which is quoted by Frank) clearly restates that men and women should pursue the same tasks. Both when they are staying in the city and going out to war, they must guard and hunt together like dogs. He then puts it unequivocally that *by* doing this (Bloom translates "in doing this," but the meaning is the same), they are doing nothing contrary to the nature of the female in her relationship to the male, "nothing contrary to the natural community of the two with each other."[41]

The generous interpretation of Frank's misreading is that in his zeal to preserve the conventional relation of the sexes, as formulated in Jewish law and custom, he finds it hard to face that Plato genuinely stated the contrary. The fact, however, is that in this passage Plato is asserting precisely that since other animals share in aggression and ruling, such joint participation is in fact natural.

Leo Strauss, a highly influential commentator and a frequent target of feminist attacks in the 1970s, attributes crucial importance to this Platonic claim that joint rule would be natural. But unlike others who see it as a forerunner of modern egalitarian programmes, Strauss considers it

Plato's way of showing us that the just city could never come into being. Regardless of what Socrates actually says, Plato's real intention was for us to recognize that his utopia was ultimately unrealizable.

At least Strauss sees that a revolutionary change would be required to fulfill Plato's scheme. And he finds that no matter how desirable, in the final analysis such reforms are unnatural; and therefore a just society in Plato's sense is impossible. Strauss himself accepts Plato's framework for discussing the good of societies and concludes with a realization that is intended to move us with its tragic overtones. The just city cannot come into being because absolute communism and the equality of the sexes—and that is the precise phrase he uses—"are *against* nature."[42]

Allan Bloom follows Strauss in his reasoning on the unnaturalness of the proposals. His views, too, have been subject to much criticism and controversy, and it would take us too far afield here to deal adequately with the objections to female equality which he reiterates in his defense and rejoinders to the attacks made on him. It is important to point out, however, that he joins the voices of those like Taylor and Strauss who condemn Socrates for "forgetting the importance of the body."[43] Only on the precondition of such "forgetting" could Plato have made such a proposal. For if he had considered the body and its needs correctly, he could have seen that the differences between men and women are far more crucial than Socrates allows.

Bloom also finds Plato's abolition of the family unsatisfactory. For the family, by which he evidently means our current Western notion of a nuclear family, is "surely somehow natural."[44] The father, if he is anything, is the one who engenders the child. The strength of what Anna Freud has called "psychological parenting," so that in her view the parent is not necessarily the one who contributes the sperm but the one who nurtures the child emotionally, is not even considered. Nor does he consider animal evidence. We know there are biological species where there is no parental investment in the offspring, as well as animals where the young are cared for by what we would call foster parents. I am not suggesting that animal data is ultimately decisive. However, any commentator in the 1960s who wishes to pronounce on the naturalness of parental feeling, and therefore on the impossibility of communal rearing for males at least—he mentions only fathers—might be expected to adduce anthropological or biological information to support his view. Instead, his assumptions are baldly stated; he appeals evidently to common sense.

An interesting contrast to Bloom written at approximately the same time is a little-known commentary written in Hong Kong. I include this study because the fact that it is addressed to students culturally different from the audience of the other commentators requires a less dogmatic approach to the naturalness of any given kind of family. N. E. Fehl's *Guide to the Study of Plato's Republic* is addressed to Chinese students at Chung Chi College to whom he declares, "Plato is our contemporary here within these green hills so close to the border [*sic*] of China."[45] His analysis revolves much less around what is natural and relies much more on the varying arrangements that have actually existed. He discusses how the family types in ancient China differed from those of fourth-century Athens and points to the similarity between the Greek schema and the Hindu caste system. He also describes the varying foundations of marriage in what he calls tribal and religious societies, the difference between the Catholic and Protestant views of the purposes of sexual union.

Fehl's own view is hard to determine because of the question and answer format he uses to stimulate students. The importance of his discussion, however, is that unlike Taylor, Strauss, Bloom, and others, he cannot call upon an assumed unanimity or self-evidence for his own views about mating, incest, and the importance of the body. He can still, however, assume certain shared assumptions about the preeminence of the male sex. So he tells his Chinese theological students at a Christian college that just as Eve was an afterthought of Yaweh, so women and the family are dealt with in a parenthesis in Plato's dream of the ideal society.[46] This disparaging of the issue no doubt has as much to do with Fehl's own bias as it does with a correct interpretation of the text.

On the other hand, his anthropological perspective, with its emphasis on the typology of family structures, leads him to consider seriously Plato's alternatives. Fehl distinguishes three types of family: the consanguine, the conjugal, and the communal. The first, which Plato took for granted, consists of a large family which includes not only parents and children, but grandparents and the male descendants of the grandparents and their wives and children. This was also the structure of ancient China and was in fact an obstacle to the development of a strong central government. Fehl sees Plato as suggesting another kind of family which he calls the communal. The third alternative, what he terms the conjugal family, where the structure is centered in the ego-spouse relation, he seems to agree with contemporary radical feminists is undesirable.

This conjugal family is the modern urban family in which frequently both mother and father are employed away from home. This type may be a necessity of urban industrial society, he states, using Hong Kong, I assume, as his model. Fehl asks whether this urban nuclear family is not worse than Plato's suggestion.[47] He thus implies that no one kind of family is more "natural" than another. As we have seen, this is not the view of the majority of the commentators from 1870 to 1970. The pervasive attitude is rather the one expressed by Desmond Lee in the introduction to his frequently reissued translation. He tells us that both the desirability and the very possibility of exact similarity of role are questionable: "To sweep aside the physiological differences as unimportant and ignore the psychological differences they *entail* is to be in danger of ignoring women's special excellences"[48] (my emphasis). He warns that if you merely expect women to do the same things as men, they are likely, as Plato in effect said, to end up as inferior men. Is it not better to recognize the difference rather than pretend it does not exist, he asks.[49]

This solicitous concern that women might "end up" as lesser men, a concern shared by Jowett and others, has persisted into the 1980s. The important issue here is the dogmatism of Lee's final formulation. For the chain beginning with the suggestions that differences "cut deep," are profound, alter women's entire being, and several other metaphorical expressions alluding to women's diverse abilities, ends with a conviction of logically entailed consequences of biology. Lee gives us no hint of what those special excellences are which Plato denies women to possess. Nor does he expand on how female physiology inevitably produces psychological differences, nor why these differences exclude women from a leadership role.

The commentators we have been dealing with all share the assumption that women's nature is ascertainable, that it is other than Plato describes it. They all find the proposals of Book V in some sense unnatural and use this either as an automatic justification for the undesirability of gender equality or at the very least as strong evidence against its advisability Twenty-four hundred years ago Plato realized that it would be a struggle to convince his male audience to consider seriously the potential of half the human race. As I have shown, the tradition of Plato studies illustrates just how difficult that struggle has been. Fortunately today, despite women's continued powerlessness, many female and male scholars are at last offering wholehearted support for Plato's argument in favor of women as political and intellectual leaders.

Notes

1. Bruni, *Epistolae,* lx, 4. "Multa sunt in iis libris abhorrentia a moribus nostris, quae pro honore Platonis tacere satius est, quam proferre." Quoted in G. Holmes, *The Florentine Enlightenment: 1400–1450* (New York, 1969), 114. Even three centuries later H. Spens in the first translation of the *Republic* into English in 1763 exhibits the same attitude. R. Gannett remarks in his preface to the reissued edition that in Spen's analysis, "the delicate question of the community of women is evaded." H. Spens, *Republic of Plato* (London, 1906), xi.

2. For an account of Greek misogyny see, for example, Sarah Pomeroy, *Goddesses, Whores, Wives, and Slaves: Women in Classical Antiquity* (New York, 1975). M. R. Lefkowitz and M. B. Fant present excellent documentary evidence of Greek attitudes. They provide numerous examples including an excerpt from Aristotle's will (taken from Diogenes Laertius) to show that "restrictions of women's rights to own property and to determine the course of their own lives" illustrate the Athenian male's low estimation of females' capabilities and general value (*Women in Greece and Rome* [Toronto, 1977]), 19. Plato uses the adjective "womanish" to mean "without courage" and in the *Timaeus* myth offers a punishment for a man who has lived an immoral life that he be reborn as a woman. Although scholars do not agree on the extent to which the myths represent Plato's true views, the psychoanalyst H. Kelson believes that the myths reveal that Plato "recognizes in the masculine principle the good, and in the feminine the evil." Hans Kelson, "Platonic Love," *American Imago* 3 (April 1942): 14. See also Dorothea Wender, "Plato: Misogynist, Paedophile, and Feminist," *Arethusa,* 6, no. 1 (1973).

3. My discussion here treats only commentators writing before this period. In *Women and the Ideal Society: Plato's "Republic" and Modern Myths of Gender* (Amherst: University of Massachusetts, 1987), I deal extensively with the great outpouring of articles and book chapters after 1972 on gender equality in Plato. Among the best are those by Julia Annas, "Plato's Republic and Feminism," *Philosophy* 51 (1976); Brian Calvert, "Plato and the Equality of Women," *Phoenix* 29, no. 3 (1975); Susan Okin, *Women and Western Political Thought* (Princeton, 1977); Christine Pierce, "Equality: *Republic,* V," *Monist,* 57 (1973): 1–11.

4. Jean B. Elshtain entitles her section on Plato and women "Divine Plato, Down to Earth" and attempts to set his feminist defenders straight. See *Public Man, Private Woman* (Princeton, 1981).

5. 454e. All quotations are from Allan Bloom's translation, *The Republic of Plato, with Interpretive Essay* (New York, 1968).

6. *Averroës Commentary on Plato's Republic,* ed. E.I.J. Rosenthal (Cambridge, 1966). Rosenthal here stresses Averroës's regret that no proper use is made of women in the service of the community. See also his "The Place of Politics in the Philosophy of Ibn Rushd," *Bulletin of the London School of African Studies* 15, no. 2 (n.d.), 252. In my view the fact that Averroës in his explication of Plato introduces such ideas as "melodies are perfect if men invent them and women perform them" (454) suggest that his egalitarianism, though remarkable, is not so total as Rosenthal maintains. For no matter how important and necessary performance is, invention—the male activity—is surely superior.

7. *Averroës,* 451e, 9, p. 166.

8. *Averroës,* 454, p. 166.

9. F.E.D. Schleiermacher, *Introductions to the Dialogues of Plato* (New York, 1973), 379.

10. This is B. Bosanquet's view. In *The Education of the Young in the Republic of Plato* (Cambridge, 1900), 11, he speaks of "the violence of the revolution" which Plato advocated.

11. V. F. Asmus, ed., *Platon: Sochinenia v Trekh Tomakh Tom 3 Chast I* (Moscow, 1971), 606. Asmus comments on the divergence between Plato's abolition of private property and the Marxist "scientific" rather than utopian view; but despite the Soviet lip service to egalitarian gender reforms, he makes no comment on female leadership. Z. Diesendruck, writing in the late 1930s in what was then Palestine refers in his introduction to the current importance of Plato in the face of the "sinking of human culture." But he makes no comment on the suggestion for equality of the sexes despite the fact that the kibbutz system was founded on just such joint leadership. Nor does he bother to note any similarity between the original settlers' provision of communal child care and the Platonic proposal for communal rearing. See *The Republic: Translated into Hebrew With Introduction and Notes* (Tel Aviv, 1953), 3 (Gimel).

12. Popper finds the *Republic* without any redeeming humanitarian features and accuses Plato of wanting to return "to the tribal *patriarchy* of the time before the Fall." *The Open Society and Its Enemies* (London, 1945), 307 (my emphasis).

13. Strauss introduces the thesis that Plato's proposals are "manifestly akin" to the comedy of Aristophanes' *Ecclesiazusae* (*Assembly of Women*), *The City and Man* (Chicago, 1964), 61. Bloom takes up this view, emphasizing that the whole book "*can only be understood* as Socrates' response to his most dangerous accuser, Aristophanes." Plato is trying to produce "a comedy which is more fantastic, more innovative, more comic" (*Republic, Interpretive Essay*), 381 (my emphasis). This would mean that almost everyone from Aristotle on has failed in their understanding. Bloom rejects all scholarship which denies that Plato is alluding to the very different comedy by Aristophanes in which there is role reversal, that is, the women rule men. In my *Women and the Ideal Society: Plato's Republic and Modern Myths of Gender* (Amherst, 1987), I deal at length with Bloom's contention that the idea of women leaders is clearly a joke.

14. *Hitlers Kampf and Platons Staat* (Berlin, 1933).

15. *The Dialogues of Plato* (Oxford, 1875), 3:62.

16. Charles Bakewell, in his introduction to *Plato: The Republic* (New York, 1928), xli.

17. *Les idées de Platon sur la condition de la femme* (Parts, 1931), 154 (my translation).

18. Ibid.

19. *Greek Political Theory: Plato and His Predecessors* (London, 1947), vi. He refers to the 1914–17 World War which was taking place as he wrote.

20. *Greek Political Theory,* 261. In the same vein he wrote that the fact of a woman's sex colors her whole being; "it makes her able indeed to inspire noble enthusiasms, but not to direct a policy or drill a regiment as Plato would require his woman-ruler or woman soldier to do." *The Political Thought of Plato and Aristotle* (New York, 1959), 148. Werner Jaeger has a similar view and notes that Plato "does not expect as we should do" that women "will make their creative contribution to the community through family life." *Paideia* (London, 1943), 2:244.

21. *Political Thought of Plato and Aristotle,* 244. This is an earlier, longer version of *Greek Political Theory.*

22. See, for example, *Politics* 125b. "The male is by nature superior, and the female inferior, and the one rules, and the other is ruled. This principle, of necessity, extends to all mankind." See also 1259b, 1260a.

23. The explanatory comment on *Republic* 452c appears in the annotated edition begun in the 1860s that Jowett did not live to complete. It was published after his death as B. Jowett and L. Campbell, eds., *Plato's Republic: The Greek Text,* with notes and essays (Oxford, 1894).

24. *Plato's Republic: Greek Text,* 3:215–16.

25. *Greek Text,* 216. His wording here is ambiguous and I am not certain I have correctly interpreted his statement that Plato did not consider "the other differences to which the difference of sex gives rise in mind and feeling." He may be referring only to the fact that biological differences cause men to *think* and *feel* differently about each sex. On this alternative interpretation women's differences would not be innate but rather universally acquired.

26. *Greek Text,* 216. Jowett identifies Plato's view with the line "woman is the lesser man," which he quotes merely from "the poet." The unidentified line is no doubt from A. Tennyson's "Locksley Hall"; but, considering the context, the British poet's view is actually more reminiscent of the misogyny of Socrates' audience. For in the lines immediately preceding Jowett's quote, Tennyson describes women thus: "Nature made them blinder motions/bounded in a shallower brain." *The Poetical Works of Alfred Lord Tennyson* (Boston, n.d.), 60.

27. *Republic,* introduction and analysis, in *The Dialogue of Plato,* trans. into English, 3d ed. (Oxford, 1892), lxxxix. He does comment in *Greek Text,* 234, on the singular nature of "the infrequency of the opportunity for nuptial intercourse."

28. *Greek Homosexuality* (New York, 1978), 154.

29. *Plato and Platonism* (London, 1910), 257.

30. *Platonism,* 248.

31. Ibid. He does not deny that the proposals are consistent with animal "nature"; in fact, he sees the family arrangements as "a movement backwards, to a barbarious or merely animal grade of existence" (257). And he says of women guardians that if we see them as a reinstatement of the Amazon we must condemn them as "a survival from a half-animal world," which adult reason has long since overcome (259).

32. *Education in the Republic,* 11.

33. *A Companion to Plato's Republic* (London, 1925), 182.

34. *Plato: The Man and His Work* (New York, 1956), 278.

35. Demosthenes, lix, 122. Dover insists we cannot consider this *the* decisive fourth-century view. See *Greek Popular Morality in the Time of Plato and Aristotle* (Berkeley and Los Angeles, 1974), 14.

36. *Plato: Man and Work,* 278.

37. *Greek Homosexuality,* vii.

38. This was the view of John Stuart Mill writing in the 1860s. He denied that "anyone knows, or can know, the nature of the two sexes, as long as they have only been seen in their present relation to one another." We cannot possibly know the capabilities of women, he says, because "most of them have never been called out." His discussion at this point is still stirring and applicable today. See "The Subjection of Women," in *The Feminist Papers,* ed. Alice S. Rossi (New York, 1974), 203, 204. Richard Jenkyns thinks Plato's "striking feminism" must have encouraged Mill and perhaps guided him, but provides no evidence for this speculation. *The Victorians and Ancient Greece* (Cambridge, 1980), 230.

39. In R. C. Lodge, *Plato's Theory of Education,* with an appendix on the education of women according to Plato, by Rabbi Solomon Frank (London, 1947).

40. *Theory of Education,* 307.

41. *Republic,* Bloom trans., 466d, p. 146.

42. *The City and the Man* (Chicago, 1964), 127.

43. *Republic, Interpretive Essay,* 382.

44. *Republic,* 385.

45. *A Guide to the Study of Plato's Republic* (Hong Kong, 1961), 1.

46. *Guide,* 50.

47. *Guide,* 53.

48. *The Republic,* trans. with introduction (London, 1974), 47.

49. In all this litany of hostility to identical roles for women three scholars stand out as notable exceptions. One is George Grote, the distinguished historian and pupil of Bentham, who summarizes Plato's views sympathetically and accurately. See *Plato and the Other Companions of Socrates* (London, 1888), 4:170–206 passim. Another, Theodor Gomperz, who vigorously applauds Plato for recognizing women's unused capacities, and writes at the turn of the century that women's presumed inferiority may well be due to "the pressure of unfavorable circumstances rather than to any deficiency of talent." *Greek Thinkers* (London, 1905), 3:126. The third exception is Adela Adam, the only female to write about the proposals before the New Wave of commentators in the 1970s. Writing in 1913 she uses the term "philosopher-queens" so far as I can determine for the first time. But even she assumes that only "gifted women" (as her better known scholar-husband first described Plato's elite females) would be interested in roles equal in status to men. And she makes no objection to what she calls Plato's "half-unconscious" reservation of certain duties for women. Nursing and social welfare are the kind of jobs that she predicts will always absorb the energies of most women. Nevertheless she praises Plato for seeing "that the work of bearing children to uphold the State . . . cannot possibly occupy a woman's whole life." *Plato: Moral and Political Ideals* (New York, 1913), 131.

Part Two

Plato and the Feminine

Introduction

> When she saw us she uttered a cry and burst out in true feminine fashion. . . . Socrates turned to Crito and said: "Crito, let someone take her home."
>
> —(*Phaedo* 60a)

I begin the second part of this book with Page duBois's "The Platonic Appropriation of Motherhood" (from her *Sowing the Body: Psychoanalysis and Ancient Representations of Women* [Chicago: University of Chicago Press, 1988]), which refocuses the discussion of Plato's feminism by shifting attention from Plato's treatment of women to the role of the feminine in the Platonic metaphysic. DuBois's book is devoted to uncovering and analyzing an important moment in the "conception of woman." It is duBois's position that the pre-Platonic metaphysic included an image of woman as wholly other than man, whereas by the time of Aristotle there had occurred a shift in the metaphysic such that woman came to be seen as like man, but inferior. DuBois argues that Plato's texts are at the crux of this transition.

DuBois further contends that the pre-Platonic image of woman as other is grounded in reproductive imagery. Woman's difference from man is located in her reproductive capacity, referred to in terms of images such as fertile fields and plowed furrows. DuBois argues that Plato participates in a "change in the situation of the female in the world" through his appropriation of reproductive metaphors (page 140).

Rather than the *Republic* and the *Laws*, duBois analyzes the *Phaedrus*, *Theaetetus*, and *Symposium* to show that Plato reinscribes the reproductive power of woman onto the male philosopher. In these dialogues, Plato characterizes philosophy as a seductive and erotic search for truth, and depicts the philosopher as a lover, inseminator, fertile field, and midwife, thereby blurring the separation between feminine and masculine and appropriating the power of reproduction for the male philosopher.[1] In a sense, duBois's analysis can be viewed as an inverted mirror image of Arlene W. Saxonhouse's concerns. While Saxonhouse attends to the implications of denying women their reproductive roles, duBois examines the same denial in terms of symbolic appropriation.

DuBois asks us to attend not to the absence of women in these texts, but to the presence of the female through mimesis, particularly in the person of Socrates who is cloaked in the mantle of the female.[2] Plato's Socrates is the midwife, whose speech feminizes young men. He is Bacchante, who speaks the words of women. DuBois argues that this veiled Socrates arises out of Plato's desire to reinscribe the powers of the female within the male in order to engender a purely masculine reproduction giving rise to offspring of the mind rather than the body. This symbolic generation confers to the philosopher a prominence that transcends the significance of the reproductive labors of women and carries with it a new description of sexual difference in which "the female, stripped of her metaphorical otherness, becomes a defective male, defined by lack" (page 155).

Wendy Brown's analysis provides an interesting counterpoint to duBois's interpretation. Like duBois, Brown calls attention to the presence of the feminine within the Platonic conception of truth and the person of the philosopher. However, Brown does not see the presence of the feminine as having any bearing on women, not even upon the metaphysical conception of woman. She argues rather that Plato employs feminine traits in describing truth and wisdom in order to criticize and reject the masculine ethos of Greek ontology and epistemology. Brown notes that Plato's effeminization is selective. The traditional masculine virtues of temperance, courage, and justice, for example, are not called into question. It is only in the realms of the political and the epistemological that Plato attempts to subvert the masculine.

Brown would have us see the ascription of reproductive abilities to the philosopher as a part of Plato's attempt to redefine the pursuit of knowledge as an erotic endeavor caused by and leading to the same types of frenzied passion found in one who is possessed by love. Plato transforms truth into a woman not because of a desire to appropriate the power of women, but because of his need to redefine wisdom as going beyond reason into the realm of inspired possession.

But if our images of wisdom must be reconceived, so too must our conception of the philosopher be transformed. The lover of wisdom must eschew the ethos of manhood that would dictate Sophistic speech and agonistic political action and don instead the mantle of the feminine. Thus we find Brown, like duBois, directing our attention to the feminization of Socrates. The question raised by the juxtaposition of these two articles is whether the presence of the feminine in Plato's texts should be viewed as an appropriation of the powers of women or an attempt to subvert the dominance of masculine values and discourse.

Any attempt to answer this question would have to involve a close analysis of Plato's *Symposium.* Through the figure of Diotima and her theory of love as invoked by Socrates, Plato draws a complicated web of connections between wisdom and the feminine. It is to the figure and words of Diotima that Luce Irigaray and Andrea Nye turn their attention. Plato scholars have often debated the question of why Plato presents his discourse about eros through the figure of a woman, the question being raised as to whether Diotima's gender is an accidental fact, unconnected to her teaching, or a condition of her doctrine.[3] Both Irigaray and Nye see Diotima's gender as essential to understanding Diotima's philosophy and Plato's use of her voice.

Irigaray's reading of the *Symposium* offers various perspectives on the figure of Diotima. There is, on the one hand, the Diotima whose dialectical teaching rests upon the notion of the intermediary in which the opposition between two terms is resolved through the disclosure of a third term, an intermediary, "that is already there and that permits progression" (page 181). This Diotima depicts love as the mediator between ignorance and knowledge, but a mediator that is not abolished in the dialectic, but rather evolves. Irigaray presents this Diotima as providing an alternative to the masculine ethos. This Diotima emphasizes the connections between terms, rather than a destructive synthesis that undoes the closure of opposing terms and that calls our certainty into question and replaces it with love.

But Irigaray also calls our attention to a Diotima whose method changes, who substitutes an image of love as a means to immortality rather than a mediary. This Diotima's love becomes fixed in the character of the beloved, no longer the fluid evolution of the lover of the other Diotima. This Diotima looks to the child, the act, the beautiful for immortality, no longer mocking those who overlook the importance of our continual regeneration in the present. Her love is qualified and hierarchized, a means not an intermediary.

Throughout her essay Irigaray reminds us who is speaking. Diotima is not present; it is Plato speaking through Socrates who discloses her method. Always there is the reminder of Diotima's presence and her absence, suggesting that the tension in the Diotimas presented may reflect who in fact is speaking. "That, surprisingly, is the view of Diotima. At least as translated through the words uttered by Socrates" (page 192).

Nye's reading of Diotima augments duBois's hypothesis of a pre-Platonic metaphysic different than that developing out of Platonic philosophy. Nye argues that although Plato reports the ideas of Diotima through the character of Socrates, he does not steal her voice. Nye offers a Diotima who presents a philosophy of love quite different from the Platonic theory of forms. She rejects Irigaray's claim that Socrates' Diotima presents incompatible positions and provides a reading of her philosophy that unifies it into an alternative to Plato's.

Nye argues that Diotima develops a philosophy that celebrates bodily love as the ultimate source of knowledge and creativity. Her Diotima would not reject physical love, including its manifestation in sexual love for a "higher" spiritual love, but would argue for a more inclusive love, "an expansion of loving intercourse that will bear fruit in new thoughts, new knowledge, and new ways of living with others, as well as in physical children" (page 199). But this Diotima's knowledge is lived, not abstract and universal, and is always rooted in the physical world. Nye's Diotima provides a philosophy in tension with a Platonic metaphysic, but compatible with the type of metaphysic developing out of some contemporary feminist theories that reject an individuated conception of both self and knowledge.[4]

Nye interprets Irigaray's failure to understand Diotima as being due to a misreading of aspects of Diotima's philosophy as Platonist and the imposition of a Freudian and Lacanian distinction between masculine and feminine sexuality. Nye insists that any reading of Diotima that is historically grounded would reject such a distinction as inapplicable, for Diotima provides a theory of love that is the same for women and men, and in which desire is not gendered. The lesson of Nye's essay is that we must not repeat Plato's treatment of Diotima. We must not make her the hidden host of the *Symposium* whose ideas have been sabotaged and converted to our own purposes. We must learn to hear Diotima's philosophy as a reflection of an alternative metaphysic that Plato fed on in creating his own.

Hampton provides yet a third perspective on the controversy raised by Irigaray and Nye. Hampton would embrace their concern to read Plato in the context of his relation to an earlier metaphysic. Her reading of Plato, however, is more sympathetic in that she depicts him as better attuned to this earlier tradition and thus more resistant to the developing masculinist ontology. Hampton focuses her analysis on Plato's treatment of dualism, arguing that his philosophy contains important traces of ancient concerns with unity and connection.

Cynthia Hampton, like Nye and Irigaray, focuses on Plato's notion of the intermediary. Hampton, however, argues that the intermediary is a notion embraced by Plato as a way to overcome the dualisms of the one and the many and the limited and unlimited inherited from the pre-Socratic tradition. She would agree with Nye that Plato borrowed from Diotima as representative of this ancient metaphysic the notion of the intermediary, but Hampton's account is more charitable in that she contends that Plato was not simply parasitic, but rather employed this notion in a sustained effort to overcome dualism.

Hampton turns from the *Symposium* to an examination of Plato's use of the mediary in the *Philebus*. Hampton sees this dialogue as Plato's effort to develop a worldview that privileges unity, continuity, and plurality in an attempt to overcome the dichotomous thinking of the pre-Socratics. She reads the *Philebus* as offering three important intermediaries: Beauty, Proportion, and Truth. Hampton finds in Plato's *Philebus* a holism that affirms the importance of connection. In other words, Hampton unlike duBois or Irigaray, reads Plato reconstructively as offering a metaphysic useful to feminists in their attempt to reject dichotomous thinking. Hampton, then, would see the presence of the intermediary, a presence she labels feminine, as an attempt to subvert the dominance of masculine values and discourse, rather than an appropriation of the feminine.

I close this section with my own attempt (co-authored with William Cowling) to explore the complexity of the roles of the feminine within Plato's theory of knowledge, focusing specifically on his metaphor of the cave and his doctrine of eros in the *Symposium*. In it Cowling and I attempt to subvert contemporary philosophical narratives that privilege a disembodied, authorial voice by casting the study as a performance and employing a multiplicity of voices.

While embracing Brown's insight that Plato appropriates aspects of the feminine while denigrating others, we reach the opposite conclusion that his philosophy has much to say about women—and about the construction of men. In fact, our performance weaves together insights gleaned from each of the essays in this section. To them we add our concern to make clear the workings of the feminine, both as a presence and as an absence, in the philosophy of Plato. And like Diotima, we embrace the importance of the mediary.

Notes

1. To the contention that Plato was simply offering an alternative epistemology in which reason and truth arise out of love, eros, and spiritual generation (see Brown, Chapter 8), duBois would turn our attention to the fact that such powers are limited to a homoerotic movement of the soul which excludes women.

2. DuBois here consciously rejects the analysis of those who argue for the absence of the feminine in Platonic texts and, in particular, the position of Derrida in "Plato's Pharmacy" in his *Dissemination,* trans. Barbara Johnson (Chicago: University of Chicago Press, 1981), 66–171.

3. For an interesting overview of explanations offered by scholars for Diotima's presence in the *Symposium,* see David Halperin's "Why Is Diotima a Woman?" in his *One Hundred Years of Homosexuality and Other Essays on Greek Love* (New York: Routledge, 1990), 113–51. Halperin adds to the scholarship by offering two additional explanations of her role.

4. See, for example, Catherine Keller, *From a Broken Web: Separation, Sexism, and Self* (Boston: Beacon, 1986) and Lynn Hankinson Nelson, *Who Knows: From Quine to a Feminist Empiricism* (Philadelphia: Temple University Press, 1990).

7

The Platonic Appropriation of Reproduction

Page duBois

The metaphorical system I have described, mapping only a part of a larger network that situates the female in ancient Greek culture, focuses on the female body as a space of reproduction and of thesaurization. It locates the female as a potential for producing goods or for protecting them. She becomes the locus of inscription, the folded papyrus that signifies the potential for deception. This potential is alienated from the earth and made dependent on the male Athenian citizen. The very fact of the network's metaphoricity links it with the practices of Athenian democracy, which described itself in relation to various others in terms of opposition.

After the political, social, and economic crisis of the Athenian defeat in the Peloponnesian War, Athens abandoned some of the most radical features of democratic practice. Forced at first into a new and repressive oligarchy by the Spartans, it subsequently developed into a restored democracy, which, like that of the fifth century, in our terms would be called an oligarchy. Many writers of the late fifth and early fourth centuries joined in condemning democracy and its ideology of equality;

the texts of the fourth century establish new terms for the location of the female.

Of particular interest in the fourth century, among the works of new comedy, legal orations, histories, and philosophical texts, are the dialogues of Plato, which create not only a new genre but establish the terms of philosophical intercourse for centuries to come. Plato's texts are at the origin of the tradition of Western metaphysics. Perhaps due to violent misreadings, failure to recognize the ironic aspects of his works or the subtleties of the interactions of his dialecticians, a particular representation of his views—an advocacy of idealism and metaphysics—has marked philosophical discourse since the fourth century.[1]

I am interested here in a particular aspect of the Platonic text and in certain dialogues. I am interested in the ways in which Plato participates in or produces a change in the situation of the female in the world. This may seem to be a minor aspect of Platonic philosophy, especially since women are never present in the Platonic setting. Yet, I believe that Plato's appropriation of the reproductive metaphors of Greek culture used to describe the place of women and his use of this metaphorical network to authorize the male philosopher are linked to a metaphorical project—to the task of monistic metaphysics, the positing of a one—father, sun, god—who is the source and origin of the good. In certain dialogues—especially in the *Theaetetus*, the *Symposium*, and the *Phaedrus*—Plato uses the metaphorical language formerly employed to locate the female and makes a new philosopher of it.

The *Phaedrus*, as a text of seduction aimed at drawing the reader toward erotic life and therefore toward philosophy, plays on the Greek definitions of male and female, using the vocabulary of sexual difference in Greek culture to establish a new portrait of the philosopher as lover, inseminator, and fertile field.

My reading of the *Phaedrus* is concerned with the presence and appropriation of the female in the dialogue; Jacques Derrida's "La pharmacie de Platon" and his reading of this dialogue have influenced my understanding of Plato and of the place of his work in the philosophical tradition. Derrida's essay discusses the *Phaedrus* as a text establishing what he elsewhere calls a metaphysics of "presence."[2] He describes Plato's work as "logocentric," focusing on presence as opposed to absence, the living voice as opposed to writing, life opposed to death, soul opposed to body. The stronger term of various dualist oppositions is in Plato's work valorized through the use of what Derrida calls a "supplement"—here, writing, called a *pharmakon,* both poison and cure. Writing is an exemplary supplement, the not-valorized side of an opposition used to establish the centrality and the value of speaking. Derrida describes the project of Platonic writing as the production of the son after the father's death: "the disappearance of the good-father-capital-sun is . . . the precondition of discourse. . . . The disappearance of truth as presence, the withdrawal of the present origin of presence, is the condition of all (manifestation of) truth."[3] Derrida regards Plato, in his emphasis on truth, presence, and speaking, as aware of, yet caught in, the same contradiction as all thinkers who follow him. He insists on the truth of the living voice, yet writes; insists on the living presence of Socrates, yet writes only after Socrates' death. Furthermore, and wrongly, I think, Derrida describes what he sees as the exclusively masculine Platonic lineage of philosophy, a phallocentric model of philosophical discourse where the inheritance of dialectic passes patrilineally, from father to son. Derrida says:

> It is all about fathers and sons, about bastards unaided by any public assistance, about glorious, legitimate sons, about inheritance, sperm, sterility. Nothing is said of the mother, but this will not be held against us. And if one looks hard enough as at those pictures in which a second picture faintly can be made out, one might be able to discern her unstable form, drawn upside-down in the foliage, at the back of the garden. In the gardon of Adonis, *eis Adonidos kepous.* (276b; p. 143)

Although Derrida's reading is brilliant and illuminating, it is, I think, blind to its own phallocentrism to the extent that it fails to acknowledge Plato's desire to appropriate maternity to the male philosopher, to incorporate into the portrait of the philosopher the very metaphors traditionally used to represent the female in classical culture.

An analysis of the historical shape of logocentrism and of phallocentrism is necessary for real understanding of the text and of its relationship, first to Greek society, then to the lineage of philosophy to which Derrida refers. Derrida "misreads" the *Phaedrus,* at least at the level of sexual difference. The particular shape of Greek misogyny, because Greek society excluded women so radically from participation in intellectual life, made the form of Plato's sexual politics different from that of those who follow him. In the *Phaedrus,* there is, I will argue, as there is in the *Theaetetus* and the *Symposium*, a mimesis of the female, so that in the homoerotic movement of the dialogue, the female is perhaps more present than she is in later texts of the tradition where the less absolute social oppression of women leaves space for philosophy to be more radically phallocentric, to abandon the reproductive metaphors used of the female, and to describe her entirely in terms of lack.

The homoerotics of the *Phaedrus*, explicit and implicit, seem to center on relations between men. The result appears to be the exclusion of women from true eros, and therefore from philosophy, from access to the truth. Plato's misogyny can be demonstrated polemically from a variety of sources; it is possible to find many passages such as this one from the *Timaeus*, where the character Timaeus includes in his account of creation, almost as an afterthought, a discussion of the creation of women that is expressive of contempt and mistrust:

> According to the probable account, all those creatures generated as men who proved themselves cowardly and spent their lives in wrong-doing were transformed, at their second incarnation, into women. And it was for this reason that the gods at that time contrived the love of sexual intercourse by constructing an animate creature of one kind in us men, and of another kind in women. . . . in men the nature of the genital organs is disobedient and self-willed, like a creature that is deaf to reason, and it attempts to dominate all because of its frenzied lusts. And in women, again, owing to the same causes, whenever the matrix or womb, which is an indwelling creature desirous of child-bearing—remains without fruit long beyond the due season, it is vexed and takes it ill; and by straying all ways through the body and blocking up the passages of the breath and preventing respiration it casts the body in the uttermost distress, and causes, moreover, all kinds of maladies, until the desire and love of the two sexes unite them. . . .
>
> In this fashion, then, women and the whole female sex have come into existence. (91a–d)

Thus, at least according to Timaeus, the necessity for women and the torments of sexual desire came about originally because of the failure of men to live bravely and justly. As Pandora was sent to punish Prometheus for his deception of Zeus, so women are the result of men's inability to behave philosophically.[4]

The fantasy of masculine *autarkeia,* self-sufficiency, was a persistent theme in Greek culture. In Hesiod's myth of the time before the division between men and gods—before work, cooking, and sacrifice—women had no place. Men were contented and sufficient unto themselves. In the fifth century, the fantasy of single-sex, masculine culture appeared in the vehement wishes of Euripides' Jason and Hippolytus.[5]

The desire to "abject" the female, to use Julia Kristeva's term, to see her as pollution, to cast her outside, is part of the character of the obsessively chaste, Artemisian Hippolytus.[6] But it is a traditional strain of Greek social relations as well. Women were normally hidden away inside their houses, but they were also often, in ritual, "cast out" of normal social life. While their reproductive powers were necessary, women's bodies could be seen to endanger the city through their miasma.

Plato has seemed to some to share the fantasy of an exclusively male world. Philosophy, in the Platonic description (with the possible rare exception of an Aspasia or a Diotima, though never represented directly in the text), is a masculine endeavor. Women, whose wombs wander, who are dominated by the unphilosophical parts of their souls, do not appear. The dominant literary genres of fifth century, tragedy, comedy, and history, in which individual women are portrayed, are in the fourth century joined, perhaps dominated, by legal orations in which only men speak and by the dialogues—accounts of men talking to each other.

Although in the *Republic* Plato says women are to be created of every class, to reproduce, to be the companions of men at every level of the state, they are nonetheless consistently described as by nature weaker, more abandoned, and less philosophical than men.[7] The implicit desire of masculine *autarkeia* is present also, perhaps especially in the *Phaedrus,* where seduction is an issue between man and man, where philosophy and the approach toward the good are the business of male lovers. Reproduction is there ascribed exclusively to men; they will inseminate each other with philosophy in a sexual act in which women have no place.

One can read a misogynist, phallocentric Plato who has a vision, especially in the *Phaedrus,* of a homoerotics based on absolute rejection of women from intercourse with men and based on the practice of philosophy that exiles women. Yet I want to identify a countercurrent in the *Phaedrus,* an undertext of dialectical movement between the sexes, a recognition that a definition of sexual identity in terms of contradictories, although argued for in the Platonic corpus, is not satisfactory. In the *Phaedrus,* Plato employs the fluid boundary between the sexes with great seductive power, especially in his portrait of Socrates. And he appropriates traditional metaphors—the descriptions of the female as defined by inner potentiality, by reproductive interiority—to the person of the male philosopher.

The female in the *Phaedrus,* although not characterized individually, is more than an "unstable form . . . at the back of the garden." She may be seen as another supplement that Plato delicately tries to control and appropriate in order to center on the male and thus on a homoerotic model for philosophy. Rather than enacting a rigid *diaeresis* between the sexes, Plato's text plays erotically with boundaries, with edges, with the space between one thing and its opposite, moving through separation to collection and back again. Plato uses the tension between the sexes in Greek culture to assert the authority of the male at the scene of philosophy, but also and more important, his own desire to appropriate the powers of the female makes that authority a very provisional one and marks the Platonic text as the threshold of a new description of sexual difference. If Plato appropriates the female powers of reproduction to the male philosopher, the philosophical tradition after him stresses the autonomy of that male, his self-sufficiency, his privileged access to the divine and the one, and that tradition describes the female as a defective male, a creature distanced from the absolute presence and union with the divine.

The *Phaedrus* is a text of seduction. It acts to allure the imaginary *erōmenos* whom Lysias desires to seduce with the first discourse.[8] Socrates offers two speeches designed at least in part to seduce his companion Phaedrus. The *Phaedrus*'s movements of alternation and exchange make it a drama of sexual encounter between two men and between the reader and the text. Phaedrus comes with a gift from Lysias, shares it with Socrates, who remarks frequently and admiringly on Phaedrus's beauty and enthusiasm; they share in this conversation outside the boundaries of the city a seductive moment of intimacy. The themes of *diaeresis* and *synagogē,* central for the character Socrates in this dialogue, offer a model of erotic contact and separation. Socrates says, "I myself am a *lover* of these processes of division and bringing together" (*egōge autos te erastēs . . . to diaireseōn kai synagagōn* [266b]). The alternation between collection, the *synousia* of intercourse, and division, the *diaeresis,* glosses the comic myth of the *Symposium* (189d–193a), where Aristophanes tells of the original unity of the human body and its cutting, its division, into male/male, male/female, and female/female halves.[9] The act of intercourse is for Aristophanes an attempt to "re-collect," to reform the fragmented body in which we live.

The description of the logical method Socrates advocates has a polymorphously erotic dimension. The possibility of "collection," *synagogē, synousia,* between the two characters, between reader and writer, is at the heart of the dialogue. Spectator and reader are swept up in Socrates' ecstatic vision of the winged soul in a scene of great metaphysical resonance. And at the end of the drama there is a reassertion of difference, of separation, as Phaedrus promises to return to Lysias. The problematic mention of Isocrates, called Socrates' *paidika* (his "darling" [270b]), seems on one level an attempt to establish a symmetry and distance between Phaedrus and Socrates. Isocrates is to Socrates as Lysias is to Phaedrus; the two older lovers return to their younger *erōmenoi* after playing with the possibility of connection between them on this sunny afternoon.

The logic of collection and division is not restricted to relations between men, however. If there is often in Plato's text a compulsive identification of the male as A and the female as not-A—an attempt to establish boundaries with an excluded middle, an obsessive movement of separation, of *diaeresis* between female and male—there is also in the *Phaedrus* an implicit and subversive argument for collection, for movement between contradictories as well. It is the tension between these movements that provides much of the erotic pleasure of reading the *Phaedrus.* And this is what makes this an important moment in the narrative I am making: the moment of the appropriation and eventual "metonymizing" of the female body.

Plato's text itself engages in an erotic metamorphosis that appears to obscure the evident misogyny in Greek culture, but it in fact reinscribes the female by locating her powers within the male. In the *Phaedrus* this reinscription occurs through a sort of Socratic transvestism, through a shifting between the opposites of male and female.[10] The language of the *Phaedrus* enacts this androgyny, this dialogue between sexual identities, in Socrates as he speaks. Socrates, for example, several times evokes the Bacchantes. In speaking of the lovers inspired by Zeus, drawing their liquid from Zeus, he says, using the feminine article and the masculine participle, that "if they draw the waters of their inspiration from Zeus, like the Bacchantes, they pour it out upon the beloved and make him, so far as possible, like their god" (*k'an ek Dios arutōsin, hōsper hai bakkhai, epi tēn tou erōmenou psuchēn epantlountes poiousin hōs dunaton homoiotaton tōi spheterōi theōi* [253a]). The simile mixes the female sexual identity of the Bacchantes with the action of irrigation in the passage where Socrates describes the moistening of the soul's wings. There he plays with the connection between erection and the growth of wings: "and as the nourishment streams upon him, the quills of the feathers swell and begin to grow from the roots over all the form of the soul" (251b–c). The *trophē,* like mother's milk, is implicitly compared to an ejaculatory stream that meets a corresponding erection in the beloved, causing the buds of his wings to sprout. Both male and female are present in the insemination and nurturing of the wings; the Zeus-inspired Bacchantes are emblematic of the crossing of the sexes.

Socrates says, after hearing Phaedrus' discourse, that he *synebakkheusa* with Phaedrus, that he joined him in Bacchic frenzy (234d). DeVries in his commentary compares this with *ton synkorubantionta* (228b), pointing out the irony of this response to Lysias's precious discourse.[11] The later mention of the Bacchae is also ironic, yet it suggests a connection between the characters in the dialogue and the worshippers of Dionysos, probably most often women, who left their cities for anarchic celebration in the mountains, living outside the boundaries not only of the polis but of their sexual identity. They resemble Socrates, who is, in the *Phaedrus, exō teichous,* "outside the (city) walls," wandering through the liquid stream of the Ilissos, which threatens to dissolve his nature (229a). He says: "I investigate . . . myself, to know whether I am a monster (*thērion*) more complicated and more furious than Typhon, or a gentler and simpler creature" (230a). The mocking description of his self-examination is a prelude to his playing a hybrid of another sort.

Socrates speaks his first discourse *egkalupsamenos* (237a), veiled as one near death, or as a woman. He plays on the ambiguity of the veil, as does Socrates at the end of the *Trachiniae* (1071–80), where Herakles, veiled and dying, calls himself female, *thēlus,* in his weakness. Michael Nagler has elucidated the relation between the veil and the female chastity in the Homeric text: ". . . in the epic tradition, one encounters the veil as projector of sexual *charis* (note its visual epithets *liparos, sigaloeis,* "shiny, bright"), as hider of these attractive qualities for purposes of modesty (*kalumma, kaluptre,* etc.), and in various combinations and syntheses of these polar opposites."[12] Veiled, Socrates is a woman, both seductive and chaste; with head bared, he is both a violated woman and a man.

In the tradition of poets from Homer and Hesiod on, Socrates speaks in the *Phaedrus* of being inspired by the Muses and by the Nymphs. The state of "enthusiasm," having the god or goddess in one, can connote a shifting of sexual identity. Cassandra, after having been possessed physically by Apollo and refusing him a child, is possessed once again, inhabited by the male god as she speaks his prophecy in the *Agamemnon* (1200–1210). The chorus calls her arts *tekhnaisin entheois;* the god, breathing delight (*pneōn kharin*), inspired her and entered her as the Muses and the Nymphs can enter and inspire and blur the identity of the poet. Socrates speaks ironically of the danger of being himself possessed by the Nymphs (*hupo tōn Nymphōn . . . enthousiasō* [241e]). He recites a catalogue of cross-sex "enthusiasm," of the priestesses at Dodona who prophesy in their madness, of the Sibyl and others who, using "possessed prophecy" (*mantikēi entheōi*), foretell many things. These forms of ecstasy blur sexual contradictories; they suggest that double-sexed creature imagined by Aristophanes in the *Symposium.* Cross-sexed possession by the gods both erases the boundaries of sexual identity and, by crossing the edges of sexual difference, enacts a mimesis of intercourse.

Socrates' allusions to possession by divine figures are echoed in the text by a version of Socratic transvestism or ventriloquism, realized literarily. In the myth of the charioteer and his two horses (246a ff.), Socrates allusively mimes a character from another drama: Atossa, queen of Aeschylus's *Persians.* The image of the chariot probably alludes to Parmenides (28b1) and to representations in art, but the image of two horses, one docile, one anarchic, suggests the dream of Atossa as well (*The Persians* 181–99). Atossa says of the women of Xerxes' chariot: "One . . . towers/proud, her mouth obedient to the reins" (192–93). Socrates' good horse "needs no whip, but is guided only by the word of command and by reason" (*Phaedrus* 253a). In the Persian queen's dream, "the other stamps, annoyed, and rends apart/Her trappings in her hands; unbridled, seizes/The car and snaps its yoke in two" (*xunarpazei bia/aneu khalinōn kai zugon thrauei meson* [*The Persians* 194–96]). Socrates' dark horse, at the sight of the beloved, "struggling (*biazomenos*) . . . and pulling, he forces them . . . he lowers his head, raises his tail, takes the bit in his teeth (*endakōn ton khalinon*) and pulls shamelessly" (*Phaedrus* 254d). Socrates, in his description of the charioteer, as *hupokritēs,* expounder and actor, puts himself in the place of Atossa. The intertextuality allows as well for an allusive identification between the internal parts of the soul, the horses, and the females yoked to Xerxes' chariot in Atossa's dream.

The ritual drama of Athens, tragedy and comedy, was just one occasion of sacred transvestism in the religious life of the city. Cross-dressing seems to have been especially prominent in rituals of puberty and adolescence. During the Oschophoria, a festival celebrated during the month of Pyanepsion, two well-born young men wearing female robes headed a procession from Athens to Phaleron, supposedly in memory of a trick the hero Theseus played on Minos.[13] Jean-Pierre Vernant interprets the ritual exchange of dress as a temporary participation in the other sex that preceded the distinct separation of the sexes in adulthood. I would argue further that in Greek culture, so repressive to women, where women were the paradigmatic "others," the temptation to play the other must have been a suppressed but enduring and powerful motive. Pentheus, in the *Bacchae,* is seduced into transvestism by his fascination with women's secrets.[14] The mantic powers of Teiresias himself were perhaps derived from the years he lived in the body of a woman.

One further mask that Socrates assumes in the *Phaedrus* is that of Sappho. His mention of the poets Sappho and Anacreon prepares the way for a later assumption of her lyric voice (235c). He says that he has heard something better than Lysias' discourse from Anacreon or from Sappho—called *kalēs,* perhaps to prepare for the unlovely Socrates who will assume her place. Then after his first, impious *logos* (251b), he offers a description of the effects of *erōs,* shadowed with allusion to Sappho 31 (*phainetai moi . . .*). Sappho there speaks of trembling, (*tromos*), of cold sweat (*idrōs psuchros*), of the gaze at her lover, of a flame beneath the flesh. Socrates says: "And as he looks upon him a reaction from his shuddering [*phrikēs*] comes over him, with sweat [*hidrōs*] and unwonted heat; for as the effluence of beauty enters him through the eyes he is warmed." Sappho's was perhaps the canonical description of desire, with its brilliant evocation of heat, cold, trembling. To echo her response so deftly is to be possessed by her, to become the lyric poet possessed by the lyric poetess, to blur once again the line between the sexes by dressing oneself in the words and images of the other. In Sappho's poem, another homoerotic text, there is the curious phenomenon of desire suggesting a change of sexual identity. The gaze at her lover and at her lover's companion—the other, the male—makes Sappho set herself in his place. She undergoes a transforming identification that involved the physical metamorphosis described in the poem. The situation of homoerotic desire ensures the mimetic presence of the other sex in the *erastēs,* the lover.[15]

Socrates' transvestism, delicate and allusive as it is, is consistent with a pattern of the Greek male's fascination with and gradual appropriation of the socially suppressed female other. The mimesis of the female in the *Phaedrus* is perhaps a way of implicitly suggesting the theme of intercourse between Socrates and Phaedrus, by establishing a difference between them, one displaced from the *erastēs/erōmenos* (lover/beloved) difference, since both presumably are *erastai,* lovers (236b, 257b). But this taking on a female identity also plays with the possibility of the woman's presence at the scene of philosophy, a presence that is allusively represented in a strategy devoted to stabilizing the practice of philosophy around the central figure of the male.

A passage at the end of the dialogue (after the discussion of the *pharmakon* [writing]) illuminates the movement of the appropriation of the female and shows how the traditional metaphors of description are transformed in the Platonic text. The field, the furrow—the dominant metaphors used for reproductive intercourse from the time of Homer—are here assimilated to a situation of pederasty and philosophy. Socrates transforms the commonplaces of poetry, marriage, and social practice and converts them to his own ends, a seduction of the soul of the lover toward beauty and philosophy.

After pointing out the futility of sowing one's seeds in a garden of Adonis (276b), Socrates describes a proper garden, one where words, like seeds, will flourish: "serious discourse about them [justice, etc., 276c] is far nobler, when one employs the dialectic method and plants and sows in a fitting soul intelligent words which are able to help themselves and him who planted them, which are not fruitless, but yield seed [*sperma*] from which there spring up in other minds other words capable of continuing the process forever" (276e–277a). The themes of the garden of Adonis and of the citizen-woman as a field for reproduction of the citizen-male's family have been brilliantly analyzed by Marcel Detienne in *Les jardins d'Adonis.* Here in answer to Phaedrus, whom Socrates jokingly calls *murrinousiou* (244a, perhaps referring punningly to Myrrha, Adonis's mother), Socrates alters the botanical code that opposed Adonis's gardening and Demeter's agriculture. He uses the imagery associated with Demeter, goddess of grain, of cereals, of fruitful human increase, of the furrow, the woman's sexual organs to be ploughed by her husband. Here the imagery of the fruitful field, characteristically used of women, crosses the sexes once again. This field yields not human children, a new generation to populate the polis, but *sperma,* seed. The philosopher who erotically implants his seed, his words, in the soul of the beloved will begin an endless process of purely masculine reproduction, where the produce is more words, more seeds.[16]

This passage demonstrates the gesture of appropriation of the network of metaphors associated with women and with their role in the city. The metaphor of the fertile field, of the furrow ploughed by the husband, used by Sophocles to describe Jocasta and, in the fifth century, connected with the myth of Thebes, is here reinscribed into the relationship of pederasty. The older philosopher, erotically bound to his beloved, plants not the seeds of the family, but the words of philosophy. He transfers the power of reproduction to the art of philosophy. The metaphor of inscription; also connected in the fifth century with the mind and body of the female, is linked here to the practices of pederasty and of philosophy. The female body is no longer the site of ploughing and sowing, of inscription and marking; it has been replaced by the soul of the male philosopher.

In other texts, Plato employs metaphors elsewhere associated with the act of heterosexual intercourse, or the metaphor of stones. In the *Theaetetus,* Socrates repeatedly refers to himself as a midwife (149a ff.). This dialogue's narrative frame is a conversation between Euclides and Terpsion, who took notes on a Socratic report of a conversation he once had with Theodorus and Theaetetus. It is an aporetic dialogue that considers what knowledge is and ends without an answer. The whole text resonates with the metaphors described earlier as "locating" the woman and her body. In a consideration of the Protagorean utterance, "man is the measure of all things," Socrates describes how a theory of knowledge consistent with this view might evolve. He uses the language of reproduction to account for perception:

> Their [those who follow Protagoras] first principle, on which all that we said just now depends, is that the universe really is motion and nothing else. And there are two kinds of motion. Of each kind there are any number of instances, but they differ in that the one kind has the power of acting, the other of being

> acted upon. From the intercourse and friction of these with one another arise offspring, endless in number, but in pairs of twins. (156a)

The model of generation is abstracted from a gendered, reproductive act to describe the process of perception; gender is here erased.

Later in the text, in an attempt to account for false judgment, Socrates develops the analogy between the mind and a wax tablet:

> Imagine, then, for the sake of argument, that our minds contain a block of wax. . . . Let us call it the gift of the Muses' mother, Memory, and say that whenever we wish to remember something we see or hear or conceive in our own minds, we hold this wax under the perceptions or ideas and imprint them on it as we might stamp the impression of a seal ring. (191c–d)

The rich and suggestive metaphor of the tablet, used in the fifth century for the mind but also frequently employed by such authors as Sophocles and Aristophanes to stand for the woman's body, has here been enlisted once again to describe a universal process, a gift of the Muses' mother, memory.

Socrates accounts for the differences in judgment by *evaluating* different minds' wax; of course, the philosopher's wax would be of excellent quality:

> When a man has in his mind a good thick slab of wax, smooth and kneaded to the right consistency, and the impressions that come through the senses are stamped on these tables of the "heart" [*Iliad* 2.851; 16.554]—Homer's word hints at the mind's likeness to wax—then the imprints are clear and deep enough to last a long time. (194c)

Others, less fortunate, have muddy, impure, oversoft, or hard wax, and therefore judge falsely. Socrates finds the analogy with imprinting more satisfactory than the description of intercourse between the perceived and the perceiving.

Throughout this dialogue, Socrates refers to himself as a midwife who is bringing Theaetetus to give birth to ideas—some worthy of death by exposure, some more valuable. He says he is like a barren woman, beyond the age of childbirth, who can help others to reproduce: "How absurd of you, never to have heard that I am the son of a midwife, a fine buxom woman called Phaenarete!" (149a). This section is usually cited as an example of Socratic humility and irony; I would rather connect it with a subtext in this dialogue and elsewhere that allies the philosopher with the woman.

Socrates continues, associating the skills of the midwife with those of husbandry: "Consider the knowledge of the sort of plant or seed that should be sown in any given soil. Does not that go together with skill in tending and harvesting the fruits of the earth? . . . And so with a woman; skill in the sowing is not to be separated from skill in the harvesting?" (149e). The woman, the midwife, can be a matchmaker because, like the farmer, she knows the right seed for a particular plot of ground. Socrates claims that his skills are like his mother's: "My art of midwifery is in general like theirs; the only difference is that my patients are men, not women, and my concern is not with the body but with the soul that is in travail of birth" (150b). Not only is Socrates himself a midwife, a woman, although one past childbirth, but the young men who converse with him are feminized by their conversation with him: "And in yet another way those who seek my company have the same experience as a woman with child; they suffer the pains of labor and, by night and day, are full of distress far greater than a woman's, and my art has power to bring on these pangs or to allay them," (151a–b). This is *appropriation of female experience,* of the female body; it recalls Medea's cry:

> What they say of us is that we have a peaceful time
> Living at home, while they do the fighting in war.
> How wrong they are! I would very much rather stand
> Three times in the front of battle than bear one child.
> (*Medea* 248–51)

Socrates, no longer contrasting men's life in war with women's role at home of reproducing, reinscribes the act of generation, of reproduction, and transfers it to the philosopher, whose experience in labor and birth is idealized and made to transcend that of women.

At the end of the *Theaetetus,* Socrates returns to the description of himself as midwife. Just before referring to the indictment brought up by Meletus, which will bring about his death, he says: "this midwife's art is a gift from heaven; my mother had it for women, and I for young men of a generous spirit and for all in whom beauty dwells" (210c). This dialogue is of particular interest in part because it contains an elaborate description of philosopher's difference from and superiority to all other mortals; for example: ". . . from their youth up they [the leaders in philosophy] have never known the way to market place or law court or Council Chamber or any other place of public assembly; they never hear a decree read out or look at the text of a law. To take any interest in the rivalries of political cliques, in meetings, dinners, and merrymakings with flute girls, never occurs to them even in dreams" (173d).

Thus the philosopher, the very exemplar used by Foucault to typify the Greek in his "history of sexuality," has contempt for politics, for the workings of democracy, even for ordinary heterosexual pleasure. A place above triviality and frivolity is established as the scene of philosophy; the female is both excluded and assimilated to a theory of monistic homoerotics.

In the *Symposium,* too, Plato uses the vocabulary associated with sexual difference in his description of Socrates. In his reaction to the discourse of Agathon, Socrates evokes the myth of Medusa, mocking Agathon's excess of rhetoric: "his speech reminded me so strongly of that master of rhetoric, Gorgias, that I couldn't help thinking of Odysseus, and his fear that Medusa would rise from the lower world among the ghosts, and I was afraid that when Agathon got near the end he would arm his speech against mine with the Gorgon's head of Gorgias' eloquence, and strike me as dumb as a stone" (198b–c). The dialogue returns again to the theme of the stone image.

In this conversation within conversation, in a highly elaborate rhetorical frame of reportage, Socrates speaks the words of a woman, takes her place, acts her part in this dialogue that replaces the embodiment of the voice of the woman in the theater, which engaged in another form of transvestism with the male actor playing the part of the woman. In ancient Athens, in the theater, in ritual, in the philosophical dialogue, male actors played out the role of female in varieties of costume. And their exchange of identities, the transgression and movement across the boundary between the sexes, constituted an erotic pleasure. Plato uses that movement to play, to seduce, and finally to contain the female other. Here it is the philosopher who echoes the words of Diotima, "a Mantinean woman . . . who was deeply versed in this and many other fields of knowledge" (201d). Diotima instructs Socrates about love, and he repeats her discourse: "All men are pregnant (*kuousi*), Socrates, both in body and in soul" (206c); "those whose procreancy is of the body turn to woman as the object of their love, and raise a family. . . . But those whose procreancy is of the spirit rather than of the flesh—and they are not unknown, Socrates—conceive and bear the things of the spirit" (208e–209a).

Socrates is made privy to the secrets of reproduction, and he shares his knowledge by engaging in a literary mimesis of this wisest of women. She teaches him that the philosophical intercourse, conception, pregnancy, and delivery of male lovers are superior to the corporeal acts of human women: "he and his friend will help each other rear the issue of their friendship—and so the bond between them will be more binding, and their communion even more complete, than that which comes of bringing children up, because they have created something lovelier and less mortal than human seed" (209c). Socrates repeats at length the words of his teacher Diotima; her words are contained, enclosed, locked within his own discourse as a "Mantinean," mantic, secret truth. Socrates' assumption of the place of the prophetess lies at the heart of his doctrine.

In the speech of Alcibiades, spoken not in praise of love but in praise of Socrates himself, who thus "is" love, the association between the philosopher and the woman recurs. Alcibiades compares the effect Socrates has on him to the effects visible in a Corybant, a worshiper of the great mother: "For the moment I hear him speak I am smitten with a kind of sacred rage, worse than any Corybant" (215d); he compares Socrates to a Siren.

In an elaborate simile, an example of the "likening" game played by the Athenians, Alcibiades compares Socrates to a statue. His words suggest an analogy between this simile and the place of Diotima enclosed within the earlier discourse of Socrates: "What he reminds me of more than anything is one of those little sileni that you see on the statuaries' stalls; you know the ones I mean—they're modeled with pipes or flutes in their hands, and when you open them down the middle there are little figures of the gods inside" (215a–b).

He returns to this simile later: "I don't know whether anybody else has ever opened him up when he's been being serious, and seen the little images inside, but I saw them once, and they looked so godlike, so golden, so beautiful, and so utterly amazing that there was nothing for it but to do exactly what he told me" (216e–217a). The imagery echoes the pregnancy motif in Diotima's speech and again appropriates the vocabulary of female reproductive powers to the philosopher. He is masculine, most masculine, a silenus, a satyr, with an Apollo inside; these are figures associated with libidinality, with heterosexual and homosexual eros. But the notion of male pregnancy draws on the representation of the female; as Diotima is enclosed within Socrates' speech, as he is pregnant with her, with her teachings, so Alcibiades sees Socrates as pregnant, as entreasuring, as stone enclosing the riches of the gods.

The reinscriptions of the Platonic text convert the metaphorical network of the fifth century to a new prominence for the male, the philosopher, the figure whom Michel Foucault sees as the figure of mastery, the center of philosophical and erotic practices from this moment on. And they establish a space for a new inscription, the metonymic placing of the female in relation to her superior and inferior. This occurs in the text of Aristotle and defines her place for centuries. The male philosopher becomes the site of metaphorical reproduction, the subject of philosophical generation; the female, stripped of her metaphorical otherness, becomes a defective male, defined by lack.

Notes

1. See Harry Berger, "Plato's Flying Philosopher," *Philosophical Forum* 13, no. 4 (1982): 385–407.

2. Jacques Derrida, *Of Grammatology*, trans. Gayatri Spivak (Baltimore: Johns Hopkins University Press, 1976), 6–13.

3. Jacques Derrida, "Plato's Pharmacy," in his *Dissemination*, trans. Barbara Johnson (Chicago: University of Chicago Press, 1981), 168.

4. See Pietro Pucci, *Hesoid and the Language of Poetry* (Baltimore: Johns Hopkins University Press, 1977); and Nicole Loraux, "Sur la race des femmes et quelques-unes de ses tribus," in *Women in the Ancient World*, ed. John Peradotto and J. P. Sullivan, special issue of *Aresthusa* 11, nos. 1, 2 (1978): 43–87.

5. On utopianism in the fifth century, see F. Solmsen, *Intellectual Experiments of the Greek Enlightenment* (Princeton: Princeton University Press, 1975). See also Marylin Arthur, "The Dream of a World without Women: Poetics and the Circles of Order in the *Theogony* Prooemium," *Arethusa* 16 (1983): 97–116.

6. Julia Kristeva, *Powers of Horror: An Essay on Abjection*, trans. L. S. Roudiez (New York: Columbia University Press, 1982). See also Froma Zeitlin, "The Power of Aphrodite: Eros and the Boundaries of the Self in the *Hippolytus*," in *Directions in Euripidean Criticism*, ed. P. Burian (Durham, N.C.: Duke University Press, 1985), 52–110.

7. On the question of Plato's attitudes toward women, see, among many others, Dorothea Wender, "Plato: Misogynist, Paedophile, and Feminist," *Arethusa* 6, no. 1 (1973): 75–90; Julia Annas, "Plato's *Republic* and Feminism," *Philosophy* 51 (1976): 307–21; Mary O'Brien,

The Politics of Reproduction (London: Routledge and Kegan Paul, 1981); and Nancy Hartsock, *Money, Sex, and Power: Toward a Feminist Historical Materialism* (New York: Longman, 1983).

In the *Timaeus,* Plato's character Timaeus uses the metaphor of sexual difference to talk about the parts of the soul:

> Within the chest, they fastened the mortal kind of soul. And inasmuch as one part thereof is better, and one worse, they built a division within the cavity of the thorax—as if to fence off two separate chambers, for men and for women—by placing the midriff between them as a screen. (69e–70a)

The manly part is closer to the head, obedient to reason, while the heart must be cooled by the lungs in order that it "be subservient to the reason (*logōi*) in time of passion." Women are associated with the heart's blood, which like the womb moves throughout the body and threatens anarchy.

8. On the institution of pederasty in ancient Greece, see K. J. Dover, *Greek Homosexuality* (Cambridge, Mass.: Harvard University Press, 1978).

9. On the *Symposium,* see John Brenkman, "The Other and the One: Psychoanalysis, Reading, *The Symposium,*" in *Literature and Psychoanalysis, the Question of Reading: Otherwise,* ed. Shoshana Felman (Baltimore: Johns Hopkins University Press, 1982), 396–456.

10. On transvestism, see Froma Zeitlin, "Travesties of Gender and Genre in Aristophanes' *Thesmophoriazousae,*" in *Reflections of Women in Antiquity,* ed. Helene P. Foley (New York: Gordon and Breach, 1981), 169–217.

11. G. J. DeVries, *A Commentary on the "Phaedrus" of Plato* (Amsterdam: Adolf M. Hakkert, 1959).

12. Michael N. Nagler, *Spontaneity and Tradition: A Study in the Oral Art of Homer* (Berkeley and Los Angeles: University of California Press, 1974).

13. H. W. Parke, *Festivals of the Athenians* (London: Thames and Hudson, 1977).

14. See Charles Segal, *Dionysiac Poetics and Euripides' "Bacchae"* (Princeton: Princeton University Press, 1982).

15. On Sappho, see Jack Winkler, "Gardens of Nymphs: Public and Private in Sappho's Lyrics," *Women's Studies* 8, nos. 1, 2 (1981): 65–91; Anne Giacomelli, "The Justice of Aphrodite in Sappho Fr. 1," *Transactions of the American Philological Association* 110 (1980): 135–42; and W. W. Fortenbaugh, "Plato *Phaedrus* 253c3," *Classical Philology* 61 (1966): 108–9.

16. See H. D. Rankin, "On *ADIAPLASTA ZOIA,*" *Philologus* 107 (1963): 138–45; see also Miles Burnyeat, "Socratic Midwivery, Platonic Inspiration," *Bulletin of the Institute for Classical Studies* 24 (1977): 7–16; and Paul Plass, "Plato's Pregnant Lover," *Symbolae Osloenses* 53 (1978): 47–55.

8

"Supposing Truth Were a Woman . . .": Plato's Subversion of Masculine Discourse

Wendy Brown

> What is found at the historical beginnings of things is not the inviolable identity of their origin; it is the dissention of other things. It is disparity.
>
> —Michel Foucault

Plato is the founder of Western philosophic rationalism. Nietzsche and Derrida insist upon this, and even those who despair of these modern thinkers largely agree. I shall argue that this is a misreading of Plato; intertwined with his development and defense of rationalism are challenges and contradictions to rationalism, indications of its limits, and intimations of a quite different conception of knowledge. These challenges and intimations are marked, at times lightly, with gender. Plato's hesitations about rationalism are often spoken through a subtle subversion of conventional gender identities, especially manhood, in a curiously gendered discourse on epistemology.

Plato's sexing of an important but ambiguous strain of his epistemological arguments does not mean that he is feminist nor am I concerned

With the exception of the *Republic,* all citations of Plato's works are from *Plato: Collected Dialogues,* ed. Edith Hamilton and Huntington Cairns (Princeton: Princeton University Press, 1963). Passages from the *Republic* are quoted from Allan Bloom's translation (New York: Basic Books, 1968).

with the question of whether his philosophical relation to gender fulfills contemporary political standards of feminism. Rather, this essay explores the way in which, for reasons largely irrelevant to the situation of women, Plato engages in a critique of the socially male modes of thinking, speaking, and acting prevalent in his epoch and milieu. Explored also are the tensions this critique produces in Plato's thought; insofar as his assault upon the masculinist features of Greek culture is partial, equivocal, and bound by antinomies that he revalues but does not jettison, Plato raises a problem that he ultimately cannot settle, a critique whose resolution he cannot provide.

While the political thought of Plato has generated a substantial amount of feminist commentary in recent years, discussion of Plato's treatment of gender has been mostly limited to his explicit utterances about women and his program for "equal opportunity" put forth in Book V of the *Republic.*[1] In this essay, gender in Plato's thought will be examined in terms of his depiction of the nature of wisdom and philosophizing, the relation of philosophy to power, and the "politics" of the *Republic.* The guiding thread is Plato's personification of truth and philosophy as female. Why does Plato refer to philosophy as a woman? Why are the souls that finally glimpse truth named female as well? What subversion of Greek conceptions and practices of manhood is being assayed in these moves? And what are the limitations and paradoxes of this subversiveness?[2]

I

Socrates criticizes styles and practices, not merely ideas and institutions. This is what makes him a thoroughly *political* philosopher—he discerns and explores elements of power, corruption, and formative influence where others may see only benign custom or fancy. Two of the practices Socrates criticizes, Sophistic speech and agonistic political action, are particularly fundamental to the masculine ethos of the Athenian polis.[3] In attacking and ultimately rejecting these practices, Socrates is challenging classical notions, embodiments, and expressions of manhood.

Socrates' denunciation of the political education and discourse practiced by the Sophists (*Republic* 492a–493d; *Sophist* 222a–226b) is usually interpreted as a critique of the Sophists' relativism, professionalism, and explicit devotion to training aspirants to power and reputation. Socrates does indeed seek to separate "true philosophy" from each of these elements—to cleanse it of both ethical relativism and practical opportunism. But underlying these concerns is an even more thoroughgoing critique of the *mode* of discourse. Socrates ascribes to the Sophists and their students, a mode that is distinctly *agonistic* and at odds with both justice and wisdom precisely because it is agonistic. For Socrates, when thinking and speaking become a game or contest undertaken for extrinsic purposes, they cease to contribute to the discovery of wisdom and to the founding of justice. Thus in criticizing the Sophists' relationship to power, Socrates depicts the agonistic style of Sophistic discourse as both a root and a symptom of what is wrong with the content of Sophistic teachings (*Theaetetus* 167–168c). Socrates distinguishes himself from the Sophists through the claim that the aim and therefore the mode of his inquiry is nothing other than wisdom—by his account, neither considerations of power nor reputation distort the pursuit (*Republic* 499a).

On one level, of course, Socrates' posture of imperviousness to power and reputation is pure subterfuge: There may be no finer historical instance of the discursive "will to power" than the person of Socrates. This does not, however, fully undermine his attempt to distance himself from the Sophists, nor is his refusal to "set himself up as a teacher" and be remunerated for his conversations all that sets him apart from them (*Crito* 33a–b). Even if one can detect "sophistry" within Socrates' philosophical work, this work is located on radically different terrain from that of the Sophists. Socrates seeks alternative political truths to those structuring fourth-century B.C. Athens; Sophists, often by their own admission, are indifferent to truth and teach instead the pursuit of political power in any context, no matter how corrupt. Socrates entreats his friends to seek after knowledge in order to become just and virtuous; Sophists teach their students how to persuade, exploit opportunity, and win an argument (*Euthydemus* 271c–272b). Indeed, the consequence of Socrates' "purification" of the philosophic vocation, his friendly Athenian critics argue, is the cultivation of impotent virtue while the Sophists create winners (*Republic* 358b–367c, 487d). For them, Socrates' attack on the teachings of the Sophists amounts to a useless and impotent reprimand of the powerful because it issues from outside the (male) world in which power is generated and exploited. In the words of Socrates' companion Adeimantus, genuine philosophers, if not "queer or vicious," are "useless to cities" (*Republic* 487d). In the words of contemporary interpreter Arlene Saxonhouse, "the philosopher and the female share a common alienation from the city," a common irrelevance to the world of political power.[4]

Parallel and related to Socrates' attack on Athens' agonistic mode of speech and education is his critique of its agonistic mode of political action and political power. His infamous battle with Thrasymachus in the first book of the *Republic* (337a–354c), his critique of Pericles (*Gorgias* 515d–516d), his attack on the values and practices of timocracy and democracy (*Republic* 548a–550b, 557a–562a), and most important, his own ideal city's dominant characteristics of harmony, humility, sufficiency, and quietude (*Republic* 443d–e)—these are but a few instances of his protest against the agonistic character of Athenian politics. As the Sophists are enemies of wisdom and a virtuous intelligence, champions of the heroic ethic in politics are enemies of justice and a virtuous bearing in action.

In the first book of the *Republic,* Plato makes clear that agonistic power politics and sophistic political discourse are two faces—actually the body and the voice—of a single ethic. They merge in the person of Thrasymachus, a fiercely combative Sophist who upholds a politics in which justice is the outcome of a battle for power—"the interest of the stronger" (*Republic* 338d). Plato's critique of the Sophists and agonistic politics also come together in an interesting way in his assault on epic poetry (*Republic* 603c–608c). What Plato spies and is determined to expose in his beloved Homer is the extent to which heroic greatness in the Athenian tradition is bound up with ethical weakness. The "justice" Homeric heroes evince and embody is the justice Thrasymachus declares—the prevalence of the strong over the weak, accomplished for the sake of the advantages this prevalence brings. In Plato's view, Homer and the Sophists alike teach that no one does what is right voluntarily but only under compulsion of necessity or desire for gain.[5] When heroism is at stake, knowledge, speech, and deed will necessarily acquire an instrumental character; virtue will be sacrificed to concerns of power qua domination, wisdom and justice will be subjected to political contingency and necessity.

Both the Sophistic mode of speech and the heroic ethic of political deed constitute a specifically masculine ethos in the Greek popular ontology—the agonistic element contained in both was expressly linked to manhood—and this is the ontology in which the Socratic challenges are situated.[6] Consequently, Socrates' manliness is occasionally questioned or impugned by his interlocutors. In the *Republic,* Thrasymachus seeks to defeat Socrates' argument about justice by humiliating him as a wimp: "Tell me Socrates, do you have a wetnurse?" (*Republic* 343a). And in the *Gorgias,* Callicles chides Socrates in similar fashion:

> Philosophy, you know, Socrates, is a pretty thing if you engage in it moderately in your youth; but if you continue in it longer than you should, it is the ruin of any man. For if a man is exceptionally gifted and yet pursues philosophy far on in life, he must prove entirely unacquainted with all the accomplishments requisite for a gentleman and a man of distinction. . . . When a man who is now growing older still studies philosophy, the situation becomes ridiculous and I feel toward philosophers very much as I do toward those who lisp and play the child. . . . When one hears a grown man . . . playing the child, it looks unmanly and worthy of a beating. . . . Such a man, even if exceptionally gifted, is doomed to prove less than a man, shunning the city center and market place, in which the poet said that men win distinction, and living the rest of his life sunk in a corner and whispering with three or four boys, and incapable of any utterance that is free and lofty and brilliant. (*Gorgias* 484d–485d)

Innuendoes about Socrates' adequacy as a man are not limited to attacks upon his *vocation* as a philosopher. Indeed, the *content* of his philosophy, aimed as it is against the prevailing ethic of heroic action and agonistic striving, is also the occasion for ridicule and charges of effeminacy. Thrasymachus directly, Glaucon and Adeimantus more obliquely, suggest that while Socrates' account of justice and virtue may be pretty, it is hardly appropriate or helpful to men concerned with manly things—honor, power, wealth, or reputation (*Republic* 338–367).

While Socrates is thus quite clearly launching a good deal of his critical fire at Athenian males and the Athenian ethos of manhood, a problem arises in discerning from just what standpoint this attack is made. The critique does not issue simply from a "defense of the feminine" or from the "standpoint of the female," as, for example, Arlene Saxonhouse suggests.[7] For Plato opposes some, but by no means all, conventions of masculinity, and he perpetuates some of the most severe elements of Greek misogyny even while lancing others. He does not reject or cast aside the traditional masculine virtues of the Greeks—temperance, courage, wisdom, and justice.[8] To the contrary, he repeatedly defines, refines, and defends these virtues. Moreover, his repudiation of bodily, sentient, and sensual experience as ways of knowing and his uneasiness about the body's everyday needs, demands, and desires would seem to land him firmly in masculinist terrain.[9] To the extent that the characterological distinction between female and male has already begun to be explained in terms of a division between creatures ruled by mind and those ruled by body, Socrates (and Plato to an even greater degree) clearly aligns himself with and develops the male side of this invidious antinomy.[10] For both philosophers, being enslaved to the body in any way is just that, a condition of unfreedom, especially problematic for the mind that must be free if it is to attain to truth (*Phaedo* 65,81; *Phaedrus* 258e). In this regard, Socrates may be scoffed at by his contemporaries as an aesthete, but certainly not as an effeminate weakling or hedonistic sensualist.

Plato's challenges to Athenian masculine practices are thus complicated by their equivocal character and because these challenges are delivered not from the standpoint of masculinity's "opposite," that is, femininity, but from somewhere more ambiguous, shifting, and fraught with tension. Plato's quarrel with the Athenian construction of masculinity is rooted in a concern with its consequences for an ethical politics and philosophy, not its consequences for women. To the extent that Plato sometimes valorizes or even identifies with the characteristics or situation of women, it is not, as Saxonhouse suggests, to establish an opposition between male and female, politics and philosophy.[11] Rather, his *aim* is to *reduce* the distance between them and thereby subvert the conventional standing of masculinity, politics, and political discourse, a standing predicated upon distance from qualities identified with women and femininity. Plato's revaluation of conventional gender construction is undertaken to recast politics in a more philosophical vein, and, at the same time, to relocate knowledge, knowing, and philosophy to a sphere less soaked by masculinist political power than the one it currently inhabits.

In short, Plato features gender in discussions of epistemology and the nature of philosophy only in part because gender is at issue and not at all out of concern with gender justice. While Plato perceives conventional constructions of masculinity as problematic, equally important is that subversion of conventional constructions or valuations of gender always entails a more general subversion of the ontological and epistemological underpinnings of a human order. When gender constructions (as opposed to mere gender roles) are thrown into question, the fundamental modes, ordering principles, and locations of most cultural practices are turned belly up for examination as well. Thus for Plato to cast the problem of philosophy and politics in terms of gender is a sign that a radical conceptual reordering of the human universe is in store. Plato's subversion of conventional assumptions about gender is deployed to disturb a larger web of assumptions about political life and philosophical endeavor.

II

The heart of Plato's challenge to masculine discourse lies beneath the aforementioned attacks upon agonistic modes of speech and action and resides, rather, in his formulation of knowledge, knowing, and teaching. It lies in those features of his thought that have been obscured by those who insist that Plato is the founder of Western philosophic rationalism, "the banishing of the senses, betraying a state of emergency" in Nietzsche's intonation or "logocentrism" in Derrida's more succinct if less evocative turn of phrase.[12] Plato does, indeed, bind philosophy to abstract mathematical reasoning, assert the supremacy of mind, call the senses deceivers, and declare the body a sickness or tomb of the soul (*Phaedo* 65, 81; *Cratylus* 400c). But there is another dimension of Plato that, if attended to, illuminates the enormous tensions entailed in this effort to establish rationalism. There is Plato the poet, the celebrant of eros, the dreamer, the maker of myths and allegories. Accounts given of Plato's theory of knowledge most often note these features of Plato's character of mind as something that lends a note of pathos, irony, or even contradiction to his rationalism from outside the rationalism itself. If, instead, we locate the poet, the mythmaker, and the erotic inside the supposed rationalism, as I will argue Plato himself does, we will see a rather different Plato—less formally rational, less "logocentric," and more subversive of a masculine mode of discourse.

For Plato, human wisdom is acquired through a process of recovery or recollection. In the *Republic*, *Phaedrus*, and *Meno*, he insists that the true educator does not transmit knowledge but, rather, brings to birth what is already present in a "student's" mind or soul.[13] This argument derives from Plato's conviction that all souls are immortal and that prior to their residence in our mortal bodies, they had full knowledge of "true being" as it is manifest in the heavens (*Phaedrus* 247c–e). Philosophizing and educating are therefore a process of "turning the soul toward truth"; the soul is turned away from its perceptions and attachments in the phenomenal world and toward the true nature of things, a truth it already—latently or intuitively—knows but with which it must be reconnected (*Republic* 519c–d). Thus Socrates calls himself a "midwife" of philosophy, one who brings to birth wisdom and truth in others through *elenchus* or dialectical reasoning (*Theaetetus* 149a–151d).

If truth is latent in every soul and omnipresent in the heavens, what, for Plato, is the role of dialectical reasoning in apprehending it? First, we need to note what reason does not do: It does not actually name or describe the truth embodied by the Forms. This first becomes evident in Plato's diatribes against philosophical writing in the *Phaedrus* and the *Seventh Letter,* in which he insists that any attempt to purvey wisdom through writing is certain to sacrifice the truth character of an insight: "Once a thing is put in writing, the composition . . . whatever it may be, drifts all over the place, getting into the hands not only of those who understand it but equally of those who have no business with it; it doesn't know how to address the right people, and not address the wrong. And when it is ill-treated and unfairly abused it always needs its parent to come to its help, being unable to defend or help itself" (*Phaedrus* 275e). While wisdom and truth have a universal standing in Plato's epistemology, they must be approached and grasped in highly particular, individual ways. For Plato, important things are not learned simply with the brain but from an ordering of desires, the body, sensibilities, and even—although he sometimes rails against it—experience. This ordering is inescapably particularistic, and the universal quality of Platonic truth is therefore an entirely separate matter from the *process* of knowing, from *learning.* Because the highest truth cannot be put into words, the latter category comprises *all* written and spoken discourse.

The world of *discursive* reason is therefore not a world of absolute truths but of awakening, reminding, or recollecting, and these things must be utterly personalized to be of value. The problem with writing is that it addresses abstract or generalized audiences; the particularity of a road to truth characteristic of Socrates' tailor-made conversations with his interlocutors is utterly impossible in written discourse. To render the matter in modern terms, the written word cannot address the highly intersubjective elements of learning of which Socrates is supremely appreciative. By contrast, philosophical conversation between lovers or good friends represents the highest possibility for glimpsing wisdom (*Symposium* 209). Yet as already noted, speech, too, always falls short of grasping or expressing the truth. When, in the *Republic*, Glaucon and Socrates are ready to discuss the nature of the Good, Socrates breaks off, telling Glaucon "you would no longer be able to follow . . . you would no longer be seeing an image of what we are saying, but rather, truth itself" (*Republic* 533a). Words make images or representations of the truth, they serve as the bases of hypotheses or as stepping-stones toward the truth, but they cannot ultimately present or embody the truth (*Republic* 511c).[14]

If discursive reason neither produces nor expresses truth, what is its precise nature and relationship to truth; why is it important at all? It is in the *Republic* that Plato most clearly sets out what might appropriately be called the "function" of dialectical reasoning. "When the eye of the soul is really buried in a barbaric bog," Socrates explains to Glaucon, "dialectic gently draws it forth and leads it up above" (*Republic* 533d). Dialectic is a trustworthy assistant on the journey of a soul toward truth—it "has the power to release and leads what is best in the soul up to the contemplation of what is best in the things that are" (*Republic* 532c). Dialectic, paradoxically, both liberates and directs the mind, but dialectical reasoning is not itself truth, productive of truth, or expressive of truth. It is at best an instrument, a noble and excellent one when rightly used but capable as well of being tremendously abused.

Plato's recognition of the dangers inherent in the use of dialectic is worth lingering over for a moment. While Plato praises dialectic as among the highest and most powerful forms of thinking, he also knows that it can be vulgarized into mere debate, eristic, or pointless games of contradiction (*Republic* 454a). More important politically, dialectic can serve to corrupt rather than develop untrained minds. In the wrong hands, the use of dialectic can lead to debunking law and religion out of sheer fascination with the mind's power and can foster a reckless, irresponsible relativism. "How great is the harm coming from the practice of dialectic these days . . . surely its students are filled with lawlessness," Socrates declares to Glaucon in the *Republic* (537e).

"Haven't you noticed when lads get their first taste of arguments, they misuse them as though it were play, always using them to contradict . . . like puppies enjoying pulling and tearing with argument at those who happen to be near?" (*Republic* 539b–c). But even when dialectic is in hands presumably as responsible and virtuous as those of Socrates, a danger inheres. Dialectical inquiry can restrict imagination, deter hunches, arrest intuition, bring premature conclusions, and fix the boundaries of an argument in ways that lead not toward but away from wisdom (*Theaetetus* 166a–b).[15] It can intimidate and hush the human experience, indeed, the very human being participating in dialectical discourse.

Socrates seems well aware of the dangers and limitations entailed in the use of dialectic. And he frequently breaks off from the dialectical mode of inquiry when he senses that his companions in conversation are losing the thread of the argument or are beginning to feel coerced and badgered. When one is no longer being "turned" toward the truth but only herded or dragged, the eye of the soul does not see for itself what Socrates is trying to illuminate, and there is no point in going on. When such an impasse is reached, Socrates frequently introduces an image, a myth, or an allegory. But in so doing, he does not leave behind his former concerns or arguments. Rather, the image or allegory assists and develops the argument by opening it up again, recalling its purpose, its human dimensions and worldly, political characteristics.[16] Socrates' introduction of allegory thus appeases his comrades in conversation by calling them back to themselves, to their own reference points and experiential knowledge of the world. They are relieved from the growing frustration of simply chasing along behind Socrates and are permitted instead to reenlist as his ally in the pursuit of truth.

It is here that we come upon the first of several ways in which the limitations of Plato's rationalism and his attendant assault on a masculine mode of discourse become evident. Plato sometimes abandons dialectical inquiry and takes up an allegorical mode, not merely because most of Socrates' interlocutors (and presumably Plato's reading audience) are too dim-witted to follow a chain of pure abstract reasoning, but because as thinkers and actors, humans are more than merely reasoning beings. Our mental universe is shaped by logic, causal relations, and immediate necessity but also by imagination, dream, and desire. And for all of Plato's railing against the appetitive or desirous, the fanciful or poetic, he does not and cannot jettison these parts of our being. Socrates and

Plato must awaken and inspire precisely these dimensions of us because they are involved in a political struggle to loosen our engagement with the immediate world of necessity and move our minds into a radically different, imaginative domain. They must break the conservative hold of the present and incite us to envision an order of existence and values utterly unlike our own yet identifiably human and livable. This cannot be accomplished merely by reasoning with us; rather, the sensuous, longing, appetitive elements of our being must be touched and drawn into the project. In this regard, Socrates and Plato know what many theorists of revolution after them may have inadequately appreciated: People are never moved to become revolutionaries through logic alone because it is not solely the reasoning part of us that feels and knows what is wrong with this world nor yearns for a different one.

In different language, the point is a familiar one to postmodern scholars of political theory: Platonic epistemology and pedagogy are intricately bound to Platonic politics. The *content* of Platonic truth, its *political* radicalism, is in part why the road to truth is not paved solely with dialectic, reason, or logic. The myths, allegories, stories, and images in the dialogues appeal to the dimensions of Socrates' companions that are not necessarily articulate but that feel, sense, and yearn. They touch what cannot be put into words, and what is therefore most important hermeneutically is not the textual details but the evocative power of the story, its capacity to *resound* within the listener. Quite simply, Plato knows what many of his contemporary students may not: The storyteller reaches and moves places inside human beings that will forever elude the analytic philosopher.

It is because dialectic is a springboard for glimpsing the truth but not what actually makes the leap (*Republic* 511b) that Plato places so much importance upon nurturing philosophical studies in souls of innately good character that have been properly reared and trained. Many can reason brilliantly who will fall drastically short of being philosophers; in this important sense, philosophy can never be reduced to a *science* of argument. In the *Republic,* Socrates declares that the true lover of knowledge must be just, moderate, courageous, graceful, and indifferent to material and sensual pleasure (*Republic* 485a–487a). Or, as Plato casts the matter in the *Seventh Letter,* "natural intelligence and a good memory are equally powerless to aid the man who has not an inborn affinity with the subject." He then names "justice and all the other noble ideals" as constitutive of this "inborn affinity" (*Seventh Letter* 344a). It is in the

Phaedrus, however, that Plato offers the richest account of the complex, organic process of learning and instructing others in the pursuit of wisdom: "The dialectician selects a soul of the right type, and in it he plants and sows his words founded on knowledge, words which can defend both themselves and him who planted them, words which instead of remaining barren contain a seed whence new words grow up in new characters, whereby the seed is vouchsafed immortality, and its possessor the fullest measure of blessedness that man can attain unto" (*Phaedrus* 277a).

Even with virtuous souls for students, particular individuals must be taught or drawn toward truth in the fashion appropriate to the character and capacities of that individual. A Thrasymachus is not spoken to in the same way as a Glaucon, a musical soul is initiated into knowledge differently from an erotic or spirited one. "You must discover the type of speech appropriate to each nature, and arrange your discourse accordingly, addressing a variegated soul in a variegated style that ranges over the whole gamut of tones and a simple soul in a simple style" (*Phaedrus* 277c). The point again is that for Socrates, thinking, speaking, and sharing knowledge are activities done for the sake of an individual's acquisition of virtue, not for extrinsic, instrumental purposes. Individuals must never be addressed as potential objects or instruments of power and reputation but, rather, each must be individually nurtured as a living, active embodiment of justice and virtue. This kind of pedagogy and politics, which some might call "maternal" in its attention to particular needs, comprises a direct assault on the instrumentalism of Athenian politics—the politics of agonistic speech and deed in which others are tools or impediments to one's own or the polis' glory.

III

If dialectic is but an instrument for approaching the truth, how does one actually grasp it, what is the experience or phenomenon of seeing it? Here we arrive at the historically neglected aspect of Plato's theory of knowledge.[17] For the experience of actually seeing the truth is nothing short of an experience which witnesses will perceive as madness. It is an inspired, speechless, incommunicable experience in which the philosopher or poet is literally "possessed" by the truth and is rebuked by others as being "out of his wits" (*Phaedrus* 249d). Dialectic leads the way but "at last in a flash, understanding . . . blazes up, and the mind, as it exerts all its powers to the limit of human capacity, is flooded with light" (*Seventh Letter* 344b).

For Plato, recovery or recollection of truth is the soul's recovery of its "wings," the wings it had in its prior existence in the heavens but loses upon descending into a mortal body. "The natural property of a wing is to raise that which is heavy and carry it aloft to the region where the gods dwell" (*Phaedrus* 246e). Thus, when a student of wisdom begins to draw near the truth, the soul "throbs with ferment in every part, and even as a teething child feels an aching . . . in its gums when a tooth has just come through, so does the soul of him who is beginning to grow his wings feel a ferment and a painful irritation" (*Phaedrus* 251c). Actually coming together with that which is being beheld releases a "flood of passion" whereby the soul is "warmed and fostered," given respite from its anguish and filled with joy (*Phaedrus* 251c).

What is remarkable and revealing in this highly sexual account of the experience of beholding "true being" is that Socrates is speaking simultaneously of the experience of love of wisdom and love of another human being. Here, as in the *Symposium,* he is suggesting not merely similarity but potential identity or accord between loving truth and loving a person. Pursuit of knowledge is, ultimately, an erotic endeavor and brings the pursuer to the same heights of frenzied rapture as love of a human creature does. The greatest blessings, Plato insists, come by way of madness, "indeed of madness that is heaven-sent." This divine "madness" is always superior to man-made sanity and one should therefore "prefer the friendship of the passionate to that of the sane" (*Phaedrus* 244b–245b). For Plato, madness is nothing more and nothing less than divine inspiration—only in this state does the poet or rhapsodist express beauty, the philosopher encounter wisdom, and the lover know the fullness and meaning of love (*Ion* 534a–535c; *Phaedrus* 249d–e). Socrates speaks of this state as one of being literally "held" or possessed by the gods—the soul has recovered its participation in true being by being born aloft into the place where true being resides, that is, in the heavens. This is a condition of madness because the soul has taken leave of the earthly realm of things, language, persons, customs, and activity. Here is Socrates' description in the *Phaedrus:*

> The soul of the philosopher alone recovers her wings, for she . . . is ever near in memory to those things a god's nearness whereunto

> makes him truly god. . . . Standing aside from the busy doings of mankind, and drawing nigh to the divine, he is rebuked by the multitude as being out of his wits, for they know not that he is possessed by a deity. . . . When he that loves beauty is touched by such madness he is called a lover. Such a one, as soon as he beholds the beauty of this world, is reminded of true beauty, and his wings begin to grow; then he is fain to lift his wings and fly upward; yet he has not the power, but inasmuch as he gazes upward like a bird, and cares nothing for the world beneath, men charge it upon him that he is demented. (*Phaedrus* 249d–e)

Hardly a depiction of logocentrism or male rationalism have we here: speechless rapture, frenzied passion, gazing upward like a bird, possessed by the gods—these are the characteristics of one who is beholding the truth. We have also, of course, encountered Socrates himself, as he is caricatured by Aristophanes, as he is depicted by Aristodemus at the beginning of the *Symposium,* as he speaks of his state when he first begins to discuss love with Phaedrus—"you must not be surprised if, as my speech proceeds, I become as one possessed" (*Phaedrus* 238d; *Symposium* 175). Not Socrates the dialectician but Socrates the lover of wisdom is before us, Socrates who speaks of philosophy as a lover and who insists that the most divine progeny are born of erotic discourse (*Gorgias* 481d–482d). In the *Republic,* Socrates develops the image of the passionately sexual, monogamous, possessive, and procreative lover of wisdom in a passage that moves from the sexual act to procreation and birth in a split second:

> The real lover of learning . . . does not tarry by each of the many things opined to be but goes forward and does not lose the keenness of his passionate love nor cease from it before he grasps the nature itself of each thing which is with the part of the soul fit to grasp a thing of that sort; and it is the part akin to it that is fit. And once near it and coupled with what really is, having begotten intelligence and truth, he knows and lives truly, is nourished and so ceases from his labor pains, but not before. (*Republic* 490b)

Plato's insistence upon the procreative dimension of true philosophizing is open to several possible interpretations. One kind of feminist reading might cast it as simply another instance of men seeking to appropriate for themselves women's distinctive capacity for procreation. Whether men envy, fear, or despise women for their unique capacity to generate and deliver new life into the world, men will attempt to resolve their uneasiness about this capacity through socially controlling women and reproduction, on the one hand, and ideologically appropriating this power, on the other. The process of appropriation involves men depicting themselves as progenitors of ideas and truths, and declaring their progeny to be vastly superior to the "mere life" offered up by women. "And I ask you, who would not prefer such fatherhood to merely human propagation?" (*Symposium*, 209d).[18]

A more sympathetic feminist reading of Plato's rendering of philosophizing as procreative is also possible. In contradistinction to an agonistic context for philosophizing, in which glory, reputation, and power are preeminently at stake in espousing wisdom, Plato locates philosophy in the realm of love, nurturance, and procreation. The birth and cultivation of new ideas are the natural product of a well-chosen union between two virtuous human beings (*Symposium* 209c). Philosophical truth is thus situated in the context of love, attachment, and desire for Good. Conversely, truth escapes the seeker's grasp when the struggle for it occurs in a context of individual striving for recognition, fame, or power (*Republic* 496a).[19]

Plato's depiction of philosophizing as a procreative activity is also subject to a third interpretation, one that draws from both of the other two. Socrates occupies a social-sexual milieu of male homosexuality, inarguably a nonprocreative milieu. Moreover, while most Athenian citizens married and fathered children, this did not generally entail attachment to the *oikos*, celebration of intercourse with women, or passionate involvement with them. Thus what we might be seeing in Plato's treatment of philosophy is a justification of male homosexuality through an attempt to imbue it with some natural telos such that the highest form of procreation is cast as the procreation of ideas between male lovers. "And so the bond between them will be more binding, and their communion even more complete, than that which comes of bringing children up, because they have created something lovelier and less mortal than human seed" (*Symposium* 209c).[20] One problem with this interpretation is that Plato ultimately proscribes male homosexual intercourse and Socrates refuses the sexual advances of his beloved

Alcibiades (*Symposium* 219). Another problem with it is that Plato personifies philosophy as female.

The importance of Plato's personification of philosophy as a woman can be appreciated only in the context of the stages of divinely inspired love depicted in the *Symposium.* For it is not the mortal beloved (male) but the pursuit of wisdom or true being that constitutes the highest stage and is sought after by the truly philosophical lover. This pursuit is facilitated through loving another's beauty, but it is not consummated by that love (*Symposium* 211c). The highest love is love of truth, love of the woman, Philosophy (*Symposium* 210c–d). And it is through intercourse with her that beautiful children (true ideas) are produced. Listen to the way Socrates speaks of Philosophy's would-be lovers in the corrupt Athens of his own day:

> Men for whom philosophy is most suitable go into exile and leave her abandoned and unconsummated . . . while other unworthy men come to her and disgrace her. Of those who have intercourse with her, some are worthless and the many worthy of bad things. . . . When men unworthy of education come near her and keep her company in an unworthy way, what sort of notions and opinions will we say they beget? Won't they be truly fit to be called sophisms, connected with nothing genuine or worthy of true prudence? (*Republic* 495c, 496a)

True being, philosophy, and wisdom, are depicted as female just as it is a woman, Diotima, who taught Socrates what he knows about the relationship between Eros and Wisdom (*Symposium* 201d). Truth is what fulfills and perfects a man in Plato's account, and Truth is a woman, something that lies well beyond all the agonistic striving and straining of the Athenian ethos but something that lies beyond reason as well.

And here, I think, is the heart of the matter: The ephemeral, mad, speechless, erotic, procreative, and blessed nature of true philosophic insight in Plato's account culminates in an opposition to maleness, to socially male characteristics of mind and action. Socrates teaches his friends to recognize philosophers by their soothing, gentle character and to reject as unphilosophical those who "burst in like drunken revelers, abusing one another and indulging in a taste for quarreling" (*Republic* 500b). In the development and right employment of dialectic, philosophy has its "masculine moment," but its culmination or consummation is a caricatured female precisely in the Greek but also larger Western sense of being irrational, unfathomable to most men, powerless to express itself in the language of men, subversive of established order, and procreative. Truth itself is female, and the souls worthy of her have shed their embeddedness in male practices, styles, and ambitions in order to approach her. The Eros of philosophizing, the connection between the philosopher and "her" object of study, is also female: Feminine souls are depicted as lusting for female beauty, a search that culminates in a strange sexual hybrid of frenzied rapture (*jouissance?*) and procreation. What do men know of such eros? This would be precisely the point: Plato is radically revaluing and resituating both the activity and the content of philosophy; to signify this radicality, he renders the knower, the known, and the quality of their relation in dramatically foreign terms. He makes strange by making female the entire philosophical endeavor, thereby seeking not only to divest philosophy and politics of the socially male qualities to which he objects but also to rupture, more generally, the ground of existing ontological and epistemological assumptions about knowledge and power.

Plato locates truth in a realm unfathomable and inaccessible to men bent upon political or material advantage, not only the Sophists and their students, but any whose temperament leans to the pursuit of individual gain or glory, public display, or agonistic rivalry. Those who love and are deserving of philosophy will not be regarded as real men by their Greek peers. They will abrogate both the "macho" posturing and much of the misogyny constitutive of Greek manhood, and they will be disparaged in gendered terms by their peers for doing so. Moreover, as I shall argue in the next section, Plato's formulation of philosophy, philosophers, and truth are unmanly in their relation to institutional political power.

IV

It is a commonplace that Plato experiences great difficulty in reconciling philosophy with political power, yet he must achieve this reconciliation for philosophy to achieve the bearing and status he seeks for it in the city. The *Republic* itself can be read as a prolonged (and ultimately unsuccessful) effort to wrestle this problem to the ground. I want to consider here an aspect of this problem that reveals an equivocal relationship to gender at its core. Both Socrates and Plato, albeit in somewhat different ways, are ensconced in and advocate what can be regarded as an antimasculine relationship to power. With Socrates, the focus is upon his privatization of the philosophical vocation, his valuation of friends and the city of Athens over abstract principles, and his personal eschewal of political power. With Plato, the focus is upon the "politics" of the *Republic* itself, that is, the structures of power and the animating values of the ideal city.

Although Socrates served in Athenian political and military offices when called to do so, he located his vocation as philosopher in the "private" sphere. He explicitly shied away from political life, refused to make a genuinely public activity out of his work or "calling," and eschewed the honors, material reward, and formal power that his intellectual talents have earned him. Socrates' own account of this choice is offered in the *Apology*, where he insists that engaging in politics would have "long ago cost me my life, without doing any good either to you or to myself" (*Apology* 31d). Instead of bringing his concerns with justice and goodness to political life, Socrates explains, he has "busied himself on his [fellow citizens'] behalf, going like a father or an elder brother to see each one of you privately and urging you to set your thoughts on goodness" (*Apology* 31d). What Socrates makes quite clear in this discussion is that he considers his efforts at improving individual souls in the city the most important work a person can do, far more important than the business of politics. Thus he does not reject politics merely because he is ill-suited for it but because it is a superficial and corrupt affair compared to the activity in which he is engaged, an activity described best by Socrates himself:

> So long as I draw breath and have my faculties, I shall never stop practicing philosophy and exhorting you and elucidating the truth for everyone that I meet. I shall go on saying, in my usual way, My very good friend, you are an Athenian and belong to a city which is the greatest and most famous in the world for its wisdom and strength. Are you not ashamed that you give your attention to acquiring as much money as possible, and similarly with reputation and honor, and give no attention or thought to truth and understanding and the perfection of your soul? (*Apology* 29e)

Socrates does not simply refuse the inconveniences and constraints of political life as a location for his work, he refuses the relevance of political life to virtue and justice. Yet Socrates does not reject Athens. Rather, he recasts the political entity, Athens, as a *familial* body to which he feels obligation, indeed a profound familial obligation. His commitment is to improving the souls and the virtue of individual Athenians as if he were a "father or elder brother" to each of them; his civic identity is not democratic or heroic but familial. Ultimately, he even sacrifices himself for this family; he chooses Athens over his own life and chooses to die at Athens' hands rather than live apart from her. Socrates' life and death embody the values he consistently espouses: He acts according to love of city-as-family, virtue, and truth, he concerns himself with the concrete effects of his actions on others, and he shuns political power, property, prestige, and glory. In the Greek sense at least, Socrates is no man.

Yet if Socrates has little use for public life, neither has he much interest in genuine private life—*oikos* or family affairs. He openly acknowledges his personal "neglect of family" and the hardships created for them by his choice of poverty (*Apology* 31b). Socrates lives in the streets and the bars; he lives for the wisdom and understanding he can acquire and disseminate in these places. Thus Socrates leads neither a personal life nor, in the established sense, a political life; he leads the life of the citizen-philosopher. If he is no man in the sense of sharing in political power, neither is he an *idios* in the sense of being tied to the realm of *oikos*. Again, Socrates' subversion of masculine values and discourse issues from somewhere other than masculinity's formal "opposite."

While Socrates does not situate his opposition to the masculine values of the polis in its traditional antinomy, there is a respect in which his relationship to politics and to the city can be seen as womanly. For Socrates works with Athenian citizens much as women are said to work—by trying to shape men in the private sphere, beseeching and remonstrating them in places outside the purview of political power and performance.[21] He rejects the masculine penchant for wielding institutional power in which individuals become relatively more abstract in favor of the typically feminine mode of addressing the interiors of individuals to develop or manipulate them. Socrates tries to nourish virtue in the men who are or will be controlling and shaping the world. He avoids reaching into the realm of power itself and avoids particular questions of policy. He adopts a posture of ignorance and disinterest toward the internal workings of conventional political practices and machinations. He moralizes while other men act. However, he does not therefore view himself as irrelevant to politics. Rather, he regards what he does as the only truly worthy political work. His avoidance of Athenian public life is a criticism of public political life itself and hence a criticism of the male raison d'être in Athens.

Plato's effort to dramatically recast political life and power is moored in precisely this Socratic critique. In the *Republic,* politics is ostensibly about virtue, wisdom, and the collective good, not power, struggle, and interest. Plato strives to expunge the sources and causes of power struggles from every corner of his ideal city. He abolishes private families, property, and the governing bodies familiar to Athenian democrats, thereby seeking to eliminate the battles and tensions issuing from private ownership on one hand and public participation or debate on the other. In a move absolutely counter to the traditional masculine thrust of politics, Plato strives to purge the city of all conflict and to bind it together as the most close-knit (and idealized) family ever conceived, where each is sister or brother to every other. "The city best governed is that which is most like a single human being" (*Republic* 462d).[22] When all of this is accomplished, the only power issue remaining is the ultimate one—control or rule of the city itself. And here Plato chooses "those who least want to rule," philosophers, as captains of the ship. Only philosophers will place love of truth and love of the city over personal gain. Only philosophers disdain power as much as they love beauty and truth. Only philosophers will succeed in replacing politics as Athenians knew it with politics as Socrates conceived it, politics as the cultivation of individual virtue and the virtuous community.

The *structure* of the ideal city is effeminate in its replacement of political faction and public assembly with relations of familial hierarchy and accord. For Plato, harmonious interdependence is a more sublime value than individual glory; each individual finds fulfillment as a strand in the family web rather than through independent identity or endeavor. The *leadership* of this city is effeminate in its unfamiliarity with and dislike of political power. Philosophers, like the typically socialized female, may have to be dragged to the reins of power. "If there is one thing women are queasy about, it is *actually taking power.*"[23] Like philosophers, women need political power—both to protect themselves and to advance their vision of the world, and like philosophers, women are often extremely uncomfortable with seeking or holding power.[24] Finally, the *ethos* of this city is effeminate in valorizing harmony and stability over glory and risk, "fullness" or fulfillment over striving and ambition. For Plato, not freedom but belonging is the basis of happiness (*Republic* 520a).

In naming Socrates' approach to philosophy and Plato's approach to politics "effeminate," I am not praising them, for they have fallen into precisely the error of some contemporary feminists: Upon contemplating the horrors or even the limitations of the masculine political world, one strain of feminism repudiates politics and glorifies traditionally female activities rather than seek a transformed political life. If Plato is remarkable for his profound recognition of "the personal as political," he is limited in his recognition of the value and possibilities of a reconstituted *public* life. Like such feminists, he runs from and shuns public power, conflict, striving, and struggle rather than seeking to liberate these things from their problematic masculine habitat.[25]

To glimpse the problem another way, despite their consciousness of the constructed nature of both gender and politics, and despite their attempt to subvert the conventional constructions, there is a respect in which Socrates and Plato end up reinforcing Athenian constructions of politics as irredeemably male and corrupt while glorifying philosophy as female, powerless, and pure. As such, there is no place for philosophy in existing cities (Plato's great lament) and no place for existing cities in philosophy (the lament of Plato's loyal critics). In short, Plato's infamy as purveyor of the "death" of politics at the hands of philosophy arises from his limited vision regarding the reconciliation of attributes historically divided between male and female. Elements of soul, temperament, ethics, thought, and politics, which existed in an antinomous (and gender-specific) relation in Plato's own milieu, he accepted as inherent antinomies. Thus, despite Socrates' erotic nature and pedagogy, Plato devises his nurturant, virtuous community by suppressing individual bodies on the one hand and the "body politic" on the other.[26] The body and the body politic alike constitute a danger to the eternally stable, harmonious soul or city. And, although his political philosophy required it and he struggled to formulate it, he could not finally conjure a "sensuous rationality" but only mind ruling sensual being or sensual being ruling mind. Similarly, he could not imagine a dynamic and striving moral community but only vital corruption or static virtue. He could not imagine power that was not domination but only the dominance of the powerful or collective powerlessness. He could only negate or subvert; he could not synthesize or rearrange, he could not plumb the depths of the malleability, the fully constructed nature, of gender and politics.

Notes

1. Two notable exceptions to the feminist focus on Book V are Mary O'Brien, *Politics of Reproduction* (Boston: Routledge and Kegan Paul, 1981), 124–36, and Arlene Saxonhouse, "The Philosopher and the Female in the Political Thought of Plato," *Political Theory* 4, no. 2 (1976): 195–212, or the revised version in *Women in the History of Political Thought: Ancient Greece to Machiavelli* (New York: Praeger, 1985), chap. 3 (also repr. Chapter 4, this volume).

2. In this essay, I have not attempted to sort out the problem of "who's who" between Socrates and Plato; yet my subject does not permit simply eschewing the matter. In fact, it could be argued that Plato's introduction of the Forms and his development of an epistemology that jettisons the distinctly erotic element imbued to philosophy by Socrates sharply attenuates the subversion of masculine discourse in which Socrates was engaged. Plato appears to thwart both the democratic and the sensual elements of Socrates' mode of philosophizing; he moves away from Socrates' attempt to *embed* philosophizing in the city, in individuals, in the whole of human existence, and instead, renders philosophy a distant, methodical search for Truth.

Indeed, Plato can be seen as the partial "Thermidor" of the revolution in thought opened up by Socrates: He proffers truth claims that are certain and universal (the *eidos*) as opposed to Socrates' more tentative and situational ones; he develops a pedagogy that is distanced and institutionalized (in the Academy) as opposed to Socrates' personalized conversations with friends; and his mode of inquiry is directed and controlled, rather than vulnerable in its absence of clear boundaries.

Notwithstanding these possible differences between Plato and Socrates, my primary concern in this essay lies with a feature of the Platonic dialogues other than the Plato–Socrates problem. Moreover, it is ultimately impossible to accurately separate the author of the dialogues from his favorite protagonist—the separations suggested above are as speculative as such attempts always are. Consequently, my argument about Plato's subversion of masculine discourse does not devolve upon the Socrates–Plato distinction, and while I sometimes distinguish the two philosophers from one another, at other times I treat them interchangeably or under the simple rubric, "Plato."

3. On what grounds can the teachings of the Sophists be termed "fundamental" to the Athenian political ethos? Although the Sophists whom Plato criticizes were foreigners, and appear to have been generally disliked by the Athenian political establishment, they "had no difficulty in finding pupils to pay their high fees, or audiences for their public lectures and displays" (W. K. C. Gutherie, *The Sophists* [Cambridge: Cambridge University Press, 1971], 38). Thus, while the Sophists themselves did not share political power, and were reviled by some of those in power, public disparagement of them was not merely opposition to a group of professional intellectuals but rather to a central feature of Athenian public life. For similar reasons, Plato's critique of the Sophists cannot be reduced entirely to intellectual rivalry. For Plato, the Sophists were a symptom of their age: "They were doing no more than mirror the lusts and passions of the existing democracy" (Gutherie 21).

4. Saxonhouse, *Women in the History of Political Thought*, 38.

5. Hans-Georg Gadamer, *Dialogue and Dialectic*, trans. by P. C. Smith (New Haven: Yale University Press, 1980), 50.

6. In *The Human Condition,* Hannah Arendt offers an uncritical account of the "masculinism" of this ontology (Chicago: Chicago University Press, 1958), chap. 2. Nancy Hartsock offers a feminist interpretation in *Money, Sex, and Power: Toward a Feminist Materialism* (Boston: Northeastern University Press, 1983), chaps. 7 and 8.

7. Saxonhouse, *Women in the History of Political Thought,* 38, 49, 51.

8. Of course, there is nothing intrinsically masculine about these virtues but with the obvious exception of Plato in Book V of the *Republic,* they were commonly held to be virtues that not only designated manliness but in which women could not share. Lacking the capacity for complete wisdom, women could not be just; lacking a domain for the expression of courage, they could not develop it; and lacking the mastery of body by mind, they are necessarily less temperate and continent. See Michael Shaw, "The Female Intruder: Women in Fifth-Century Drama," *Classical Philology* (October 1975), esp. 256–257.

9. In chapter 4 of *Manhood and Politics: A Feminist Reading in Political Theory* (Totowa, N.J.: Rowman and Littlefield, 1988), I discuss more extensively the gendered foundation of the ancient Athenian view of the body, in which the body was simultaneously celebrated as an artifact of beauty and athletic marvel and repudiated as animalistic in its ordinary needs and expressions.

10. The issue here is whether humans control or are controlled by their physiological aspect. In most Greek texts, women and male slaves are depicted as ontologically derivative from their physiology and bodily functions. Aristotle and Arendt attempt to make a systematic political metaphysic out of this often faintly articulated assumption and use this principle to divide the human from the less than human. That Plato rejects this depiction of women does not mean that he rejects the distinction: indeed, his argument in Book V is that when women are not engaged in reproduction, they need not be controlled by their bodies. In other words, when not engaged in reproduction, women can be just like men.

11. Saxonhouse, *Women in the History of Political Thought,* 49.

12. Friedrich Nietzsche, "Twilight of the Idols," in *The Portable Nietzsche,* trans. W. Kaufman (New York: Penguin, 1976), 478, 480. Jacques Derrida, *Disseminations,* trans. B. Johnson (Chicago: University of Chicago Press, 1981).

13. Plato's strongest effort to establish this is contained in the *Meno,* wherein Socrates "proves" that an uneducated slave has a latent knowledge of geometry that a skilled "teacher" can draw forth from him. Socrates: "And the spontaneous recovery of knowledge that is in him is recollection, isn't it?" (*Meno* 85d).

14. On this point, see Hans-Georg Gadamer, *Truth and Method* (New York: Seabury, 1975), 367–70.

15. In November 1976, at the University of California, Santa Cruz, John Schaar offered a splendid reading of Plato in which the myths and allegories were treated not as mere supplements to the chain of reasoning but as revelatory of an entire mode of political thought and philosophical conversation. I long ago incorporated parts of this reading into my own work and cannot footnote precisely; suffice to say, I hope, that Schaar's lecture is the basis of this portion of my argument.

16. John Schaar, 1976 lecture (see note 15).

17. A recent example of this neglect is Mary Nichols, who ignores the "mad" and "speechless" qualities of the philosophical encounter with truth in her otherwise rich account of the two types of philosophy in the *Republic.* "The Republic's Two Alternatives: Philosopher-Kings and Socrates," *Political Theory* (May 1984): 252–74.

18. This is the kind of interpretation one might associate with the feminism of Mary O'Brien, *Politics of Reproduction.*

19. This is the kind of interpretation one might associate with the feminism of Carol Gilligan, *In a Different Voice* (Cambridge: Harvard University Press, 1982) or Sara Ruddick,

"Maternal Thinking," in *Mothering: Essays in Feminist Theory,* ed. Joyce Trebilcot (Totowa, N.J.: Rowman and Allanheld, 1983), 213–20.

20. In "Love and Sex in Plato's Epistemology," Evelyn Fox Keller offers a fascinating interpretation of the relationship between Plato's epistemology and his male homosexual milieu. *Reflections on Gender and Science* (New Haven: Yale University Press, 1985), chap. 1.

21. While my point is that this is a nearly universal stereotype of women and by no means particular to ancient Greece, *Lysistrata* is a Greek example of the female attempt to influence public power from the private sphere.

22. This is one of those places in which Plato and Socrates move in a common direction but according to rather different visions. While both treat the family as a model for relations among citizens, Socrates' version of the family is a far more liberated, egalitarian, and playful one than is Plato's. Socrates, "familial" relation to Athens was characterized by openness, equality, and devotion to its members as genuine friends. Plato, on the other hand, offers something more like an idealized patriarchal family in the *Republic:* philosopher-rulers know what is best for all, and the rest of the city's inhabitants are meant to find fulfillment in serving the "higher good" of the city as a whole. Similarly, Socrates seems to revel in human diversity and incorporate it into his approach to familial relations with Athens while Plato strives to reduce diversity in the family that is the "ideal city" of the *Republic.*

23. Marilyn Frye, "On Separatism and Power," *The Politics of Reality: Essays in Feminist Theory* (Trumansburg, N.Y.: Crossing, 1983), 107.

24. Helene Moglen, "Power and Empowerment," *Women's Studies International Forum* (Spring 1983): 133.

25. Since political power has been historically constructed and engaged by men, and since it often imperils the lives it has been women's task to nourish and protect, many radical feminists conjure a vision of collective life "beyond" political power. Marilyn French makes the project evident in the very title of her magnum opus on feminism, *Beyond Power* (New York: Summit, 1985).

26. This move, too, is paralleled by some contemporary feminists. Because of the historically oppressive organization of female sexuality and reproduction, women's oppression may *appear* to be inherently grounded in the body. Some feminists have therefore cast the metaphysical or technological overcoming of the body as fundamental to women's entry into humanity and history. Two classic examples of this problematic tendency within feminism are Simone de Beauvoir, *The Second Sex* (New York: Knopf, 1952) and Shulamith Firestone, *The Dialectic of Sex* (New York: Bantam, 1971). Andrea Dworkin carries on the tradition in her recent work *Intercourse* (New York: Free Press, 1987).

9

Sorcerer Love: A Reading of Plato's *Symposium*, Diotima's Speech[1]

Luce Irigaray

Translated by Eleanor H. Kuykendall

In the *Symposium,* the dialogue on love, when Socrates finishes speaking, he gives the floor to a woman: Diotima. She does not participate in these exchanges or in this meal among men. She is not there. She herself does not speak. Socrates reports or recounts her views. He borrows her wisdom and power, declares her his initiator, his pedagogue, on matters of love, but she is not invited to teach or to eat. Unless she did not want to accept an invitation? But Socrates says nothing about that. And Diotima is not the only example of a woman whose wisdom, above all in love, is reported in her absence by a man.

Diotima's teaching will be very dialectical—but different from what we usually call dialectical. Unlike Hegel's, her dialectic does not work by opposition to transform the first term into the second, in order to arrive at a synthesis of the two. At the very outset, she establishes the *intermediary* and she never abandons it as a mere way or means. Her method is not, then, a propaedeutic of the *destruction* or *destructuration* of two terms in order to establish a synthesis which is neither one nor the other. She presents, uncovers, unveils the existence of a third that is already there and that permits progression: from poverty to wealth, from ignorance to wisdom, from mortality to immortality. For her, this progression always leads to a greater perfection of and in love.

But, contrary to the usual dialectical methods, love ought not to be abandoned for the sake of becoming wise or learned. It is love that leads to knowledge—both practical and metaphysical. It is love that is both the guide and the way, above all a mediator.

Love is designated as a theme, but love is also perpetually enacted, dramatized, in the exposition of the theme.

So Diotima immediately rebuts the claims that love is a great God and that it is the love of beautiful things. At the risk of offending the Gods, Diotima also asserts that love is neither beautiful nor good. This leads her interlocutor to suppose immediately that love is ugly and bad, incapable as he is of grasping the existence or instance of what is held *between*, what permits the passage between ignorance and knowledge. If we did not, at each moment, have something to learn in the encounter with reality, between reality and already established knowledge, we would not perfect ourselves in wisdom. And not to become wiser means to become more ignorant.

Therefore, between knowledge and reality, there is an intermediary which permits the meeting and transmutation or transvaluation between the two. The dialectic of Diotima is in *four terms,* at least: the here, the two poles of the meeting, the beyond, but a beyond which never abolishes the here. And so on, indefinitely. The mediator is never abolished in an infallible knowledge. Everything is always in movement, in becoming. And the mediator of everything is, among other things, or exemplarily, love. Never completed, always evolving.

And, in response to the protestation of Socrates that love is a great God, that *everyone says so or thinks so,* she *laughs.* Her retort is not at all angry, balancing between contradictories; it is laughter from elsewhere. Laughing, then, she asks Socrates who this *everyone* is. Just as she ceaselessly undoes the assurance or the *closure* of opposing terms, so she rejects every ensemble of unities reduced to a similitude in order to constitute a whole:

> "You mean, by all who do not know?" said she, "or by all who know as well?" "Absolutely all." At that she laughed. (202)[2]
>
> ("Ce tout le monde dont tu parles, sont-ce, dit-elle, ceux qui savent ou ceux qui ne savent pas?—Tous en général, ma foi!" Elle se mit à rire.)

The tension between opposites thus abated, she shows, demonstrates, that "everyone" does not exist, nor does the position of love as *eternally* a great God. Does she teach nothing that is already defined? A method of becoming wise, learned, more perfect in love and in art (*l'art*). She ceaselessly questions Socrates on his positions but without, like a master, positing already constituted truths. Instead, she teaches the renunciation of already established truths. And each time that Socrates thinks that he can take something as certain, she undoes his certainty. All entities, substantives, adverbs, sentences are patiently, and joyously, called into question.

For love, the demonstration is not so difficult to establish. For, if love possessed all that he desired, he would desire no more.[3] He must lack, therefore, in order to desire still. But, if love had nothing at all to do with beautiful and good things, he could not desire them either. Thus, he is an *intermediary* in a very specific sense. Does he therefore lose his status as a God? Not necessarily. He is neither mortal nor immortal: he is between the one and the other. Which qualifies him as demonic. Love is a *demon*—his function is to transmit to the gods what comes from men and to men what comes from the gods. Like everything else that is demonic, love is complementary to gods and to men in such a way as to join everything with itself. There must be a being of middling nature in order for men and gods to enter into relations, into conversation, while awake or asleep. Which makes love a kind of divination, priestly knowledge of things connected with sacrifice, initiation, incantation, prediction in general and magic.

The demons who serve as mediators between men and gods are numerous and very diverse. Love is one of them. And Love's parentage is very particular: child of *Plenty* (himself son of *Invention*) and of *Poverty*, conceived the day the birth of Aphrodite was celebrated. Thus love is always poor and

> . . . rough, unkempt, unshod, and homeless, ever couching on the ground uncovered, sleeping beneath the open sky by doors and in the streets, because he has the nature of his mother. . . . But again, in keeping with his father, he has designs upon the beautiful and good, for he is bold, headlong, and intense, a mighty hunter, always weaving some device or other, eager in invention and resourceful, searching after wisdom all through life, terrible as a magician, sorcerer, and sophist. Further, in his

nature he is not immortal, nor yet mortal. No, on a given day, now he flourishes and lives, when things go well with him, and again he dies, but through the nature of his sire revives again. Yet his gain for ever slips away from him, so that Eros never is without resources, nor is ever rich.

As for ignorance and knowledge, here again he is midway between them. The case stands thus. No god seeks after wisdom, or wishes to grow wise (for he already is so), no more than anybody else seeks after wisdom if he has it. Nor, again, do ignorant folk seek after wisdom or long to grow wise; for here is just the trouble about ignorance, that what is neither beautiful and good, nor yet intelligent, to itself seems good enough. Accordingly, the man who does not think himself in need has no desire for what he does not think himself in need of.

[*Socrates.*] The seekers after knowledge, Diotima! If they are not the wise, nor yet the ignorant (said I), who are they, then?

[*Diotima.*] The point (said she) is obvious even to a child, that they are persons intermediate between these two, and that Eros is among them; for wisdom falls within the class of the most beautiful, while Eros is an eros for the beautiful. And hence it follows necessarily that Eros is a seeker after wisdom [a philosopher], and being a philosopher, is midway between wise and ignorant. (203–4)

(rude et malpropre; un va-nu-pieds qui n'a point de domicile, dormant à la belle étoile sur le pas des portes ou dans la rue selon la nature de sa mére. Mais, en revanche, guettant, sans cesse, embusqué les choses belles et bonnes, chasseur habile et ourdissant continûment quelque ruse, curieux de pensée et riche d'expédient, passant toute sa vie à philosopher, habile comme sorcier, comme inventeur de philtres magiques, comme sophiste, selon la nature de son père. De plus, sa nature n'est ni d'un mortel ni d'un immortel, mais, le même jour, tantôt, quand ses expédients ont réussi, il est en fleur, il a de la vie; tantôt au contraire il est mourant; puis, derechef, il revient à la vie grace au naturel de son père, tandis que, d'autre part, coule de ses mains le fruit de ses expédients! Ainsi, ni jamais Amour n'est indigent, ni jamais il est riche! Entre savoir et ignorance, maintenant, Amour est intermédiare. Voici ce qui en est. Parmi les

Dieux, il n'y en a aucun qui ait envie de devenir sage, car il l'est; ne s'emploie pas non plus à philosopher quiconque d'autre est sage. Mais pas davantage les ignorants ne s'emploient, de leur côté, à philosopher, et ils n'ont pas envie de devenir sages; car, ce qu'il y a precisement de fâcheux dans l'ignorance, c'est que quelqu'un, qui n'est pas un homme accompli et qui n'est pas non plus intelligent, se figure l'être dans la mesure voulue; c'est que celui qui ne croit pas être depourvu n'a point envie de ce dont il ne croit pas avoir besoin d'etre pourvu. —Quels sont donc alors, Diotime, m'écriai-je, ceux qui s'emploient à philosopher si ce ne sont ni les sages ni les ignorants? —La chose est claire, ditelle, et même déjà pour un enfant! Ce sont ceux qui sont intermèdiares entre ces deux extrêmes, et au nombre desquels doit aussi se trouver Amour. La sagesse, en effet, est évidemment parmi les plus belles choses, et c'est au beau qu'Amour rapporte son amour; d'où il suit que, forcément, Amour est philosophe, et, étant philosophe, qu'il est intermédiare entre le savant et l'ignorant.)

Eros is therefore *intermediary* between couples of opposites: poverty-plenty, ignorance-wisdom, ugliness-beauty, dirtiness-cleanliness, death-life, etc. And that would be inscribed in love's nature as a result of his genealogy and date of conception. And love is a philosopher, love is philosophy. Philosophy is not formal knowledge, fixed, abstracted from all feeling. It is the search for love, love of beauty, love of wisdom, which is one of the most beautiful things. Like love, the philosopher would be someone poor, dirty, a bit of a bum, always an outsider, sleeping under the stars but very curious, adept in ruses and devices of all kinds, reflecting ceaselessly, a sorcerer, a sophist, sometimes flourishing, sometimes expiring. Nothing like the representation of the philosopher we generally give: learned, correctly dressed, with good manners, understanding everything, pedantically instructing us in a corpus of already codified doctrine. The philosopher is nothing like that. He is barefoot, going out under the stars in search of an encounter with reality, seeking the embrace, the acquaintance (*connaissance*) [co-birthing, *co-naissance*] of whatever gentleness of soul, beauty, wisdom might be found there. This incessant quest he inherits from his mother. He is a philosopher through his mother, an adept in invention through his father. But his passion for love, for beauty, for wisdom, comes to him from his mother, and from the date when he was conceived. Desired and wanted, besides, by his mother.

How is it that love and the philosopher are generally represented otherwise? Because they are imagined as *beloved* and not as *lovers*. As beloved Love, both like and unlike the philosopher, is imagined to be of unparalleled beauty, delicate, perfect, happy. Yet the lover has an entirely different nature. He goes toward what is kind, beautiful, perfect, etc. He does not possess these. He is poor, unhappy, always in search of . . . But what does he seek or love? That beautiful things become his—this is Socrates' answer. But what will happen to him if these things become his? To this question of Diotima's, Socrates has no answer. Switching "good" for "beautiful," she asks her question again. "That the good may be his," ("Qu'elles devienne siennes") Socrates repeats.

> "And what happens to the man when the good things become his?" "On this," said [Socrates], "I am more than ready with an answer: that he will be happy." (204–5)

> ("Et qu'en sera-t-il pour celui a qui il arrivera que les choses bonnes soient devenues siennes?" "Voilà, dit Socrate, à quoi je serai plus à mon aise pour répondre! Il sera heureux.")

And happiness seems to put an ultimate end to this dialogical repetition between Diotima and Socrates.

Socrates asks: what should we call what pertains to lovers? "By what manner of pursuit and in what activity does the eagerness and straining for the object get the name of Eros? And what may this action really be?" ("Quel est le genre d'existence, le mode d'activité pour lesquels à leur zèle, à leur effort soutenu conviendrait le nom d'amour, dis-moi? En quoi peu bien consister cet acte?") And Diotima replies: "This action is engendering in beauty, with relation both to body and to soul." (205, 206) ("C'est un enfantement dans la beauté et selon le corps et selon l'âme.") But Socrates understands nothing of another, equally clear, revelation . . . He understands nothing about fecundity in relation both to body and to soul:

> The union of a man and woman is, in fact, a generation; this is a thing divine; in a living creature that is mortal, it is an element of immortality, this fecundity and generation. (206)

(L'union de l'homme et de la femme est en effet un enfantement et c'est une affaire divine, c'est, dans le vivant mortel, la présence de ce qui est immortel: la fécondité et la procréation.)

This statement of Diotima's never seems to have been understood. Besides, she herself will go on to emphasize the procreative aspect of love. But first she stresses the character of *divine generation in every union between man and woman,* the presence of the immortal in the living mortal. All love would be creation, potentially divine, a path between the condition of the mortal and that of the immortal. Love is fecund before all procreation. And it has a *mediumlike, demonic* fecundity. Assuring everyone, male and female, the immortal becoming of the living. But there cannot be procreation of a divine nature in what is not in harmony. And harmony with the divine is not possible for the ugly, but only for the beautiful. Thus, according to Diotima, love between man and woman is beautiful, harmonious, divine. It must be in order for procreation to take place. It is not procreation that is beautiful and that constitutes the aim of love. The aim of love is to realize the immortality in the mortality between lovers. And the expansion which produces the child follows the joy at the approach of a beautiful object. But an ugly object leads to a turning back, the shriveling up of fecundity, the painfully borne weight of the desire to procreate. Procreation and generation in beauty—these are the aim of love, because it is thus that the eternity and imperishability of a mortal being manifest themselves.

Fecundity of love between lovers, regeneration of one by the other, passage to immortality in one another, through one another—these seem to become the condition, not the cause, of procreation. Certainly, Diotima tells Socrates that the creation of beauty, of a work of art (*l'oeuvre*) (solitary creation this time?) is insufficient, that it is necessary to give birth together to a child, that this wisdom is inscribed in the animal world itself. She continues to laugh at the way he goes looking for his truths beyond the most obvious everyday reality, which he does not see or even perceive. She mocks the way his dialectical or dialogical method forgets the most elementary truths. The way his discourse on love neglects to look at, to inform itself about, the amorous state and to inquire about its cause.

Diotima speaks of *cause* in a surprising way. We could note that her method does not enter into a chain of causalities, a chain that skips over or often forgets the intermediary as generative milieu. Usually, causality is not part of her reasoning. She borrows it from the animal world and evokes it, or invokes it, with respect to procreation. Instead of allowing the child to germinate or develop in the milieu of love and fecundity between man and woman, she seeks a cause of love in the animal world: procreation.

Diotima's method miscarries here. From here on, she leads love into a schism between mortal and immortal. Love loses its demonic character. Is this the founding act of the metaphysical? There will be lovers in body and lovers in soul. But the perpetual passage from mortal to immortal that lovers confer on one another is put aside. Love loses its divinity, its mediumlike, alchemical qualities between couples of opposites. The intermediary becomes the child, and no longer love. Occupying the place of love, the child can no longer be a lover. It is put in the place of the incessant movement of love. Beloved, no doubt; but how be beloved without being a lover? And is not love trapped *in the beloved,* contrary to what Diotima wanted in the first place? A beloved who is an end is substituted for love between men and women. A beloved who is a *will,* even a *duty,* and a *means* of attaining immortality. Lovers can neither attain nor advance that between themselves. That is the weakness of love, for the child as well. If the couple of lovers cannot care for the place of love like a third term between them, then they will not remain lovers and they cannot give birth to lovers. Something gets solidified in space-time with the loss of a vital intermediary milieu and of an accessible, loving, transcendental. A sort of teleological triangle replaces a perpetual movement, a perpetual transvaluation, a permanent becoming. Love was the vehicle of this. But, if procreation becomes its goal, it risks losing its internal motivation, its fecundity "in itself," its slow and constant regeneration.

This error in method, in the originality of Diotima's method, is corrected shortly afterward only to be confirmed later on. Surely, once again, *she is not there. Socrates reports her views.* Perhaps he distorts them unwittingly and unknowingly.

The following paragraph takes up what was just asserted. It explains how it is that there is permanent renewal in us. How there is, in us, a ceaseless loss of the old, of the already dead, both in our most physical part—hair, bones, blood, our whole body—and in our most spiritual part: our character, our opinions, our desires, joys and pains, our fears. None of these elements is ever identical to what they were; some come into existence while others perish. The same is true for knowledges, which are acquired and forgotten—thus constantly renewed:

> "This is the fashion in which everything mortal is preserved, not in being always perfectly identical, as is divinity, but in that the disappearing and decaying object leaves behind it another new one such as it was. By this arrangement, Socrates," said she, "the mortal partakes of immortality, both in body and all else; the immortal does so in another way. So do not marvel if everything by nature prizes its own offspring; it is for the sake of immortality that every being has this urgency and love." (208)

> ("[C'est] de cette façon qu'est sauvegardé ce qui est mortel, non point comme ce qui est divin par l'identité absolue d'une existence éternelle, mais par le fait que ce qui s'en va, mine par son ancienneté, laisse après lui autre chose, du nouveau qui est pareil à ce qu'il était. C'est par ce moyen, dit-elle, qui ce qui est mortel participe à l'immortalité, dans son corps et en tout le reste. . . . Donc, ne t'émerveille pas que, ce qui est une repousse de lui-même, chaque être ait pour lui tant de sollicitude naturelle, car c'est en vue de l'immortalité que font cortège à chacun d'eux ce zèle et cet amour!")

Here, Diotima returns to her type of argumentation, including her mocking of those who suspend the present in order to search "for an eternity of time and immortal glory" ("pour l'eternité du temps une gloire immortelle"). She speaks—in a style that is loosely *woven* but never definitively *knotted*—of becoming in time, of permanent generation and regeneration here and now in each (wo)man [*chacun(e)*] of what is more corporeally and spiritually real. Without saying that one is the fruit of the other. But that, at each moment we are a "regrowth" of ourselves, in perpetual increase. No more quest for immortality through the child. But in us, ceaselessly. Diotima has returned to a path which admits love as it was defined before she evoked procreation: an intermediate terrain, a mediator, a space-time of permanent *passage* between mortal and immortal.

Next, returning to an example of the quest for immortality through fame she re-situates (the) object (of) love outside of the subject: reknown, immortal glory, etc. No more perpetual becoming-immortal in us, but rather a race toward some thing that would confer immortality. Like and unlike procreation of a child, the stake of love is placed outside the self. In the beloved and not in the lover? The lovers cited—Alcestis, Admetus, Achilles, Codros—would not have been cited unless we always remembered them. It was with the goal of eternal reknown that they loved unto death. Immortality is the object of their love. Not love itself.

> Well then (said she), when men's fecundity is of the body, they turn rather to the women, and the fashion of their love is this: through begetting children to provide themselves with immortality, reknown and happiness, as they imagine—Securing them for all time to come.
>
> But when fecundity is of the soul—for indeed there are (said she) those persons who are fecund in their souls, even more than in their bodies, fecund in what is the function of the soul to conceive and also to bring forth—what is this proper offspring? It is wisdom, along with every other spiritual value. (208–9)

> (Cela étant, dit-elle, ceux qui sont féconds selon le corps se tournent plutôt vers les femmes, et leur façon d'etre amoureux c'est, en engendrant des enfants, de se procurer à eux-mêmes, pensent-ils, pour toute la suite du temps, le bonheur d'avoir un nom dont le souvenir ne périsse pas. Quant à ceux qui sont féconds selon l'âme, car en fait il en existe, dit-elle, dont la fécondité réside dans l'âme, à un plus haut degré encore que dans le corps, pour tout ce qui appartient à une âme d'être féconde et qu'il lui appartient d'enfanter. Or, qu'est-ce cela qui lui appartient? C'est la pensée, et c'est toute autre excellence.)

What seemed to me most original in Diotima's method has disappeared once again. That irreducible intermediary milieu of love is cancelled between "subject" (an inadequate word in Plato) and "beloved reality." Amorous becoming no longer constitutes a becoming of the lover himself, of love in the (male or female) lover, between the lovers ("un devenir de l'amant lui-même, de l'amour en l'amante(e), entre amants").[4] Instead it is now a teleological quest for what is deemed the highest reality and often situated in a transcendence inaccessible to our condition as mortals. Immortality is put off until death and is not counted as one of our constant tasks as mortals, as a transmutation that is endlessly incumbent on us here and now, as a possibility inscribed in a body capable of divine becoming. Beauty of body and beauty of soul become hierarchized, and the love of women becomes the lot of those who, incapable of being creators in soul, are fecund in body and seek the immortality of their name perpetuated by their offspring.

> By far the greatest and most beautiful form of wisdom (said she) is that which has to do with regulating states and households, and has the name, no doubt, of "temperance" and "justice." (209)

> (de beaucoup la plus considérable et la plus belle manifestation de la pensée etant celle qui concerne l'ordonnance des Etats comme de tout établissement, et dont le nom, on le sait, est tempérance aussi bien que justice.)

Amorous becomings, divine, immortal, are no longer left to their intermediary current. They are qualified, hierarchized. And, in the extreme case, love dies. In the universe of determinations, there will be contests, competitions, and amorous duties—the beloved or love being the prize. The lovers disappear. Our subsequent tradition has even taught us the interdiction or the futility of being lovers outside of procreation.

Yet Diotima had begun by asserting that the most divine act is "the union of man and woman, a divine affair." What she asserted then accorded with what she said about the function of love as an intermediary remaining intermediary, a demon. It seems that in the course of her speech she reduces a bit this demonic, mediumlike function of love; so that it is no longer really a demon, but an intention, a reduction to intention, to the teleology of human will. Already subjected to a doctrine with fixed goals and not to an immanent flourishing of the divine in the flesh. Irreducible mediator, at once physical and spiritual, between lovers; and not already codified duty, will, desire. Love invoked as a demon in a method toward the beautiful and good often disappears from the speech, reappearing only in art, "painting," in the form(s) of love inciting to eroticism and, perhaps, in the shape of angels. Is love itself split between eros and agape? Yet, in order for lovers to be able to love each other, there must be, between them, Love.

There remains what has been said about the philosopher-love. But why would not philosopher Love be a lover of the other? Only of the Other? Of an inaccessible transcendent? In any case, this would already be an ideal that suppresses love qua demonic. Love becomes political wisdom, wisdom in regulating the city, not the intermediary state that inhabits lovers and transports them from the condition of mortals to that of immortals. Love becomes a sort of *raison d'état.* Love founds a family, takes care of children, including the children which citizens are. The more its objective is distanced from an individual becoming, the more valuable it is. Its stake is lost in immortal good and beauty as collective goods. The family is preferable to the generation of lovers, between lovers. Adopted children are preferable to others. This, moreover, is how it comes to pass that *love between men is superior to love between man and woman.* Carnal procreation is suspended in favor of the engendering of beautiful and good things. Immortal things. That, surprisingly, is the view of Diotima. At least as translated through the words uttered by Socrates.

The beings most gifted in wisdom go directly to that end. Most begin with physical beauty and "must love one single object [physical form of beauty], and thereof must engender fair discourses" (210) ("par n'aimer qu'un unique beau corps et par engendrer à cette occasion de beaux discours.") If the teaching is right, that must be so. But whoever becomes attached to one body must learn that beauty is in many bodies. After having pursued beauty in one perceptible form, he must learn that the same beauty resides in all bodies; he will

> abate his violent love of one, disdaining this and deeming it a trifle, and will become a lover of all fair objects. (210)

> ([devenir] un amant de tous les beaux corps et détendra l'impétuosité de son amour à l'égard d'un seul individu; car, un tel amour, il en est venu à le dédaigner et à en faire peu de cas.)

From the attraction to a single beautiful body he passes, then, to many; and thence to the beauty residing in souls. Thus he learns that beauty is not found univocally in the body and that someone of an ugly bodily appearance can be beautiful and gentle of soul; that to be just is to know how to care for that person and to engender beautiful discourses for him. Love thus passes insensibly into love of works (*oeuvres*). The passion for beautiful bodies is transmuted into the discovery of beauty in knowledges. That which liberates from the attachment to only one master opens onto the immense ocean of the beautiful, and leads to the birth of numerous and sublime discourses, as well as to thoughts inspired by a boundless love of wisdom. Until the resulting force and development permit the lover to envision a certain *unique* knowledge (210). This marvelous beauty is perceptible, perhaps, by whoever has followed the road just described, by whoever has passed through the different stages step by step. He will have, then, the vision of a beauty whose existence is "eternal, not growing up or perishing, increasing or decreasing" ([dont] l'existence est éternelle, étrangère à la génération comme à la corruption, à l'accroissement comme au décroissement") and which, besides, is *absolutely* beautiful:

> not beautiful in one point and ugly in another, nor beautiful in this place and ugly in that, as if beautiful to some, to others ugly; again, this beauty will not be revealed to him in the semblance of a face, or hands, or any other element of the body, nor in any form of speech or knowledge, nor yet as if it appertained to any other being, or creature, for example, upon earth, or in the sky, or elsewhere; no, it will be seen as beauty in and for itself, consistent with itself in uniformity for ever, whereas all other beauties share it in such fashion that, while they are ever born and perish, that eternal beauty, never waxing, never waning, never is impaired. (210–11)

> (pas belle à ce point de vue et laide à cet autre, pas davantage à tel moment et non à tel autre, ni non plus belle en comparaison avec ceci, laide en comparaison avec cela, ni non plus belle en tel lieu, laide en tel autre, en tant que belle pour certains hommes, laide pour certains autres; pas davantage encore cette beauté ne se montrera à lui pourvue par exemple d'un visage, ni de mains, ni de quoi que ce soit d'autre qui soit une partie du corps; ni non plus sous l'aspect de quelque raisonnement ou encore quelque connaissance; pas davantage comme ayant en quelque être distinct quelque part son existence, en un vivant par exemple, qu'il soit de la terre ou du ciel, ou bien en quoi que ce soit d'autre; mais bien plutôt elle se montrera à lui en elle-même, et par elle-même, éternellement unie à elle-même dans l'unicité de la nature formelle, tandis que les autres beaux objets participent tous de la nature dont il s'agit en une telle façon que, ces autres objets venant à l'existence ou cessant d'exister, il n'en

> résulte dans la réalité dont il s'agit aucune augmentation, aucune diminution, ni non plus aucune sorte d'altération.)

To attain this sublime beauty, one must begin with the love of young men. Starting with their natural beauty, one must, step by step, raise oneself to supernatural beauty: from beautiful bodies one must pass to beautiful pursuits; then to beautiful sciences, and finally to that sublime science that is supernatural beauty alone, and that allows knowledge of the essence of beauty in isolation (211). This contemplation is what gives direction and taste to life. "It will not appear to you to be according to the measure of gold and raiment, or of lovely boys and striplings" (211) ("Ni l'or ou la toilette, ni la beauté des jeunes garçons ou des jeunes hommes ne peuvent entrer en parallèle avec cette découverte.") And whoever has perceived "beauty divine in its own single nature" (211) ("le beau divin dans l'unicité de sa nature formelle"), what can he still look at? Having contemplated "the beautiful with that by which it can be seen" (211) ("le beau au moyen de ce par quoi il est visible"), beyond all simulacra, he is united with it and is *really* virtuous; since he has perceived "authentic reality" ("réel authentique") he becomes dear to the divine and immortal.

This person would, then, have perceived what I shall call a *sensible transcendental,* the material texture of beauty. He would have "seen" the very spatiality of the visible, the real before all reality, all forms, all truth of particular sensations or of constructed idealities. Would he have contemplated the "nature" (*nature*) of the divine? This is the support of the fabrication of the transcendent in its different modes, all of which, according to Diotima, are reached by the same propaedeutic: *the love of beauty.* Neither the good nor the true nor justice nor the government of the city would occur without beauty. And its strongest ally is love. Love therefore deserves to be venerated. And Diotima asks that her words be considered as a celebration and praise of Love.

In the second part of her speech, she used Love itself as a *means.* She cancelled out its intermediary function and subjected it to a telos. The power (*puissance*) of her method seems less evident to me here than at the beginning of her speech, when she made love the mediator of a becoming with no objective other than becoming. Perhaps Diotima is still saying the same thing. But her method, in the second part, risks losing its irreducible character and being replaced by a metaphysics. Unless what she proposes to contemplate, beauty itself, is understood as that which confuses the opposition between immanence and transcendence. An always already sensible horizon at the depths of which everything would appear. But it would be necessary to go back over the whole speech again to discover it in its enchantment.

Notes

1. Luce Irigaray, "L'amour Sorcier: Lecture de Platon, *Le Banquet.* Discours de Diotime. In Irigaray (1984, 27–39). Translation published by the kind permission of Les Editions de Minuit.

2. This and subsequent quotations from the *Symposium* are rendered in the English translation of Lane Cooper in Plato (1938, 252–63). References in French, which follow in parentheses, are Irigaray's citations from the French translation of Léon Robin in Plato (1950).

3. In this and subsequent passages, "Love" or "love" is rendered in English with the masculine pronoun—a translation required by French grammar. "L'Amour," capitalized, means "the God of Love"—Cupid or Eros, and is always masculine in French. "Eros" and "Love" are interchangeable in English translations of most of Diotima's speech; a similar interchangeability exists in French. Historically, "l'amour" was feminine in French until it was made conventionally masculine to accord with Latin use. In poetry, uses of "l'amour" in the feminine persist to this day; but "l'amour" was not grammatically feminine in the passages from Plato that Irigaray was citing. Irigaray's argument in this essay can be read as an exploration of the ethical implications of these grammatical points. See Grévisse (1964, 190–92). (Translator's note)

4. Irigaray is here exploiting the very characteristics of French grammar that exemplify her argument. "L'amant" must be masculine when any of the lovers is male; but it is also possible to specify that the lover is female, as in the title of her 1980 *Amante Marine* ([Female] lover from the seas). (Translator's note)

References

Grévisse, Maurice. 1964. *Le bon usage.* 8th ed. Gambloux: Editions J. Duculot.

Irigaray, Luce. 1980. *Amante Marine.* Paris: Editions de Minuit.

———. 1984. *Ethique de la différence sexuelle.* Paris: Editions de Minuit.

Plato. 1938. *Phaedrus, Ion, Gorgias, and Symposium, with Passages from the Republic and Laws.* Translated by Lane Cooper. New York: Oxford University Press.

———. 1950. *Oeuvres complètes.* Translated by Léon Robin. Paris: Gallimard (Bibliothèque de la Pléiade 58), 1.

10

Irigaray and Diotima at Plato's Symposium

Andrea Nye

Who is the "host" of that famous philosophical party described in Plato's *Symposium?* Who decided that no woman would be invited so that twenty centuries later, when Luce Irigaray decides to impose her feminine presence in her essay "L'amour sorcier" (*Hypatia* 3, no. 3 (1989); repr. Chapter 9, this volume), she can only intervene as interloper and eavesdropper? Is the host Agathon, in whose house the Symposium takes place? Is it Socrates, in whose honor the feast is held? Is it Plato, who evokes the scene for us?

The root meaning of "host" is a physical body on whose flesh parasites feed. The host is the nourishment they steal and convert to prolong their own dependent existences. The host is a sacrificed animal body offered up to placate heaven. The host is the physical bread the faithful eat at communion to become one with an insubstantial god. If we take "host" in these root senses, then, as I hope to show, it is Diotima and not Agathon, Socrates, or Plato who is the real host of the *Symposium.* And if this is true Irigaray's presence is no intrusion. She, or any woman, enters into the discussion of love with perfect right.

Irigaray, however, feels none of the confidence of an invited guest, nor does she recognize Diotima's authority. Irigaray's Diotima is not the mistress of her own house, but an alienated troubler of dichotomous categories whose success depends on being clever enough to subvert Platonic logic. Irigaray's own commitment to this "feminine operation" prevents her from understanding Diotima's teaching and its relation to Platonism.

Diotima's discourse, as reported by Socrates as reported by Plato, has always been the locus of scholarly skirmishing. In the *Symposium,* when it is his turn to speak on love, Socrates does not speak in his own voice. He repeats the teaching of his mentor, Diotima. Most scholars have found this puzzling and embarrassing. How can the great Socrates, founder of philosophy, be saying that he learned everything he knows from a woman? In a rhetorical competition between Athenian men, what is a woman doing correcting the mistakes of previous male speakers? And what is Plato doing, letting Socrates repeat respectfully the teachings of a woman, teachings not always in keeping with Plato's own?

These anomalies have been handled in a variety of ways. Some scholars have argued that Diotima is a fictional priestess invented by Plato to give divine authority to Socrates, even though this explanation must ignore the many elements in Diotima's teaching inconsistent with Platonic philosophy as well as the fact that Diotima would be the only fictional character in all of the Platonic dialogues. Others have explained her appearance by referring to the romantic subplots of the *Symposium:* Socrates wishes to correct Agathon whom he wants to seduce, but without antagonizing; therefore Socrates puts his correction in Diotima's mouth so that he may imply ingratiatingly that he too once needed instruction and had to be put right. Still others have argued that Plato includes Diotima's discourse in order to ridicule its simplistic naturalism, ignoring the fact the Socrates praises Diotima and reports *her* ridicule of his naivete and excessive abstraction. Almost universally, it is asserted without argument that Diotima is fictional. In translation and commentaries, her teachings are interpreted so as to be compatible with Platonic philosophy.[1]

In fact, Diotima's philosophy of love differs both from the theory of Forms in Plato's *Republic,* and from the mystical Pythagoreanism developed in the *Phaedrus.* Far from suggesting that the body is a degraded prison, Diotima sees bodily love as the metaphor and concrete training ground for all creative and knowledge-producing activities.[2] She argues that sexual love for one person must be outgrown, but not because it is physical and so imperfect. Rather, the lover must progress to friendship, knowledge, and politics because exclusive sexual love for one person is obsessional, narrow, and makes one servile (*Symposium* 210c–d). Diotima does not argue that heterosexual intercourse is inferior but urges an expansion of loving intercourse that will bear fruit in new thoughts, new knowledge, and new ways of living with others, as well as in physical children (209a).[3] The beauty-in-itself that the initiate in Diotima's philosophy may experience as the culmination of her training is not a transcendent Platonic Form. The initiate glimpses no universal, abstracted from imperfect particulars, but an in-dwelling immortal divine beauty, an attracting center that foments fruitful creation in all areas of existence.[4] Diotima identifies this center with the pre-Hellenic Cretan goddess, Eilethia, goddess of childbirth, and with her attendant spinner of fate, Moira (206d). To be in touch with this divinity, she says, is to live a new enlightened existence and to be a lover of the divine. Only in this way, Diotima concludes, will we be able to avoid false images of virtue and achieve real virtue (212a1–5). The initiate in Diotima's philosophy cannot dwell in the world of absolute beauty as the philosopher of Plato's *Republic* aspires to dwell in the upper sunlit world of the Forms. To cut oneself off from the natural generative center of human life, is to be content with only abstract, unreal ideas of virtue and to fail to achieve real virtue which must be lived and generated in the visible, physical world.

At first, there is much in Diotima's teaching that Irigaray approves. She applauds Diotima's mocking of Socrates' simplistic dichotomous thinking: love is either ugly or beautiful, rich or poor, etc. She accepts Diotima's view of love as an intermediary or third term that moves between two opposing terms whose logic is deconstructed. She endorses Diotima's theory of personal identity based on the realization that the self is not unitary but constantly in a process of renewal and destruction.

But then Irigaray withdraws her approval. After such a promising beginning, she charges, Diotima's method "fails" (1984, 33). Diotima searches for a "cause" for love in a natural impulse toward procreation. She sees an "issue" and not sexual pleasure as the end of sexual intercourse. She sees nonprocreative sex as only a means to the end of certain "collective goods." She sacrifices sexual pleasure to a teleological goal. She sets up a hierarchy of goods in which an abstract philosophical love of beauty is "higher" than physical love, undermining the plurality of her original deconstruction. In other words, Irigaray judges Diotima as a lapsed French feminist struggling to maintain the "correct method" against philosophical orthodoxy. Although Diotima begins well with an ironic onslaught on dualistic, hierarchical categories, she soon reverts to an orthodoxy of her own. Instead of continuing to derail Socratic logic, Diotima becomes a Platonist.

But has Irigaray listened to what Diotima says? Does she hear Diotima or the voices of Platonic scholars and commentators determined to show that Diotima is a Platonist? Irigaray works from a text glossed by many readings that shape and distort Diotima's teaching to make it compatible with Platonic dogma. For example, Irigaray complains that Diotima thinks some external acquisition such as immortality or collective happiness is the end for which love is only a means. But this popular criticism of Platonic love depends on a misleading translation and interpretation of the expression "γενέσθαι άυτῶ," literally "to come to be for someone," or "to happen to someone" (204d). Why do we love? asks Diotima. What is it that we want? We want, the Greek reads, "the beautiful to come into being for us." Irigaray, however, accepts the misleading but common translation, "We want the good to be ours" (1984, 31). Possession, however, in the sense of acquiring a property, is not what lovers crave, according to Diotima. Instead, they long for the quickening, fertilizing contact with someone beautiful in body and soul that is necessary if, together, lovers are to generate new ways of thinking and living. Diotima's lover is not the heaven-crazed lover of the *Phaedrus* who glimpses in his idol the dim reflection of an otherworldly vision *he* would like to reclaim.[5] Nor is she the Platonic teacher seeking a suitable receptacle for the *déssemination* of his own ideas.[6] Instead, according to Diotima, what we seek in love is the fruitfulness of interaction, the fecundity of dialogue. The "goods" that result are collective, not the possession of any individual.[7]

In another and even more serious misinterpretation of Diotima's teaching, Irigaray accepts a Platonic reading of Diotima's theory of beauty-in-itself. Here, she follows traditional scholarship in taking Diotima's final revelation of unchanging beauty as a less sophisticated version of Plato's theory of hierarchical Forms. In fact, the progress of Diotima's initiate is not vertical, from lower to higher, but lateral, from narrow sexual relations and an exclusive concern with one's own family, to "better" (not "higher"), more inclusive relationships.[8] The lover comes to love souls *as well as* bodies, many *as well as* one. When she finally begins to sense the creative process in all of life, she is "embarked on the wide sea of beauty," and can bear "magnificent thoughts in philosophical abundance" (201d). The final vision of a Beauty that does not change is not of a transcendent Form, seen as a rigid confining model for human excellence. It is the very opposite. The initiate senses an inner generative impulse at the heart of life, an impulse that continually foments change and decay and so prevents the settling in of rigid form. Only when she has this insight, Diotima warns, will the lover be able to give birth to true virtue and not to false images of virtue (212a1–5).[9]

Diotima does not proscribe "lower" forms of love or of thought. She does not say what Irigaray has her say: "de beaucoup la plus considerable et la plus belle manifestation de la pensée étant celle qui concerne l'ordonnonce des Etats comme de tout établissement" (by far the most important and the most beautiful expression of thought being that which concerns the government of states as of any establishment) (1984, 35). Diotima is more subtle. She says: "Much that is most important and best comes from this sort of thinking (that is, practical wisdom), both for the city and for the management of the household" (209a). The progress of Diotima's initiate, unlike that of Plato's student, never requires the renunciation of "lower" forms of engendering, only a widening circle of those with whom we have loving intercourse, and a widening of the benefits of that intercourse.

Diotima does argue that the point of love is the "goods" that come from harmonious intercourse. She does not say, however, what Plato seems to imply in the *Phaedrus:* that we use the loved one, finding in him an ideal that will assist our reascent to a Platonic heaven inhabited by ideal essences. There is no equivocation in Diotima's naturalistic view of immortality as the good we leave after us. Her goods are not preexisting eternal essences which the lover wishes to acquire or reach. Instead, loving intercourse *is* creativity: it *is* the process by which we create new forms. When these forms—a child, an idea, a new way of life, a new theory or administrative technique—are identified with a preexisting ideal, then Diotima's love disappears. The child becomes the false image of the parents' imagination, the idea a spurious abstraction, the theory an alienated intellectualism, the administrative technique a strategy of domination. For Diotima, the issue or outcome of loving harmonious relations are goods, not "The Good." Goods are simply the plurality of things that make us happy. This is so obvious, Diotima says, that no more need be said about it (205a).

According to some of the criteria used in recent works by feminist writers, Diotima's philosophy, with its denial of autonomous alienated consciousness, its recognition of the affective and collective nature of knowledge, its unwillingness to separate the practical from the theoretical, might seem to be deeply feminist. Irigaray, however, sees Diotima as capitulating to Platonic metaphysics. It is not hard to understand why classical scholars choose to interpret Diotima as a Platonist: this is one way to explain the anomaly of her appearance at the *Symposium* and to perpetuate the illusion that the foundations of culture are irrevocably male. But why Irigaray would make such a mistake needs further explanation. The source of the misunderstanding, I believe, is to be found not just in a misleading translation, but in the conceptual infrastructure of Irigaray's feminist strategy: in deconstructive method and textual practice, in "écriture féminine," and in the concept of feminine "jouissance."

Irigaray, as feminist critic of Western philosophy, adopts a textual practice, a "travail du langage." She has no naive notion of refuting male philosophers in their own terms. Instead, she approaches them as texts, that is, as internally generated, more or less ordered systems of meaning whose logical order and pretended truth may be deconstructed. The reader of a text must avoid being taken in both by an establishment of authoritative truth and by the temptation to establish a rival thesis.

> Autrement dit, l'enjeu . . . est d'enrayer la machinerie théorique elle-même, de suspendre sa prétension à la production d'un vérité et d'un sens par trop univoques. (1977, 75)
>
> (In other words, what is at stake is to jam the theoretical machinery itself, to suspend its pretension to the production of a too unitary truth and meaning.)

The source of this strategy is, of course, Jacques Derrida. For Derrida, the pretension to truth and unitary meaning is theological. Logic's claim to self-evidence, the representation of physical fact, even the presence of a human voice in spoken words, all rest on an implicit appeal to a transcendent presence. Once such a "god" is rejected, it becomes clear that speech is not relevatory of any transcendent truth but is an internally ordered phonemic graphism neither prior to nor essentially different from writing. This is not to say that we can do away with a "unitary" meaning ordered in hierarchical oppositions. These must continue, Derrida argues, to form the semantic matrix of thought. However, if, as in traditional philosophical refutation, the premises of a supposed truth are rejected as false and an alternative semantic ordering is asserted which is to be more consistent with the "facts," then the theological presence of truth is reasserted.[10]

Instead, Derrida proposes a variety of deconstructive strategies, many of them adopted by Irigaray. Hierarchical oppositions can be turned on their heads and the supposed presence exposed as a lack against which the opposing term is defined. Or, the deconstructor may read between the lines and discover ways in which the author unwittingly subverts her or his own text. Or she may discover in seemingly unimportant asides and "supplements" the core problem or issue that motivates the text. In all of these cases, deconstructive readings must not claim to find *the* meaning, *the* truth of a text, or event the author's *intended* meaning. Released from such logocentric projects, the reader may proceed to explore an infinite chain of deferrals and differences in which any supposed authoritative order is always compromised.

In *Spurs: Nietzsche's Styles,* a deconstruction of Nietzsche's misogyny, Derrida specifically identifies this subversion of the text as "feminine." For the "woman," outside masculine appropriation, there can be no truth. As feminine, she keeps an ambiguous distance, leaves open a seductive plurality of meanings, and so can play irreverently with the text, taking pleasure in overturning whatever order misogynist, truth-asserting, phallic society tries to establish.[11] Like other French feminists, Irigaray found in these strategies both a possible antidote for the paralyzing realization that sexism can be built into semantic structure, and a flattering reversal of the proverbial sexist claim that women are inferior because they are illogical and incapable of consistency. Derrida seems to suggest a way in which women, excluded from and degraded in male culture, can still undermine, if not overcome, that culture.

This method, however, so brilliantly deployed by Irigaray in her readings of Aristotle, Plato, Kant, and other male philosophers, falters when applied to Diotima.[12] In Diotima's thought, there is no hierarchical logic to expose, no masculine/presence, feminine/absence to deconstruct. Diotima's lovers are humans who must die and the motivation for their interaction does not depend on their sex. But neither can Irigaray successfully claim Diotima as a fellow deconstructionist. Diotima is not concerned with undermining an authoritative logic. Her tone with Socrates does not need to be bolstered by the defiant irony with which

Irigaray faces down her philosophical forebears. Instead, she treats him with the playful condescension due a youth who has not yet grasped the simplest of natural facts. Not only does Diotima not need to deconstruct a Platonic theory of the Forms, she has doubts that Socrates is even capable of following her discussion of the "erotica" or mysteries of love. To her exposure of his ignorance, Socrates responds humbly. Irigaray, however, does not approve the masterful way in which Diotima directs the discussion.

The reason for her disapproval can be found in the theory of language on which Irigaray's textual practice depends. That theory, derived from Derrida and from Irigaray's other mentor, Lacan, depends on a Saussurian view of language as a system of signs internally related.[13] In the Lacanian version, we do not use words to communicate; instead we "enter into" language, a fixed system of meanings structured around the master signifier, the Phallus, and its corollary, the Name of the Father. Once this view of language is accepted, Derridean deconstruction becomes the only liberatory tactic.[14] Fixed configurations of meaning must be broken up or subverted in order to insure a degree of anarchic freedom. On this view, Diotima, as speaker of a language, must enter into the hierarchical system of meaning that structures any semantics. Like Plato, or any philosopher, she must find herself trapped in a system of signifiers with phallic presence at the center. If she is not to lapse into unintelligibility, she must revert to the founding oppositions of Western metaphysics: subordination of the body to the mind, of physical appetite to rationality, of natural existence to spiritual heaven. Her only alternative would be to subvert their authority in a "feminine operation" of deconstruction. Because Irigaray accepts the Lacanian view of language as a system of signs into which we enter, whether to obey or subvert, she can only understand Diotima in the same terms. Not only must Irigaray perform a "feminine operation" in her reading of Diotima, she must evaluate Diotima's own method according to its success as an "écriture féminine."

"Ecriture de la femme" is Irigaray's version of Derrida's "feminine operation." The subversion of the text of patriarchy, she claims, requires a new kind of feminine style. This style will be always fluid, never allowing itself to be defined or restricted, never taking a fixed position. A woman writer must:

> met . . . feu aux mots fétiches, aux termes propres, aux formes bien constuites . . . et fait exploser toute forme, figure, idée, concept, solidement établis. (1977, 76)
>
> (put fire to fetish words, correct terms, well-constructed forms, and explode every solidly built form, figure, idea, concept)

This advice may be pragmatically sound for a woman struggling in a predominantly male establishment who must negotiate concepts and rules of thought devised by men that leave her little room for intelligible self-expression. Diotima, however, in a different situation, has no interest in sustaining such a style. On the contrary, although she begins with a tertiary logic that Irigaray finds promisingly elusive, Diotima proceeds to refute the views of Aristophanes and Pausanias and to expound a thesis of her own.[15] She speaks with authority, as someone who has come to knowledge through a difficult process and who can pass on that knowledge only by urging an initiate to travel the same road. Irigaray, however, judges Diotima within the context that gives meaning to her own deconstructive practice as if Diotima were a twentieth-century Parisian *intellectuelle* struggling against the authority of a male academic establishment to produce an "écriture féminine." But the institutional setting for Diotima's philosophy is not the École Normale Supérieure. The ahistorical character of Irigaray's intellectual inheritance prevents her from seeing the difference.[16]

In Lacanian and Derridean metaphysics, the distinction between natural and/or historical reality and the linguistic terms we use to interpret, represent, or criticize that reality is dissolved. For Lacan, the world outside of language is not a human world. It is the world of animal intersubjectivity and unreflective sensation. To learn to speak is not to learn to express sensations or articulate intersubjectively constituted experience, but to enter the world of the symbolic. A split in the self between watching subject and mirrored object, foundational both in the development of an individual and of human culture, allows the construction of an alienated linguistic identity. This identity is then articulated within the context of a social language, a transpersonal symbolic nexus whose central and primal signifier is the phallus. According to Lacan, our identities, as well as our understanding of any situation, are fixed only within this patrifocal symbolic order.

Although for Derrida the meanings in which we find ourselves are more ambiguous, disordered, "frayed," he also sees language as radically discontinuous with physical existence. A cry or a moan may be a natural sign, but words can never express an affective experience. History, literature, culture, everything human, is a text. There are no facts outside of language that language may express, or correctly or incorrectly represent. There is no nontextual situation out of which one may speak. The transition from physical existence to symbolic meaning is absolute and occurs outside of historical time as the precondition of culture itself.

This is not simply to say that language, as socially constructed meaning, mediates an individual's expression of her experience. If our words are never wholly our own but are taken from the mouths of others, we and they still speak from particular material situations. The Saussurian premise is more radical. Language has meaning not from its use in human expression, but from formal syntactical relations. Even when, as for Derrida, these relations are not rigidly ordered, meaning does not depend on who is speaking or where and why she says what she does. This is true because for Derrida the hierarchical oppositions against which deconstruction operates are necessary. More important, it is true because even Derridean metaphor, ambiguity, and paradox depend on formal patterning: configurations of differences and deferrals, reversals and spacings. However, to read a text in this way is to refuse to consider the institutional conditions of its production or the identity of its author. Therefore, Irigaray cannot place Diotima's thought within a particular material historical context. Whatever her circumstances or her identity, Diotima, as speaker, has entered the world of the text and has left material existence behind. But this is to erase the specific historical/ social setting of the Platonic dialogues.

Much has been written about the sequestered and inferior status of women in classical Greece. There has also been much feminist criticism of the misogynist thought that ratified that inferiority.[17] However, the subjugation of Greek women was not only textual, nor was it a necessary effect of the alienated origins of symbolic thought. Instead, it was the outcome of more than a millenium of social change in the Aegean and Mediterranean areas. Beginning about 2000 B.C., Greek-speaking invaders and emigrants began to arrive in mainland Greece. These invaders brought with them the male-dominated social structures of a nomadic, illiterate, warrior society: political hierarchy, the worship of a supreme sky and thunder god, the restriction of women to the domestic sphere. In Greece they found no primitive animal subsistence, but a civilization focused on a sophisticated Minoan culture. Minoan frescoes and seals document a way of life very different from that of the invaders. Women are depicted in positions of prominence, presiding at religious ceremonies, worshiping a female deity, attending festivals and entertainments, participating in the important ceremony of bull dancing.[18] In the intervening centuries—from the fall of Crete to Mycenaean dominance, through the dark ages, up to classical times—the clash continued between a theology focused on a central female divinity and natural cycles of generation on the one hand, and one focused on a supreme warrior-father-god on the other.[19] By classical time, although subjected to increasing segregation and domestic isolation, as well as to complete political disenfranchisement, women still retained some of their old power in religion. They continued to fill important sacerdotal roles as priestesses of Athena or Demeter; they participated publically in religious festivals and initiations; they celebrated women's rituals such as the Dionysian or the Thesmophorian; they performed as prophetesses at oracular shrines such as Delphi.

In historical context, then, it is neither surprising nor anomalous that Diotima would appear in an authoritative role as the teacher of Socrates.[20] As prophetess/priestess she was part of a religious order that had maintained its authority from Minoan/Mycenaean times. At Delphi, the sibyl still presided as the most respected oracle in Greece. Thousands proclaimed the benefits of initiation into the wisdom of Demeter at Eleusis. Socrates himself points out the respect due Diotima for preparing the sacrifice that rescued Athens from the plague (201d). As Mantinean prophetess, Diotima does not speak as a lone woman who has painfully managed to gain entrance to a male party. She speaks out of a tradition of female power and female thought still alive in Greek culture. When Socrates refers to the prophetic power of the sibyl or the inspired voices of the Muses in the *Phaedrus,* he taps sources that may not be available in Irigaray's Christianized late twentieth-century Paris, where the connection between divinity and masculinity is axiomatic, and the "absence" of the feminine a necessary truth.

Historically locatable psychoanalytic formulations of that necessary truth are part of the conceptual underpinning of Irigaray's feminist method. Women's sexuality, Irigaray argues, is absent from Freudian theory. In her view, women's liberation is intimately connected with the recognition of and indulgence in a specifically feminine sexual pleasure. This feminine *"jouissance"* is defined in contrast with a dominant masculine sexuality.[21] Masculine sexuality is phallic, that is, active, penetrative, aggressive, focused on orgasm. Women's pleasure, on the other hand, is self-touching, interactive, heterogeneous, plural, and flowing rather than gathering to a climax.

This view of feminine sexuality also has at its source the ideas of Lacan. Lacan corrected any lingering biologism still inherent in Freud's account of women's supposed sexual disabilities only to make those disabilities even more inaccessible to feminist reform.[22] In principle, biology can be circumvented by contraception or artificial methods of reproduction. But when Lacan locates women's disability in universal structures of linguistic meaning, he writes women's inferiority into culture itself. For Lacan, that inferiority is inscribed as a kind of nonentity, as what cannot be expressed. Lacan complained with some satisfaction that when women (including women analysts) are asked about their sexuality, "they know nothing about this pleasure" (Lacan 1975, 68).

Irigaray, like Lacan, does not question the contrast between masculine and feminine sexuality. Instead, she attempts to answer Freud's and Lacan's unanswered question—What do women want?—and to make articulate that feminine *"jouissance"* which escapes masculine logic. She supplies Lacan's "Woman", the *"pas-toute"* (not all there), with a specific presence. Women's sexuality will no longer be the simple negative, or lack of masculine phallic presence; nor will it be the ineffable ecstasy-beyond-words of Lacan's appropriation of Bernini's *Saint Thérèse.*[23] Instead, it will be an alternative kind of pleasure—describable, recoverable, and connected with a woman's different "self-touching" sexual economy.

Irigaray's neo-Lacanian account of sexuality is in sharp dissonance with Diotima's. Diotima grounds love and sexual desire in natural existence rather than in semantic configurations of meaning. Diotimean love is the same for all, women and men, and makes no distinction between feminine and masculine desire. Diotima's theory of love does not focus on pleasure; genital pleasure in the sense of a private sensation is not mentioned in her philosophy. It is not surprising, therefore, that, given Irigaray's commitment to the explanatory and liberatory power of feminine sexual pleasure, she can make no sense of Diotima's positive view. After a promising beginning, Irigaray charges, Diotima makes no distinction between our human (textual) identity and nature. She looks for a cause in natural phenomena; she leaves intact a hierarchy in which spiritual love is better than physical.

These formulations, however, do not do justice to Diotimean positions which do not share Irigaray's presuppositions. Although Diotima grounds sexual desire in a principle of nature, that principle involves neither women's reproductive organs nor men's penises. Instead, it has to do with the fact of mortality and the impulse of living things to perpetuate themselves. Our desire to transcend our mortality by leaving good after us is not limited to the engendering of children. In fact, our immortality is more secure when we produce new ways of living and thinking. Diotima makes no distinction between men and women in this respect. Both men and women come together to bring up children; in her account this is not an exclusively female activity. Both men and women enter into other kinds of loving relationships to produce virtues, ideas, new ways of management. These relationships can be between any sex, heterosexual or homosexual.[24] In every case, the impulse of desire is the same—cooperative generation of good things both for the couple and for others, both for the household and the community. The pursuit of pleasurable sensation could not be the motive for Diotima's desire; a privatized sensation of pleasure could never account for the universality and urgency of love as she sees it. For Diotima, love is not a recreation but permeates the whole of human activity.

Irigaray, however, sees in Diotima's philosophy another attempt to deprive women of their specific sexual pleasure. Although Irigaray would agree that desire motivates our activities and our thought, this is for her a textual and not a natural fact. Therefore, for her, the key to the subversion of the patriarchal order is nontextual sexual pleasure, a force outside conceptual structures, especially those generative and familial structures that have made women the container/envelope that protects and shelters the male. The maternity so important for Diotima in the lives of both men and women is, for Irigaray, only a trap from which sexual pleasure, or "jouissance," must deliver us. Diotimean love, which has issue in human goodness, knowledge, familial and institutional relationships, is anathema to Irigaray. It makes love, she says, into a "devoir" or "moyen" (a duty or means) (1984, 33). Love becomes "sagesse politique, sagesse ordre de la cité" (political wisdom, wisdom ordering the city) (1984, 36). In contrast, Irigaray's feminine pleasure involves a free, sensuous play of bodies and texts, engaged in for its own sake, opposed to the establishment of any doctrine, politics, or commitment. For Irigaray, to allow stakes in love is to cease to be feminine. It is to found an alienated masculine order. The feminine can never be foundational because its very essence is marginality, a marginality that is liberating because it provokes a constant questioning and mocking of the masculine order that restricts the free circulation of feminine desire.[25]

Diotima, on the other hand, speaks from a different perspective. As priestess, prophetess, member of a theological tradition, she finds nothing inconsistent in the idea of feminine institutions and social forms. She is not the marginalized and repressed female student of an all-powerful male philosophical and psychoanalytic establishment. She has not been painfully rejected by her master. Instead, she speaks to an audience which takes feminine divinity for granted and for which feminine religious leaders continue to command respect. As a result, she has a different sense of herself as feminine than a woman struggling for a foothold, or refusing to find a foothold, within the paranoid closed circle of Lacanian authority.[26]

Irigaray's rejection of Diotima's method is also linked to a view of the subject inherited from post-structuralist theory. In Diotima's philosophy, the self is in a constant process of change, both in mind and body (207d–208e). Therefore, it is clear that she cannot be accused of the Cartesianism that contemporary feminists have found so useful as an objection to masculinist theory (for example, Flax 1980, Irigaray 1974). At the same time, Diotima's view of the loving self, constantly open to mutilations that occur in any relationship and constantly in the process of generating new social forms, has little in common with the split subject of Lacan. Lacan understood that there could be no unitary self. Always in the self is the Other, but this Other of Lacan is not another person. It is the Other of language ruled by the Law of the Father. We are split between the polymorphous feeling "me" and a linguistic order in which we must live out our social lives as human and not animal. This "Other" we have no choice but to accept. Irigaray, like Lacan, sees institutionalization as a return to the Other, to the Law of the Father, and so must posit, as the only escape, a libidinous sensuality that language must leave behind.

Diotima, however, does not see in language a built-in normative order. For her, discourses are interchanges that initiate social orders. Talk between lovers is not a free expression of pure sensuous pleasure, nor is it a programmed lesson resulting in a predetermined definition of good. Neither of these possibilities would lead to the new ideas that Diotima claims are the fruits of love. Irigaray charges Diotima with moving away from an "individualized becoming" to "collective" goods. Indeed, Diotimean talk between lovers "never contemplates an individual becoming"; sexual desire, for Diotima is not an impulse toward self-realization. Instead, in love the mortal subject moves beyond her own individual life into the lives of others. Pregnancy and birth, whether of body or mind, occur only when there is an "engagement" (ἁρμόττον) and a "being together" (συνουσίά) (206c4–d1).

Irigaray, on the other hand, trapped in the metaphysics of Lacan's split self, cannot accept an interactional view of discourse. She sees feminist struggle as an internalized rebellion against the Law of the Father in one's own speech and thought. The goal of this struggle must be free expression of diffuse emotions and sensations, and a feminine speech that has affinities with the "illogic" of hysterics and dreamers:

> Echanges sans termes identifiables, sans comptes, sans fin. . . . Sans un(e) plus un(e), sans série, sans nombre. (1977, 193)
>
> (Exchanges without identifiable terms, without accounts, without end . . . without one plus one, without series, without number.)

This is a language that women may "parler entre-elles," but the revolutionary result is not the development of new forms of social life. It is a personal liberation that frees the subject from the symbolic Law of the Father.

For Diotima, on the other hand, there is no "subject," split or other. There are only selves in constant dissolution and renewal as they relate to each other. The enemy of the self is not an internalized conceptual order, but "ugliness," an ugliness not identified as the opposite of an ideal of perfect beauty but as that which one cannot love. Ugliness can have no issue, because it is rigid, sterile, impotent, arid (206d). Although Irigaray may be right in thinking that we have finally internalized such an ugliness, she is wrong to ignore the historical specificity of that process.

I, too, read Plato years ago with no interest in Greek geography, religion, or politics, sexual or other, I read Plato as if he were John Austin. Others read him as if he was Frege, or more recently Kripke. We all read him as if he were the practitioner of our own particular brand of rationality. Although we might have disagreed about what rationality consisted in, we were sure that it existed and that it allowed us to read Plato on our own terms. Deconstructive reading and "écriture féminine" have been a refreshing antidote. They have made us see the veneer of rationalism and the destructive misogyny of those we were taught to respect. Irigaray, performing her "feminine operation" has interrupted academic discourse, disrupted sacred Aristotelian, Platonic, and Kantian categories. She has made us see how the Law of the Father operates masked as metaphysical truth.

If, with Diotima, her usual sure touch falters, it is because Diotima does not play the feminine role as deconstruction or Lacanian psychoanalytic theory has conceived it. She is not the uninvited gatekeeper, but the host of the *Symposium.* She is the spokesperson for ways of life and thought that Greek philosophy feeds on, ways of thought whose authority Plato neutralized and converted to his own purposes.

In Plato's hands, Diotima's loving conversation becomes the Socratic *elenchus:* a programmed course of study in which pupil is guided toward a "correct" conclusion determined in advance. The generative, divine source of Beauty becomes the Form of the Good, an abstract transcendent object removed from the processes of the natural world. Diotima's concern that, unless we see and involve ourselves with real generative beauty, we may rely on false "images" of virtue is rejected and a sterile Socratic division manufactures villains and heroes. Diotima's celebration of erotic union as the divine mode for all creative activity becomes contempt for the body and for heterosexual intercourse.

Platonic philosophy is not the primal opening of metaphysical space, as Irigaray argued in *Speculum.* It is parasitic on an earlier metaphysics, whose characteristic idioms Plato borrows to build a phantasmic world of images. If Irigaray showed us the necessary flimsiness of the Platonic "symbolic," her Derridean and Lacanian heritage withheld from us the actual history of its fraudulent construction. To reduce Diotima to coopted feminine marginality is to perpetuate this deception. To reinstate her is to carry out that necessary restructuring of our perspective that Irigaray herself described so inspiringly in *Speculum de l'autre femme.*

Notes

1. K. J. Dover (1978) states the typical reasoning: it is unlikely that a woman could have taught Socrates (161 n. 11). A more recent example is Martha Nussbaum (1986) who asserts

Diotima's fictionality without argument and further reduces her status by labeling her as Plato's intellectual "mistress," a woman with whom he has mental intercourse (177).

2. At 210a, Diotima explains that to reach the first revelation one must begin while young by falling in love with beautiful bodies. At 206c, she describes the coming together of men and women to produce children as a "divinity and an immortality in the midst of human life." (Cf. *Phaedrus* 250c, where those who have forgotten the vision of beauty from their pre-earth existences go off like "beasts" and "beget offspring of the flesh.")

3. Line citations are to Bury's (1932) text of the *Symposium.* Translations are my own.

4. Most commentators have assumed the identity of Diotima's pure beauty-in-itself and the Platonic Form of Beauty as described in the *Phaedrus.* In the *Phaedrus,* the winged soul in its Pythagorean preexistence climbs a heavenly summit to glimpse the "true being" of Justice, Temperance, Beauty, etc. Once imprisoned in the body, the soul can only dimly discern vestiges of this heavenly Beauty in actual beautiful objects. For Diotima, the process is reversed. The lover begins by loving individuals and via a widening loving practice begins to discern the generative power in all the beautiful things to which she is attracted. Although Diotima's final vision is of a divine beauty not instantiated in any individual physical thing ("pure, mixed, not filled in with flesh or with the human, or with color" [211d]), there is no suggestion that it has any ghostly residence in a heaven of Forms. Instead, it is grasped as an immortal life force, independent of any individual being. The vision of absolute beauty is not an end in itself for Diotima. The goal continues to be "to bear" (τίκειυ) true virtue (212a3). (There is no good translation for "τίκτω" that can be used both of the father's and the mother's part in reproduction.)

5. Diotima refers to lovers as "he's" when generic terms are not available. Since Plato's audience and also the audience of the *Symposium* are male, it is to be expected that Plato and perhaps even Diotima herself would have adapted their presentations for that audience. There is, however, no reason to think that Diotima's teaching would have been meant only for men. The content of that teaching clearly refers to both women and men.

6. Cf. Derrida's (1981) deconstructive reading of the *Phaedrus* in which he traces the patriarchal motifs of succession from father to son.

7. Cf. 209b–c. When the "pregnant" lover comes into contact with someone beautiful, she not only embraces the loved one's body but also they converse. The new insights that are the "offspring" of this union are "brought up" by the couple together and this "common project" makes their love even stronger. There is no suggestion that only one of the couple profits from or possesses the "goods" that are generated in their relationship.

8. The one passage that seems to suggest a hierarchical progression is 211c, where Diotima says that "in order to approach the philosophy of love correctly one must, beginning from beautiful things, progress for the sake of what is eternally beautiful, like climbing stairs." In what follows, however, she explains what she means, again in nonhierarchical terms. The lover is go to "from one (beautiful body) to two, from two to many."

9. Commentators have had considerable difficulty in giving a Platonic interpretation of the conclusion of Diotima's discourse. She has been describing the final vision of beauty-in-itself, the eternal generative center inherent in everything and everyone we love. Then she adds: "But don't you think that only this person, this seeing person for whom the good is visible, will be able to 'give birth' not to images of virtue because she fastens on images, but true virtue because she fastens on true virtues?" (212a, 1–5). In fact, Diotima's conclusion can be read as an implicit warning against Platonism: if we detach ourselves from real concrete beauty, we may manufacture only empty ideas of virtue and not real virtue.

10. This is the argument of Derrida's foundational text, *Of Grammatology* (1976).

11. When Nietzsche's various pronouncements on women are examined, Derrida argues, there are several attitudes revealed. First, the woman is condemned by Nietzsche as a "figure"

of falsehood. Second, she is "censured, debased and despised" as a figure of truth. But in a third kind of statement, beyond this double negation, the woman is affirmed as having moved beyond the opposition between truth and falsity (Derrida 1978, 97).

12. This project is carried out in Irigaray's *Speculum de l'autre femme* (1974) where she reads the founding fathers of philosophy, Plato, Aristotle, Kant, Descartes, in order to exhibit and detail their sexist logic.

13. The relations between the master Lacan and Irigaray were troubled. As a Lacanian analyst on the faculty of Lacan's department at Vincennes, Irigaray's seminar was abruptly cancelled as unsuitable after the publication of *Speculum*.

14. Lacan, himself, believing that the symbolic order of the phallus was constitutive of linguistic meaning, promised no escape from the signifier. Psychoanalysis could only bring the subject back to the alienating moment of entering language and make him alive to the fragility of his symbolic existence.

15. When Diotima chides Socrates for employing a simplistic dichotomous logic (love must be ugly or beautiful), Irigaray approves her "non-Hegelian" dialectic, a "*jeu l'intermédiare*" that does not destroy two terms to establish a synthesis but that inserts a "third" that allows a progression from one state to another. (1984, 27) Her analysis, however, does not recognize the connection Diotima makes between the textual progression from term to term and the natural urge that aspires to beauty and goodness.

16. Other feminist deconstructive readings of Plato suffer from the same ahistorical assumptions. See for example, duBois's (1985) deconstruction of Derrida's deconstruction of the *Phaedrus*. Derrida missed, duBois argues, the submerged femininity in the *Phaedrus*, where Plato has Socrates turn into a king of "transvestite," speaking in the voices of priestesses and female poets. This analysis assumes the eternally degraded, libidinal feminine, excluded from, but erupting into, the eternally dominant masculine.

17. Irigaray herself is at the forefront with her brilliant deconstructive readings of Aristotle and Plato in *Speculum*.

18. Revisions of unfounded assumptions of male superiority by Sir Arthur Evans and others have been necessary. Cf., for example, Willetts (1977), who reviews the literature and describes the now overwhelming evidence that women had a preeminent position in Minoan Crete, and also Thomas (1973) for a more ideological, but still persuasive, argument.

19. The degree of survival of Minoan–Mycenean "matriarchal" traditions in Homer and the Archaic age has been controversial. Cf. Pomeroy (1973) for a discussion of the evidence and some speculation as to the causes of the virulence with which scholars have attacked the idea of a surviving matriarchy. There is, however, massive evidence for the continuation of Minoan religious traditions throughout the Archaic age and into classical times. Cf. Dietrich (1974).

20. Cf. also Aristoxenus frag. 15 (Kirk, Raven, and Schofield [1983] frags. 278, 233): "and Aristoxenus says that Pythagoras got most of his ethical doctrine from the Delphic priestess, Themistocleia."

21. Difficult to translate into English, *jouissance* implies sensuous pleasure in general, the use or possession of an object for one's own pleasure, and, in colloquial use, the specific pleasure of sexual orgasm.

22. Cf. Freud's essay on "Femininity" (1953) in which Freud argues that, even in "normal" development, the girl's sexuality will be to some extent repressed, resulting in a necessary degree of frigidity, narcissism, and failure to sublimate desire in great works.

23. Bernini's statue of Saint Teresa, pierced by the love of Christ, is the frontispiece for Lacan's seminar on love, *Encore* (1975).

24. Although Diotima's language has been adapted by Plato for a Greek male homosexual audience, and therefore sometimes seems to apply only to male lovers, the actual content of

her teaching shows that it is meant to apply to any combination of sexes. Her teaching was particularly useful for Plato who could adapt it to male homosexual love, or distort it to argue that pederasty between men was superior to heterosexual love.

25. At one place, Irigaray seems to suggest that this marginality is, to some degree, situational (1977, 125–26), the "mode d'action aujourd'hui possible pour les femmes" (the kind of action today possible for women). But in the previous paragraph Irigaray makes it clear that an unprecedented revolution in thought must occur before a woman could develop a "discours de la femme" or a "pratique politique."

26. See Catherine Clément (1981) for a sensitive description of some of the contradictions and compromises such a position could entail.

References

Bury, R. G. 1932. *The Symposium of Plato.* Cambridge: W. Heffer and Sons.

Clément, Catherine. 1981. *Vies et légendes de Jacques Lacan.* Paris: B. Grasset.

Derrida, Jacques. 1976. *Of Grammatology.* Translated by G. C. Spivak. Baltimore: Johns Hopkins University Press.

———. 1978. *Spurs: Nietzsche's Styles.* Translated by Barbara Harlow. Chicago: University of Chicago Press.

———. 1981. *Dissémination.* Translated by Barbara Johnson. Chicago: University of Chicago Press.

Dietrich, B. C. 1974. *The Origins of Greek Religion.* Berlin: Walter de Gruyter.

Dover, K. J. 1978. *Greek Homosexuality.* Cambridge: Harvard University Press.

duBois, Page. 1985. "Phallocentrism and Its Subversion in Plato's *Phaedrus.*" *Arethusa* 18: 91–103.

Flax, Jane. 1980. "Mother-Daughter Relationships: Psychodynamics, Politics and Philosophy." In *The Future of Difference,* edited by Hester Eisenstein and Allice Jardine. Boston: G. K. Hall.

Freud, Sigmund. 1953. "Femininity." In *The Standard Edition of the Complete Psychological Works.* Vol. 21. London: Hogarth.

Irigaray, Luce. 1974. *Speculum de l'autre femme.* Paris: Minuit.

———. 1977. *Ce sexe qui n'est pas un.* Paris: Minuit.

———. 1984. *Ethique de la différence sexuale.* Paris: Minuit.

Kirk, G. S., J. E. Raven, and M. Schofield, eds. 1983. *The Presocratic Philosophers.* 2d ed. Cambridge: Cambridge University Press.

Lacan, Jacques. 1966. *Ecrits I and II.* Paris: du Seuil.

———. 1975. *Encore, Le Séminaire de Jacques Lacan, Livre XX.* Paris: de Seuil.

Nussbaum, Martha. 1986. *The Fragility of Goodness: Luck and Ethics in Greek Tragedy and Philosophy.* Cambridge: Cambridge University Press.

Plato, 1932. *The Symposium.* Edited by R. G. Bury. Cambridge: W. Heffer and Sons.

Pomeroy, Sarah. 1973. "Selected Bibliography on Women." *Arethusa.* 6:2.

———. 1975. "Andromache and the Question of Matriarchy." *Revue des études Greques.* 88: 16–19.

Thomas, C. G. 1973. "Matriarchy in Early Greece: The Bronze and Dark Ages." *Arethusa.* 6: 2.

Thomson, George. 1949. *The Prehistoric Aegean.* London: Laurence and Wishart.

Willets, R. F. 1977. *The Civilization of Ancient Crete.* London: Batsford.

11

Overcoming Dualism: The Importance of the Intermediate in Plato's *Philebus**

Cynthia Hampton

Introduction

One of the features of Western philosophy that many feminists have attacked is dualism, the conceptualization of reality in pairs composed of members that are mutually exclusive and yet supposed to be complementary. These pairs include not only those drawn from the observation of the cycles in nature (for example, hot/cold, dry/wet), but also highly abstract metaphysical constructions (such as one/many and limited/unlimited), and those used in explanations of the human world (for example, male/female and soul/body). Perhaps the most famous ancient instance of Western dualism is the sixth-century B.C.E. Pythagorean Table of Opposites, which is headed by the opposition of the limited to the unlimited, and also includes odd/even, one/many, right/left, male/female, rest/motion, straight/curved, light/dark, good/bad, square/ob-

*I would like to acknowledge Pat Lull, Candice Blocker, and Bat-Ami Bar On for their comments on earlier drafts of this paper.

long.[1] Some feminists, including Caroline Whitbeck[2] and Genevieve Lloyd,[3] have suggested that not only was the first member of each dichotomous pair considered superior but that limit or form was associated with the masculine while unlimitedness or formlessness was linked to the feminine.[4] Most feminists, including me, use the terms "feminine" and "masculine" in reference to socially constructed gender identities, not to the biological conditions of being female or male. Of course, there is not complete consensus about what counts as feminine or masculine even with a single culture or tradition. But since dualism is one of the hallmarks of the formal constructions of reality found in Western cultures, which have been dominated by white men, it is fair to say that dichotomous thinking reflects a Western masculine worldview or ontology. For in the West, white men saw themselves as separate from anyone they perceived as significantly different than themselves, especially women. Yet at the same time these men needed to minimize the threat of women's "otherness" by channeling it in ways that would support their own positions of power, that is, by encouraging the so-called complementary aspects of the "opposite sex." Not surprisingly, dualism emerged early in Western philosophy, prevailed in ancient Greek thinking, and indeed has permeated Western culture.

The dominance of masculinist ontology is problematic not simply because it underrepresents women's experiences but because the overemphasis on separation and opposition characteristic of dualistic thinking leads, as many feminists—including Carol Gilligan[5] and Sara Ruddick[6]—have pointed out, to alienation and violence. But if so, why should Western canonical philosophical texts continue to be studied? One answer is provided by French feminist deconstructionists such as Luce Irigaray. The goal of the deconstructionist project is to expose the pretensions of a text's claims to transcendent or extratextual truths and unitary meanings. One way of doing this is to read between the lines for hidden agendas or for ways the author subverts her or his own text. So by ferreting out masculinist assumptions and ways feminine views have been marginalized in canonical texts, the claims of the Western tradition to universality are undermined.[7]

I propose that there is another reason for reading the canon: for the purposes of reconstruction, not just deconstruction. There are conscious struggles against dichotomous thinking within the tradition.[8] Surprisingly enough, one of the philosophical texts where the struggle to overcome dualism is most marked is in Plato's late dialogue, the *Philebus*.[9]

After some preliminary discussion of dualism in ancient Greek thinking before Plato as well as in his own earlier work. I shall focus on how the *Philebus* embodies Plato's struggle to overcome dichotomous thinking.

Although I do not think that Plato is altogether successful in his strivings, the understanding of his struggle is important as an example of how one's culture, let alone biology, is not one's destiny, at least not in any simpleminded way. Plato's resistance to masculinist dichotomous thinking is particularly noteworthy since as an aristocratic male he was the heir to a tradition where such thinking dominated. He was able to resist dualism not because he was a heroic feminist who championed the cause of women's liberation, but rather because he was attuned to feminine voices that his tradition could not altogether suppress. The specific feminine strains I have in mind are those associated with a holistic worldview that sees the interrelatedness and harmony between individuals—by they persons or abstract terms—as the primary reality.[10] As I shall explain shortly, the holism that apparently abounded in the goddess-centered mythology of preclassical times began to give way, in classical mythology and pre-Socratic philosophy, to an emphasis on separation and opposition. Nevertheless, the feminine influence never disappeared totally, and in Plato's philosophy it leaves some rather strong traces. Following these traces should provide a better understanding that a feminine alternative to dualism is a part, albeit a neglected part, of Western heritage. If philosophies like Plato's can be interpreted so they speak meaningfully to contemporary audiences, then we see that what is needed is not the wholesale rejection of the past, but a creative reshaping of it.

Dualism in Classical Greek Mythology and Pre-Socratic Philosophy

Dualistic thinking, while formalized by the ancient philosophers, appeared in classical mythology where natural forces were personified as male and female deities who were both complementary and in opposition. While there are many examples, for the sake of brevity I shall concentrate on one: the poet Hesiod's version of the story of Gaia (earth) and Ouranos (sky or heaven) in his *Theogony*, written around 750 B.C.E. The most famous part of his myth is the explanation of how the earth and sky, which were originally one, were separated. The sexual union of the two produced many children whom their father Ouranos hid within Gaia, concealed from the light. In revenge, Gaia made a sickle, which she urged their son Cronos (Time) to use to castrate Ouranos.[11] Thus the opposition between Earth and Sky results in their separation, yet they continue to be complementary since it is the rain of the Sky that impregnates the Earth who then brings forth grain.

But there is more to the story. Of course, this myth, like most, leaves out many details and at times contradicts itself; for example, how could Ouranos impregnate Gaia *after* his castration? As most classicists acknowledge, Hesiod was weaving together different versions of the same myth and so a coherent narrative was unlikely to result. Even so, there are aspects of Hesiod's account that suggest that the feminine Earth was the older and more powerful deity, and so Ouranos's crime was perhaps a form of rebellion. Besides Chaos (gap), Gaia was the first to emerge and Ouranos was simply her firstborn. Although Hesiod is quick to point out that Ouranos "matched [Gaia's] every dimension,"[12] this seems unlikely not only given the fact that she is his mother but also that she (but not he) is able to produce children parthenogenetically; she bore the Sea (Pontus) "without any sweet act of love."[13] These details of the myth suggest that parts of it are of pre-Hellenic origin. Although exact dating of prehistorical cultures is difficult to determine, the pre-Hellenic period was roughly between 2500 to 1000 or 800 B.C.E., from the flourishing of Cretan civilization to the time of the invasions of mainland Greece by the peoples of the north. During this time, Gaia was the ancient Earth-mother, a manifestation of the Great Goddess who was worshiped from India to the Mediterranean.[14]

If the Gaia myth does indeed contain fragments from the mythology of the Great Goddess, then certain details of the story such as why Ouranos hid the children, and why Gaia's revenge took the form of castration are more understandable. A closer look at the pre-Hellenic peoples who worshiped the Great Goddess and the mythology of those who invaded their lands is in order.

One reason pre-Hellenic people worshiped a female deity rather than a male might be that they assumed that females were the sole givers of life; they did not associate reproduction with sexual intercourse and so did not recognize paternality.[15] But unlike the Near and Middle Eastern peoples, the warrior peoples of the north, variously called Indo-Europeans, Indo-Iranians, Indo-Aryans, or Aryans, worshiped a supreme male deity who was often portrayed as a storm god living on a mountain blazing with the light of fire or lightning. They also associated good and evil as light and dark respectively. When these northerners invaded the Near and Middle East, they brought these ideas with them.[16] In classical Greek mythology, Ouranos's grandson Zeus is god of the thunderbolt and supreme king; his name, like his grandfather's, means "sky." Even Ouranos as the personified sky is associated with rain and so is a variation of the northern thunder-god. So perhaps Ouranos's not letting his children "into the light"[17] symbolizes the struggle between the sky god of the northern peoples to overcome the pre-Hellenics' Great Goddess, who, from their point of view, is mysteriously dark and evil.

As far as Ouranos's castration is concerned, note that castration stories can be found in Hittite, Anatolian, and Egyptian mythologies, and references can be found to eunuch priests in Sumner, Babylon, Canaan, and Anatolia.[18] Merlin Stone in her now-classic book, *When God Was a Woman,* speculates that castration might have been one of the substitute rituals for the earlier human sacrifice of the young consort of the high priestess. The priestess and her consort symbolized the union between the Great Goddess and her son/lover.[19] So the Gaia myth is one that symbolizes the struggle between the very ancient matrifocal society, which worshiped the Great Goddess, and the patriarchial culture of the invaders. Although patriarchy had become thoroughly entrenched by the time of Hesiod, his retelling of this myth still contains fragments of the earlier stories.

The first Greek philosophers attempted to replace mythological explanations of natural phenomena with "rational" ones by adopting the focus on separation and opposition present in the classical myths and representing these forces in more abstract terms. Throughout the pre-Socratic cosmogonies from the late seventh-century figure Anaximenes to Anaxagoras, who lived in the beginning of the fifth century, there exists a concern with the separation of the elements from the original undifferentiated source, and the subsequent "war of opposites" between the cold air and hot fire, the moist water and dry land.[20] As scholars widely acknowledge, all these theories were addressing the same basic question: How is the diversity, "the many," of the natural world derived from one basic source? This question is known as the problem of [the] one and [the] many. The influence of mythological thinking is revealed most explicitly by the fact that most of the pre-Socratics refer to the one source of all things as being "divine" or a "god."[21] By "divine" they, of course, do not necessarily mean a conscious being, let alone a person. Instead, the hallmark of divinity is simply its immortality. Yet even this practice perpetuates dualism since the contrast term for immortal is, of course, mortal.

The pre-Socratics' tendency to think of one and many as mutually exclusive reached its logical extreme with Parmenides (b. 515 B.C.E.) who argued that there can be only the One, that is, Being, so that the appearance of plurality is illusory. In his poem, written in imitation of Hesiod's *Theogony*, Parmenides describes the One as limited and unchanging (that is, at rest), and associates its revelation to him with light. Thus, Parmenides' description of the One echoes the limited (male) side of the Pythagorean Table of Opposites.[22] Parmenides' successors found his argument logically valid but rejected his conclusion as an outrageous assault upon common sense, even by philosophy's standards. In the attempt to find some place for ordinary experiences of time, change, and plurality, there arose all subsequent cosmologies and ontologies, including Plato's Theory of Forms or Ideas.

Plato's Struggle with Dualism Prior to the *Philebus*

Plato's general strategy for solving the problem of one and many was to distinguish between two groups. The first is a limited, unified group of immutable nonspatial and atemporal essences that are in no way qualified by their opposites. The second group is a manifestation of the first but is an unlimited collection of mutable, spatial and/or temporal sensibles that are thoroughly mixed with their opposites. The first group consists of Platonic Forms, the second, of sensibles or items of ordinary experience: trees, chairs, the color red, the patently false belief that the Cubs will win the pennant—ever.

A comparison between a Form and its sensible instances will highlight the differences between the two. Compare, for example, just laws with the Form of Justice. Through time and in many places, any number of just laws may be created and discarded, and none of them ever will be completely just; each one always will be unjust to some degree or in some respect. By contrast, the Form of Justice is simply what it is—unqualifiably and unchangingly just—and thus may be used as the standard by which to judge the degree to which any given law, institution, action, person, etc., may be considered just. In this way, the Form's function as a standard is derived from its nature as the true reality, which its sensible instances are able to approximate, by imitation or reflection, only in a partial way. For example, just persons try to embody the ideal of justice that is the Form but can never fully succeed because of the vicissitudes of human life and society. Not only are the Forms most fully real and thus most intelligible, they are also of supreme value. The scale of reality and knowledge is also a hierarchy of value with the Forms higher than their sensible instances, and one Form—variously referred to as the Good, the Beautiful, or the One—is the highest of all.[23]

Even with this bare-bones sketch it appears that Plato's theory, while an attempt to bring the one and the many together, simply falls back on the same strategy as his predecessors: divide, or separate, to conquer the tensions between dualistic pairs of opposites. Indeed, in the *Republic* he talks as if Forms and sensibles belong to two completely separate worlds[24] and in the *Phaedo* we find this separation mirrored in each human being as the dualism of body and soul.[25] Yet Plato's dialogues dramatize the struggle against dualism even as they sometimes lapse into such language. Throughout the Platonic corpus there is ample evidence, both implicit and explicit, of his striving to find intermediaries to bridge the gap between the one and the many, the Forms and sensibles, soul and body. Many scholars, including feminists, have called attention to some of this evidence. Genevieve Lloyd notes that in the *Republic*, Platonic psychology moves from a simple body/soul dualism to the more complex model of the tri-part soul.[26]

A most recent and provocative discussion of the role of the intermediate in the Platonic corpus is the one between Luce Irigaray and Andrea Nye on the subject of Diotima's method in the *Symposium*. Both feminists agree that the intermediary is the crucial element of the priestess Diotima's method, which resists, if not overcomes, dualism. I agree that while all the speakers at the symposium identify eros as a fundamental force at work in both the mortal and immortal realms, only Diotima's method reveals that eros is the intermediary between the two realms. The following of erotic desire transforms ignorance into knowledge, need into plenty, longing into union, and in general, enables humans to approximate the divine as much as possible.[27] Diotima's language closely resembles that of the mystery cults, such as the Eleusinian mysteries in which the initiate comes to identify with, and even become, the Earth-mother goddess Demeter.[28] As Nye also notes, Diotima's method is divine and fits within the Great Goddess tradition.[29] On the other hand, Diotima's method is both feminine and demonic according to Irigaray, since the feminine subverts masculine logic and language.[30] I agree that Diotima stands the masculine Olympian tradition on its head; the god Eros is not beautiful, wise, or prosperous, but rather is in between beauty and ugliness, ignorance and knowledge, poverty and plenty. Eros is not, strictly speaking, a god at all but rather a *daimon* (demon), a spirit who links mortal humans with the immortal gods.[31]

Although both Irigaray and Nye have important insights, I disagree with some of the implications of their respective analyses. I do not believe that Diotima leaps out of Plato's subconscious, like Athene out of the head of Zeus, in order to subvert her creator's conscious philosophical designs. Nor do I believe that Plato is trying to fit together, willy-nilly, his philosophy with the Great Goddess tradition. Rather, I see him summoning nondualistic images in his struggle to articulate a way out of the central dualisms of one and many, limit and unlimited, which he inherited from the pre-Socratics. For Plato, knowledge of ultimate reality is not just immediate insight but also is what can be accounted for in the prosaic language of reasoned explanation or causality. For Plato, as for most people who wish for both mystery and lucidity, the intoxicating images and symbolic language that abound in the *Symposium*—and elsewhere—need to be accompanied by the more sober reflection of philosophical discourse. Such reflection is found in Plato's late dialogue, the *Philebus*. I shall now turn to this text to show how Plato uses what might today be called the feminine approach of the intermediate in one of his most sustained efforts to overcome dualism.

The Intermediate in the *Philebus*: Our Divine Link to True Reality and Knowledge

In the *Philebus*, the intermediate—what lies between the one and the many—plays a key role. The gist of the ontology or worldview depicted in the dialogue is this: there is an ultimate One—the Good—that unifies all things via its intermediate aspects. Here—in marked contrast to Parmenides' One, which made plurality illusory—the Good in the

Philebus is a One that itself contains plurality. However, as I shall explain shortly, the Good encompasses the plurality of the sensible world only indirectly since sensible plurality is infinite in extent and indefinite in character[32] and so not fully real or knowable. What can be known are the Forms, which are the intermediates between the infinite plurality of sensibles and the all-encompassing Form of the Good. The Forms, unlike sensibles, are inherently limited and definite in nature. Since, as previously noted, sensibles approximate Forms, when one understands the Forms one will learn all that there is to comprehend about sensibles: the structure which "underlies" them.[33] Like contemporary chaos theorists, Plato believes that behind the apparent randomness of sensible phenomena lies order.

But how does one come to know these intermediate Forms and so solve the puzzle of one and many? As an answer to this question, Socrates—as the Platonic speaker of the dialogue[34]—introduces "the Divine Method." This method is grounded on the assumption that all is from one and many and everything has within it definiteness (or the limited) and indefiniteness (or unlimitedness). So the very foundation of the Divine Method is the assumption that one and many are expressed in the combinations of limit and unlimited that are an inherent part of the nature of all things.[35]

The realization that limit and unlimited are combined in all things enables Plato to transform the traditional dualistic pairs of hot/cold and wet/dry into continua of hotter-and-colder, and drier-and-wetter.[36] Plato retains the usual Greek view of seeing hot and cold as equally real; that is, cold is no more the absence of heat than vice versa[37] but he now depicts sensibles as being neither hot nor cold per se. Instead, each has some particular temperature that can be expressed as some point along the hotter-colder continuum.

The Divine Method not only enables Plato to break out of the dualisms concerned with the strictly material aspects of the sensible world; it also provides a nondualistic model for how ultimate reality is related to sensibles. This model is illuminated by the illustrations of the Divine Method: linguistic and musical sound. In the case of learning to pronounce the letters of the alphabet, for example, one realizes that although the sounds that can be vocalized are infinite, the rules of grammar that determine the number and nature of distinguishable linguistic sounds—vowels, semivowels, mutes—make linguistic sound one comprehensive unit.[38] One cannot learn to pronounce the letters in isolation from one another, but must do so by combining them. Thus the role of grammar is crucial in that it reveals the proper ways to unite the letters.[39] Presumably, letters form syllables, then nouns and verbs, then sentences.[40] What is true of language is true of everything else. Knowledge takes place when one can discern and express the pattern "behind" the indefiniteness and infinite variety of sensible phenomena.

Plato's insights into the nature of language studied by linguistics are remarkably similar to those of the contemporary language philosopher Noam Chomsky, who believes that all languages exhibit a universal grammar.[41] In his discussion of the knowledge of a language, he says that "knowledge of a language is mentally represented as a 'grammar'—that is, a finite system of rules and principles that interact to determine ('generate') an infinite class of expressions, each with a phonetic form, meaning, and associated structural properties (for example, an organization into words and phrases)."[42] Plato and Chomsky would agree that the mind is not a blank slate, and that our knowledge of universal grammar is innate. But Chomsky considers this innate knowledge to be part of our biological endowment, while Plato believes that the universal features of language point to the nature of ultimate reality. As the *Philebus* makes clear, the reason one and many are perennially present in all utterances is because language—at its deepest, most universal level—reflects the structure provided by the Forms (15d–16b). It is the business of the Divine Method to reveal this structure.

The focus of the Divine Method on the intermediates indicates that the goal of knowledge is neither contemplation of the absolute, indivisible One nor the experience of infinite variety, but the articulation of unity as it is expressed in multiplicity. That Plato uses linguistic and musical sound as his illustrations of the Divine Method is no accident, for such examples depict the basic structure of reality as an organic whole rather than a mere aggregate of individuals. Parts are not discrete units but elements that blend together like sounds that form spoken syllables or musical scales.

Plato's use of auditory examples also presents an alternative to the model of knowledge, which relies on the analogies of sight and/or touch. Such a model is prevalent in Plato's earlier works such as the *Republic*.[43] The visual/tactile model suggests that the soul directly encounters the Forms as the eyes or hand must be in the immediate presence of the sensible in order to see or grasp its properties. Such a model suggests that the ultimate objects of knowledge, the Forms, are absolute simples with no parts: they can be seen all at once or grasped in their entirety. But the auditory model suggested by spoken and musical sound emphasizes the interconnections of the Forms, which must be articulated as a system in order to be understood.

Plato's striving to overcome dualism is evident not only in his description and illustration of the Divine Method but also in the story he tells of this method's origins. According to Socrates in the *Philebus*, the Divine Method is "thrown down by the gods in a blaze of light from some Prometheus" (16c). In Plato's earlier version of this myth[44] Prometheus (whose name means "forethought"), a brother of Cronos and son of Ouranos, was the Titan who helped humanity overcome its initial condition of utter helplessness by giving it fire and wisdom in the crafts or skills. These skills include religious rituals by which we mark our kinship with the divine as well as the means for providing for our material needs (food, clothing, and shelter), and language.

As we have seen in the *Philebus,* language is used as an illustration of the Divine Method. Later in the dialogue, Socrates discusses causality as one of the main forces at work in the universe. He credits the Cause (which is here personified) with ensouling human bodies and giving them medicine and other devices, and also for implanting a kingly soul and intellectual intuition (*nous*) in Zeus (30b–d). This last description of the Cause harks back to another aspect of the Prometheus myth: the Titan's role in bringing about victory for the gods in their war against the other Titans and in the subsequent crowning of Zeus as king.

The main point Plato makes by using this myth is that the Divine Method can impart godlike power to mortals. This is symbolized by Prometheus's gift of fire, which, having been stolen from the gods, brings enlightenment to humanity. One noteworthy detail of this myth is the fact that humanity's benefactor is a deity who is older than the Olympian gods of classical Greek mythology. This fact suggests that human development depends on getting in touch with an older source of divinity, the spirit of inventiveness. As I shall explain shortly, this spirit ultimately leads to knowledge of the basic structure of reality provided by the Cause, the ultimate One or Good.

Such knowledge is possible not by contemplation of the One by itself but by identifying the presence of the one within the many. In other words, the recognition of the intermediate is what is called "divine," not the isolation of the one from the many. This recognition is not simply intellectual but includes the ability to act on the awareness of the intermediate even in securing the basic necessities of physical existence. Plato, by appropriating the Prometheus myth for his own purposes, stresses the idea that the Divine Method played a key role in the foundation of civilization. Of course, Plato's version of the myth is still androcentric in its reliance on male warrior-gods and their symbols: the fire and blaze of light, which are reminiscent of the lightning of the thunder-god. But at least he manages to use the myth to illustrate the concept of the intermediate, which is feminine in its inspiration.

The Importance of the Intermediate in the *Philebus* Conception of the Good and the Good Life

Intermediates of the Universal Good: Truth, Proportion, and Beauty

The importance of the intermediate is most apparent in the discussion at the end of the *Philebus* where the universal Good—the Form—is linked to the good life for humanity. At the end of the dialogue, Plato reveals that through the causal agency of certain intermediate aspects of the Good—Proportion, Beauty, and Truth—the good human life becomes possible. True to the general emphasis on interrelations in this dialogue, Socrates and his interlocutor Protarchus agreed early on that the good life consists of neither pleasure nor knowledge by themselves but the right mixture of the two (18e–22c).

But the question of which is the best element, knowledge or pleasure, is one that they do not consider to be answered in full even after lengthy discussion about each. The reason is that in order to make clear whether knowledge (including practical reasoning; that is, *phronesis*) or pleasure contributes more to the goodness of the good, mixed life "we must get a clear conception, or at least an outline of the Good" (61a). The outline of the Good emerges when Truth, Proportion or Measure, and Beauty are considered in terms of how they cause the mixed life of pleasure and knowledge to be a good one (65a).

Truth is said to enable the good life—or any other mixture—to come into existence (64b) as well as to become intelligible. As has been widely noted,[45] Truth here clearly is not simply a property of a statement that obtains if it describes something that really is the case (for example, the statement, "The cat is on the mat" is true if in fact the cat *is* on the mat). If this were all Plato meant by Truth then it would be a form of cognition or knowledge. However, since he has already included forms of cognition or knowledge in the good mixed life earlier in the dialogue (55c–59d), the discussion here of Truth's role in the good life indicates that Truth is something distinct from cognition or knowledge. In fact, Truth is more important than knowledge since it must be present in order for the good mixture even to exist. Truth, like sunlight, not only illuminates but is also the source of energy.[46] If it were not for Truth, there would be no knowledge and pleasure to mix together and form the good life. There would be no reality at all, at either the universal or the human level.

Proportion, or Measure, is likewise essential. Since Proportion brings unity it enables the components of the good life to compose a mixture rather than a jumbled heap. Once unified, the mixture may admit of Beauty as a higher level of organization. Thus Proportion and Beauty are intimately related though Plato is not very explicit about the nature of their relationship.

Perhaps a clue is given in his allusion to a connection between Beauty and excellence (64b). Beauty seems to bring a certain type of order, the perfect order that something displays once it has fully realized its function or achieved its excellence. The idea that every type of thing—a knife, tree, or human—has a function (that is, work it alone can do or do better than anything else) is one of the most important points Plato developed earlier in such dialogues as the *Republic* (353a–b). What enables something to function fully or perform its work well is its excellence and the good life is the one characterized by such excellences or virtues.

In this passage in the *Philebus,* Plato is applying his previous analysis of function and excellence to Proportion and Beauty. Using the example of the human body, one which Plato often employs elsewhere, will help clarify the relations between Proportion, Beauty, and excellence. The human body is composed of proportions of hotness and coldness, wetness and dryness, etc. A diseased body is one where at least some of these proportions are out of kilter; nevertheless, some degree of order is maintained. But the diseased body has lost, at least temporarily, its excellence: health. And certainly it has lost its beauty for only the well-functioning body could be considered truly beautiful.

The Greeks, naturally enough, saw their aesthetic standards as carved in stone, as in the Greek original of the Apollo Belvedere. Plato's aesthetics, like his ethics, is grounded on his idea of function. He would explain that people in their prime are physically more beautiful than those who are not by pointing out that only the former are fully realizing the body's true nature. The body's good therefore consists in its realization of its function or true nature and in this way it manifests truth, proportion, and beauty. What is true of the body would extend also to the other dimensions of human existence so that the ideal life would be one in which pleasure and knowledge are combined in a manner that exhibits all three aspects of the Good.

Application of the Intermediates to the Good Life: The Ranking of Pleasure

Of course, Plato's claim that the ideal human life is truthful, proportionate, and beautiful seems rather platitudinous. What makes all the difference is how pleasure and knowledge are to be combined in such a life. Readers of Plato's earlier work would know that he takes a dim view of the pleasures of the flesh and of flashy worldly glories. One often gets the impression, especially in the *Phaedo*, that Plato is more priggish than the most scrupulous Puritan. In this light, the fact that there is any role at all for pleasure in the good life is remarkable. In fact, as I shall demonstrate shortly, pleasure and knowledge do not simply parallel the dualism of body and soul. There are bad psychic pleasures and pure bodily ones. These are just a few foretastes of what is to come. Let those who anticipate a total salvaging of earthly delights in the *Philebus* be forewarned. In the contest between pleasure and knowledge, the latter is found to be the most like the Good in all three of its aspects: Truth, Proportion (Measure), and Beauty. Hence knowledge is declared to be the more honorable among both humans and gods (65a–b).

Worse yet, the contest seems rigged. Pleasure as a class is not compared to knowledge as a class, but to the highest type of knowledge, *nous* (intellectual intuition) and *phronesis* (practical reasoning). The comparison reveals that *nous* is either truth itself or the most like it while pleasure is the greatest of impostors (65c). Likewise, nothing is more in harmony with measure than *phronesis,* while the opposite is true of pleasure. Finally, *phronesis* and *nous* are never unseemly whereas the most intense pleasures are ridiculous or disgraceful (65e–66a). So in each case, the comparison is between the most extreme and disruptive pleasures and the highest type of knowledge.

This contest will turn out not to be as unfair as it seems. For Plato considers most pleasures to be mixed with pain and therefore contingently good at best while all types of knowledge must rest ultimately upon the foundation of *nous* and *phronesis.* In other words, pleasures by and large do not unambiguously reflect Truth, Proportion, and Beauty while knowledge of whatever type does to a greater or lesser extent. This contest is simply a summary of the entire analyses of pleasure and knowledge respectively. Before turning first to the classification of pleasure and then to knowledge, a word needs to be said about the final competition at the very end of the *Philebus.* In "the final ranking"—a kind of Academy Awards ceremony for what is valuable in life—the presenter, a personified "eternal nature" (that is, the Good)[47] does not give top honors to knowledge. Instead, first place goes to measure, the mean, fitness and their kin while the second spot is taken by proportion, beauty, completeness and sufficiency, and all of their ilk. Trailing in at a mere third place come *nous* and *phronesis,* while the lower forms of knowledge take fourth prize and the painless pleasures bring up the rear (66a–c).

The reason why knowledge, even in its highest form, does not claim first prize is that the order of the final ranking is determined by how humans can express the Good by realizing their proper place within the order of reality. This task requires an awareness of how human needs for both pleasure and knowledge can be structured so that they reflect what is objectively good; that is, what the "eternal nature" would choose. Earlier in the dialogue, Plato made it clear that limit and measure, as well as purity and truth, should be used as criteria in distinguishing between higher and lower pleasures and forms of cognition. To examine how Plato used these criteria is thus important in understanding how he fleshes out his ideal of the good life.

During the classification of pleasure, two basic kinds emerged. First are the mixed pleasures, so called because they are mixed with their opposite, pain. These pleasures are classified differently depending upon what aspects of them are being considered. In regard to their inherent capacity for extension in degree of intensity, magnitude, and number, the mixed or impure pleasures are indefinite (66a–c). This aspect of the mixed pleasures is experienced when a pleasure originates from abnormal and/or inordinate desires, be they physical or psychological (44b–51a).

The pleasures of the profligate, the homosexual prostitute, and the emotionally distressed would all fall into the indefinite category.[48] As mentioned earlier, pleasures of the soul do not necessarily fare better than those of a more physical nature. Excesses of emotion are condemned along with the usual catalogue of bodily vices. In contrast, when limit is imposed on the mixed pleasures through intelligence, then they are considered members of the class where the indefinite is mixed with the definite (31a ff.). The limited aspect of these pleasures would be experienced in connection with health and strength.[49]

The second main type of pleasure consists of the pure pleasures, which are by their very nature limited. These include not only ones free from pain (for example, the smell of a rose), but also those whose objects are relatively simple: the formal representations involved in geometry, music, and art. These latter pleasures are considered to be "divine"(51b–52c) because they are the closest link to the Forms the experience of pleasure can afford. Note that even the physical sensation of smelling can be a pure pleasure, although not a divine one.

The key to the classification of pleasure is to compare the different varieties according to the criteria of limit, purity, and truth. Those that are inherently unlimited are hopelessly impure, being mixed with their opposite, pain. These pleasures Socrates also considers to be false because their unlimitedness and indefiniteness inevitably lead to distortions of reality in one of three basic ways. The first way pleasure distorts reality is when the agent acts as if what is at best extrinsically valuable were intrinsically so, say, a miser who lives as if the acquisition of currency has value in itself. The second way involves the agent exaggerating the pleasure of satisfaction, say, when someone breaks her diet and, in an attempt to rationalize what she knows is a poor choice, exaggerates her enjoyment while eating the forbidden sweets.[50] The third type of distortion occurs when what is really in itself neither pleasant nor painful is experienced as pleasant because one has just escaped from pain; this freedom seems pleasant by comparison to the pain just experienced. An example of this is the belief someone might have that he is experiencing pleasure because the dentist has stopped drilling.

All three of these types of distortions have as their source the inherent indefiniteness of the pleasures involved. That is, the confused mixture of pleasure and pain in these situations will inevitably confuse the agent about the true value of the objects involved. By contrast, the pleasures that are intrinsically limited and pure are true; that is, they accurately reflect reality. Not surprisingly, in the final ranking the true and pure pleasures are admitted into the good life while the inherently indefinite pleasures are barred.[51] These latter are a hindrance to the pure pleasures and prevent the higher types of intelligence from coming about at all (63d–64a).

Although it is obvious enough that the pure and true pleasures are superior to the impure, mixed ones, exactly how truth and purity are related is not clear. Throughout most of the classification of pleasure, Plato uses the words "purity" and "truth" as more or less equivalent terms. But at one point (52d ff.) Socrates asks whether pure or impure pleasures are more closely related to truth. To help explain what he means by "purity," he gives an example: unmixed white.

Clearly, there is a sense in which unmixed white is more white than that which is mixed with other colors. But Socrates goes on to conclude that it is also the truest and most beautiful of all whiteness. Although he does not explain the relations between purity, truth, and beauty explicitly, he does say enough to convey the general point.

Purity is valuable, even highly valuable, in its own right and not just as the absence of impurity, which in the case of pleasure means being mixed with pain. For something to be what it is and nothing else is to be a clear reflection of the definiteness of the basic structure of reality. Even in our experiences of pleasure we may affirm our connection with the beautiful and well-proportioned whole of reality of which we are a part. This is the significance of the pure pleasures, which are true because they unambiguously exemplify the definiteness, proportion, and beauty that underlie the surface of human life.

Application of the Intermediates to the Good Life: The Ranking of Knowledge

Purity is likewise used as a criterion in the classification of knowledge, for it is equated to exactness (57b) and related to truth (57d). These criteria first are used to rank different kinds of skilled work according to the extent to which they employ arithmetic, the science of measurement and weighing. Music (that is, playing by ear), medicine, agriculture, piloting, and generalship are all examples of imprecise skills, while building is more exact because it uses a good number of measurements and instruments (55e–56c).

Furthermore, within both arithmetic and the science of measurement are two distinct kinds: those of the many and those of the philosophers. Concerning arithmetic, some reckon unequal units (say, two armies), while others insist on units that are all equal to one another. Likewise, calculation and measuring used in building and trade differ from the geometry of philosophers (56d–57a). The "philosophic" arithmetic and metrical arts surpass the more pedestrian varieties in purity, exactness and truth (57d) just as some pleasures are purer and truer than others (57b). The truest form of knowledge is the dialectic, defined as "that knowledge which has to do with being and reality and that which is always the same" (58a). It is called *nous* and *phronesis,* "the contemplation of true Being" (59d).[52] So, the extent of truth or purity involved in the various forms of skills and knowledge depends upon the definiteness of their respective objects.

Insofar as all forms of cognition are limited or definite to some extent, all are included in the final ranking of the good life. Such inclusion does not mean that all types of knowledge are on the same level, however. The objects of divine knowledge, as well as those of divine pleasure, are clearly objects of a higher ontological status—are more fully real—than those of the less pure types of pleasure and knowledge. The divine circle, sphere, etc., are at least closer than sensibles to true reality if not fully real themselves. At any rate, the knowledge of divine mathematical objects, along with *phronesis* regarding Justice itself and *nous,* is considered to be more important than the lower forms of knowledge that are needed for the practical purposes of life, so that one may "find . . . [the] way home" (62b). But practical types of knowledge are truly good only if one has divine knowledge (62b, d). The latter, called *nous* and *phronesis* in the final ranking, is put into a separate class from the lower varieties of cognition. The point is that divine knowledge or the dialectic, which earlier was identified with the Divine Method (17a), differs significantly from the lower types of cognition. Only the dialectic directly aims at the discovery of ultimate reality.

Put differently, this last aspect of the ranking is important as an instance of where an appeal to the universal, and not just the human, Good is being made. Although recognition of the crucial importance of limit in terms of obvious human goods such as health and excellence may be easy, the superiority of the dialectic to all other forms of cognition takes us beyond what we can value in strictly practical terms. The dialectic is superior in terms of both knowledge and value simply because its objects are ontologically superior. The objects of the dialectic are contrasted to those of the skills in terms of stability, purity, and truth. The dialectic's objects are "cognitively dependable,"[53] but are so, as I have argued elsewhere[54] because they, unlike sensibles, are real without qualification.

The great chain of Being is also a scale of value. "True Being" is no mere description of ultimate reality; it is an honorific title. To appreciate fully the truth, then, one must accord to everything its proper value as an expression of a true understanding of reality, both distributively and collectively. The dialectic or the Divine Method makes this understanding possible by revealing the basic structure of the realm of the Forms, which in turn explains the underlying order of the sensible world. In fact, the dialectic as the Divine Method ultimately leads to the Good.

Summary: The Role of the Intermediates in the Good Life as Imitation of the Divine

In terms of the good life, the types of pleasure and knowledge that are part of its mixture are those that admit of some measure or proportion and truth, while those pleasures that are inherently indefinite are left out. Measure or limit, as well as purity and truth, are used to rank the various types of knowledge and pleasure. The highest types are called "divine" because their objects belong, or are most akin, to the Forms, which are aspects of the Good. So when pleasure and knowledge are compared in terms of three of the Good's aspects—Truth, Proportion, and Beauty—we should not be surprised that knowledge, in particular the highest type, is once again shown to be the more important element in the good life.

The fact that the highest type of knowledge is referred to as *nous* and *phronesis* is also significant. *Nous* is related to *noesis,* the intuitive sense of the Forms.[55] Although, as has been already noted, Plato is moving away from the visual/tactile model of knowledge in the *Philebus,* the term *nous* still might refer to a type of knowledge that, once realized, is self-evident. But what is of particular interest is that *nous* is coupled with *phronesis,* practical reasoning. This coupling suggests that the highest knowledge is the most complete; it is what makes human imitation of ultimate reality and value possible by combining insight and activity. Small wonder that both these capacities are crucial for human imitation of the divine since the Cause itself, later identified with the Good, is described (28d–30e) as the producer and governor of the cosmic order according to *nous, phronesis,* and wisdom.

Thinking of the Good as the Cause or Creative agent (26e), rather than as abstract pattern set up in Platonic heaven, is more efficacious for human imitation of the divine.[56] In a sense, human beings are co-creators with the Good. Those who mix what is limited, pure, and true within themselves enhance the organic unity of their lives. In so doing, they touch the divine.

Conclusion

In sum, the *Philebus* depicts the universal order, including the ideal life for humanity, as a unity of distinct but interrelated aspects. Rigid dualism definitely loses ground in Plato's thought. Admittedly, though, most feminists would still find Plato's philosophy too masculine. After all, Plato persists not only in making abstract distinctions between different types of things but also in elevating what is more definite, limited or measured, pure and true, over what is less so. These criteria he takes to be objective: built into the nature of things.

I agree that for Plato—or anyone—to speak about the real nature of things is problematic, and that masculinist and intellectualist biases often parade under the banner of objectivity. But Plato is less guilty than it seems. First of all, he never makes a direct claim to absolute knowledge. The very fact that he writes dialogues indicates an openness to truth as it is revealed from the different perspectives voiced by the characters[57] although this feature is more prominent in earlier dialogues than it is in the *Philebus*. But even in the *Philebus*, only an "outline" of the nature of the Good is given. Plato's main concern is not arcane metaphysics as an end in itself. Rather, he urges his interlocutors, including his readers, to realize that human life is most meaningful when it points to what is beyond—and yet within—itself: the divine.

The longing for the divine is, I believe, at the root of Plato's holism, and perhaps all holistic "visions."[58] Recall that for the ancient Greeks, divinity is not limited to a conception of specific deities. "Divine" means immortal, what is not mortal. Plato's Forms are divine in this sense. To long for union with the divine, then, is to desire to participate in divinity, to be godlike. For Plato, as I have shown, this requires human beings to shape the human world so that it reflects more clearly the universal order that "underlies" all experiences.

I believe that a worldview ultimately needs to be judged in terms of the values it expresses. The religion of the Great Goddess is attractive to many feminists because it embodies and exhalts the feminine values associated with embracing diverse forms of life, welcoming and nurturing them as one's own. Yet as I have mentioned, Plato, like many people, yearns for plainer prose in addition to symbolic language. Here Plato's holism has much to recommend it; it too affirms the importance of connectedness and celebrates the presence of divinity in the natural and human world but does so in a more abstract form (or Form!). Plato's dialogues exhibit a kind of holistic thinking that combines symbolism with abstract reasoning.

All and all, I find that Plato's holism provides a good antidote not only to dichotomous thinking but also to the modern masculine values that accompany dualism: aggressive egoism in all its manifold guises. Feminists searching for ways to conceptualize human experiences in a nondualistic fashion might do well to pay closer attention to the all-embracing, spiritually charged holism of Plato.

Notes

1. We have no complete texts from the Pre-Socratics (so-called because with Socrates came a definite change of interest from what we now would call natural philosophy to more humanistic concerns). At best, we have quotations from their works preserved in the writings of later authors (these are often referred to as "fragments"). For the fragments of the Pythagoreans and the other Pre-Socratics, as well as an excellent running commentary, see G. S. Kirk, J. E. Raven, and M. Schofield, eds., *The Presocratic Philosophers,* 2d ed. (Cambridge: Cambridge University Press, 1983).

2. See Whitbeck, "Theories of Sex Difference," in *Women and Values: Readings in Recent Feminist Philosophy,* ed. Marilyn Pearsall (Belmont, Calif.: Wadsworth, 1986), and "A Different Reality: Feminist Ontology," in *Beyond Domination: New Perspectives on Women and Philosophy,* ed. Carol Gould (Totowa, N.J.: Rowman and Littlefield, 1984).

3. See Genevieve Lloyd, *The Man of Reason: "Male" and "Female" in Western Philosophy* (Minneapolis: University of Minnesota Press, 1984), 2–9.

4. See also Nancy Tuana, "The Weaker Seed: The Sexist Bias of Reproductive Theory," *Hypatia* 3, no. 1 (1988): 35–59.

5. See, for example, Gilligan's "Moral Orientation and Moral Development," in *Women and Moral Theory,* ed. Eva Meyers, Kittay Meyers, and Dianan Meyers (Totowa, N.J.: Rowman and Littlefield, 1986), 19–33.

6. See, for example, Ruddick's "Maternal Thinking," in *Women and Values,* ed. Pearsall, 340–51.

7. French feminist deconstructionists are applying the views of the philosopher Jacques Derrida, and sometimes those of psychoanalytic theorist Jacques Lacan, for feminist purposes. For a brief overview of deconstructionism, especially as practiced by Luce Irigaray, see Andrea Nye, "The Hidden Host: Irigarary and Diotima at Plato's Symposium," *Hypatia,* 3, no. 3, (1989): 45–61, esp. 49–53 (repr. Chapter 10, this volume).

8. Of course, I do not mean that Plato saw his struggle against dualism in terms of feminine versus masculine ways of thinking, or even that he considered dualism per se as the enemy. Most likely, he saw himself battling against the materialism of some of his predecessors and the relativism of the Sophists. All I am suggesting is that he was deeply committed to a holistic worldview despite the strong dualistic elements within his own tradition, including certain strains within his own theory.

9. Plato's dialogues are divided into three periods: early (from the execution of Plato's teacher, Socrates, in 399 B.C.E. to Plato's first trip to Italy and Syracuse in 388–87), middle (between his second and third trips to Syracuse at 367 and 361 respectively), and late (after his third trip to Syracuse until his death in 348/347). Exactly which dialogues belong to what period is a matter of perennial debate since there is little evidence from ancient sources to indicate their order of composition. Various methods of dating have been used. For a brief overview of these methods, see the introduction to R. E. Allen's *The Dialogues of Plato,* vol. 1 (New Haven: Yale University Press, 1984). The vast majority of scholars, however, agree that the *Philebus* is a late dialogue, probably the second to last Plato wrote (the *Laws* is the last).

Most editions of the dialogues, including translations, use a standard pagination—Stephanus pages—in the margins; these pages are subdivided according to the letters a, b, c, d, and e, according to the divisions in the original folio page. In this paper, I shall follow the customary practice of referring to the Stephanus pages in the Platonic corpus. Usually, I shall only allude to passages but when I quote directly from the *Philebus* I shall translate from the Greek text found in John Burnet, *Platonis Opera,* vol. 2 (Oxford: Oxford University Press, 1979).

10. Many feminists might agree with me that the feminine worldview is a holistic one but object that it cannot be identified with such an abstractly rational theory as Plato's. But I believe that Plato's holism—like any that tries to live up to the name—seeks to encompass as much of human experience as possible, and thus includes his inevitably clumsy attempts to capture the spiritual dimensions of life in abstractions and then explore them through reasoning. Perhaps he sometimes gets a little lost in his own abstractions but this fact does not in any way diminish his holistic aims.

11. See Richmond Lattimore, trans. *Hesiod: The Works and Days, Theogony, The Shield of Herakles* (Ann Arbor: University of Michigan Press, eighth printing, 1973), 130–35.

12. Ibid., 130, line 126.

13. Ibid., 131, line 131.

14. See Charlene Spretnak, *Lost Goddesses of Early Greece: A Collection of Pre-Hellenic Myths* (Boston: Beacon, 1984), 17–27. Worth pointing out is the fact that the importance of the Great Goddess religion is recognized not only by feminists but also by more traditional archeologists and classicists such as E. O. James (*The Cult of the Mother-Goddess,* 1959), B. C. Dietrich (*The Origins of Greek Religion,* 1974), and R. F. Willets (*The Civilization of Ancient Crete,* 1977).

15. See Merlin Stone, *When God Was a Woman* (San Diego: Harcourt Brace Jovanovich, 1976), 10–11.

16. Ibid., 66–67.

17. *Theogony,* op cit., 132, line 158.

18. Stone, *When God Was a Woman,* 148–49.

19. Ibid., 129–30.

20. The concept of opposed natural phenomena occurs in Anaximander, Heraclitus, Parmenides (who rejects it; see note 22), Empedocles, Anaxagoras, and in the Pythagoreans as early as Alcmaeon. See *The Presocratic Philosophers,* 119ff.

21. Examples of Pre-Socratics who refer to the ultimate source (*arche*) as divine or a god include: Thales, Anaximander, Anaximenes, Xenophanes, the Pythagoreans, Heraclitus, and Empedocles. See Kirk, Raven, and Schofield, *The Presocratic Philosophers.*

22. In Parmenides' poem, he journeys past the Gates of Night and Day, which alternate by way of Justice (that is, the world of ordinary experience where opposites alternate) to a highway (that is, path of thought) that leads him to two mutually exclusive paths: the Way of Truth (of true changeless Being) and the Way of Seeming (what mortal opinion holds as real: the changing world of empirical experience). Parmenides' cosmology *does* stress the interaction of the opposite powers of light and night but of course, this is only the Way of Seeming. In truth, Being is limited, unitary, and at rest. See Kirk, Raven, and Schofield, *The Presocratic Philosophers,* 239–62.

23. The Theory of Forms is characterized differently in various dialogues and sometimes even within a single work (for example, the *Phaedo*; see notes 24 and 25). For example, in the *Symposium,* the highest Form considered is the Beautiful, while in the *Republic* it is the Good, and in the *Parmenides,* the One. According to my reading of the *Philebus,* the Good turns out to be the ultimate One, and Beauty is one of its important aspects.

24. Here I am thinking of the famous Sun, Line, and Cave passages in Books VI and VII, which are often cited as evidence of Plato's "doctrine of the Two Worlds." There is also evidence in these passages that the so-called Two Worlds are continuous because the Forms encompass their sensibles, but the more popular interpretations emphasize their separation. For a useful recent summary of the standard interpretations of the Theory of Forms in the middle dialogues and elsewhere, see William J. Prior, *Unity and Development in Plato's Metaphysics* (La Salle, Ill.: Open Publishing, 1985).

25. Although there are passages in the *Phaedo* that suggest that the Forms are immanent in sensibles (in the account of causation at 100c–105c; see Prior, *Unity and Development,* 12–17), throughout most of the dialogue, the arguments for the immortality of the soul depend on recognizing the kinship of the human soul with the Forms while the human body is relegated to the sensible realm. Thus the body/soul dualism is simply one aspect of the Two Worlds doctrine (see Prior, *Unity and Development,* 33–41).

26. See Lloyd, *Man of Reason,* 18–22.

27. See *Symposium* 202b–205e.

28. See, for example, Kurt Randolph, "Mystery Religions," in *Religions of Antiquity,* ed. Robert M. Seltzer (New York: Macmillan, 1989), esp. 276–77.

29. See Andrea Nye, "Hidden Host," 53–58.

30. See Luce Irigaray, "Sorcerer Love: A Reading of Plato's *Symposium,* Diotima's Speech," trans. Eleanor H. Kuykendall, *Hypatia* 3, no. 3 (1989): 32–44 (repr. Chapter 9, this volume).

31. See *Symposium* 202d–203a.

32. The Greek word *apeiron* is ambiguous; it may mean infinite or indefinite. I maintain that it means both. As will become evident in my discussion above of true knowledge versus opinion, and true Being versus Becoming at *Philebus* 58c–58d, sensibles are indefinite *because* they are infinite in magnitude and intensity. For further details about this and all passages of the *Philebus* mentioned in this paper, see my *Knowledge, Pleasure, and Being: An Analysis of Plato's Philebus* (New York: State University of New York Press, 1990).

33. This point will become most apparent in my discussion of the Divine Method above.

34. Although there is controversy about the extent to which Socrates is the spokesperson for Plato's views throughout the dialogues, I think that Socrates does speak for Plato in the

Philebus. Or, at the very least, Socrates' role of main speaker indicates that Plato is once again focusing on his Socratic interests in the good life rather than on the epistemological and metaphysical puzzles discussed in the preceding trilogy of the *Theatetus, Sophist,* and *Statesman* where Socrates was completely absent and the main speaker was the Stranger from Elea.

35. Although clearly the purpose of the Divine Method is to help us untangle the knots of the problem of one and many, the exact nature of the problem (stated as a series of "puzzles," that is, *aporiai*) is not easy to discern. The key passage is 15b1–8, which is rather ambiguously worded; thus much controversy surrounds how to interpret the puzzles and even how many (two or three?) of them there are. For a brief overview of the controversy, see R. M. Dancy, "The One, The Many, and the Forms: *Philebus* 15B1–8," *Ancient Philosophy*, 4 (1984): 176–79. Fortunately, for the purposes of this paper, this issue need not be explored.

I also think that the units (which Plato calls "monads") are Forms that are ontologically prior to their sensible instances but to argue for this would go beyond the scope of this paper.

36. See *Philebus* 23c–26d.

37. As noted by Philip Wheelwright, *The Presocratics* (New York: Odyssey, 1966), 11.

38. Robin Waterfield notes that the Greek classification was based on how much breath it took to sound a particular letter; vowels took the most, mutes (our "stops") took the least, with the semivowels (our nasals, sibilants, and continuants) in between. See Waterfield, *Plato: Philebus* (Harmondsworth, Middlesex: Penguin, 1982), 63 n. 2. Perhaps Plato sees the letters, as well as musical notes, forming a continuum. When making the same division of letters in the *Cratylus,* Plato does draw a parallel between this division and the one of musical sound into rhythms (see 423e–425a; cited by Waterfield, ibid.) For our present purposes, the details of this account need not be determined.

39. See *Philebus* 18b–d.

40. Cf. *Cratylus* 424d–425a and *Theatetus* 203e–204a. In the latter, Socrates explicitly claims that the syllable is a single entity with a character of its own different from the letters that make it up; it is an example of a whole which is different from the aggregate of its parts.

41. See Chomsky's summary of his theory in his entry, "Language: Chomsky's Theory," in the *Oxford Companion to the Mind,* ed. Richard L. Gregory (Oxford: Oxford University Press, 1987), 419–21.

42. Ibid., 421.

43. The fact that the visual/tactile model is used throughout the middle dialogues is noted by Henry Teloh, *The Development of Plato's Metaphysics* (University Park: The Pennsylvania State University Press, 1981), 100–118. Consider how this model works in the Sun Analogy where Socrates gives an outline of the Good by comparing it to the sun. The analogy works on two levels: epistemological and ontological. The epistemological comparison is as follows. As the presence of the sun's light enables us to see and visible objects to be seen, so the Good enables us to know and for intelligible objects to be known. I consider the ontological comparison below (see note 46). See *Republic,* Book VI, 506e–509d.

44. See *Protagoras* 320c–322a.

45. I agree with Bury and Hackforth in emphasizing the close tie between truth and reality or Being. See R. G. Bury, *The Philebus of Plato* (Cambridge: Cambridge University Press, 1897), Appendix F., 201ff.; and R. Hackforth, *Plato's Examination of Pleasure* (Cambridge: University Press, 1954), 133. For a different view, see J. C. B. Gosling, *Plato: Philebus* (Oxford: Clarendon Press, 1975), 134–35; 212 seq.

46. That is, the sun's energy that enables things to generate and grow is analogous to the Truth that sustains Being. See the Sun Analogy, *Republic* 507a–509c.

47. I am translating "the eternal nature" although the text here is uncertain, as Gosling notes (*Plato: Philebus,* 137–38). The Greek supports my translation (as well as alternatives) and in context, I think "the eternal nature" refers to the Good as it did at 64c. The

personification of the Good occurs elsewhere in the *Philebus,* notably in the discussion of the Cause at 26e–31a where it is depicted as the creator of all (30e1–2), including the mixed kind (26e–27c). As I have argued elsewhere, there is no need to take the talk of the Cause's generation and production literally; see my "Plato's Late Ontology: A Riddle Unresolved," *Ancient Philosophy* 8, no. 1 (1988): 110–11; 115 n. 16). As I point out below, one reason Plato might have in using such language and for personifying the Good as a creator is to give us a representation of the Good that makes it clearer to us how we can model our own activities in imitation of the Forms.

48. Unfortunately, Plato is not terribly forthcoming with clear examples of abnormal and inordinate pleasures. One example he gives is the pleasure an invalid experiences when scratching an itch caused by a disease (44b–46b). He also alludes to a sexual experience at 46d–47a but does not indicate whether the pleasures here are abnormal, inordinate, or both. The example of the passive homosexual (the *kinaidos*) whose passivity may include "being kept" or even being a prostitute, and whose life is compared to one of perpetual scratching, I have borrowed from *Gorgias* 494e. The life of such a one is clearly thought by Plato to be disgraceful, and perhaps abnormal. As examples of pleasures that arise from psychic abnormalities and/or excesses he refers to those involving anger, fear, yearning, mourning, love, jealousy, envy, etc. (46b–48b). The only emotions he actually analyzes here are those aroused by comedy: the mixture of the pain of malice with the pleasure of laughing at the misfortunes of others (48b–50e). But discussion of this complicated case would take us too far afield from our present purpose.

49. Somewhat confusingly, Plato refers to both the pleasures that are mixed with pain, and those which are limited by intelligence, as being mixed, measured, or limited. But I take the mixture with pain to be the broader category, including both the inherently indefinite pleasures and those limited by intelligence. For the pleasures limited by intelligence still include pain; for example, the pleasures of health involve the restoration of bodily imbalances.

50. For more on these two types of false pleasure, see my "Pleasure, Truth and Being in Plato's *Philebus*: A Reply to Professor Frede," *Phronesis* 32, no. 2 (1987): 253–62, and *Pleasure, Knowledge, and Being.*

51. There remains the problem of where the pleasures that are limited by intelligence (that is, the necessary pleasures attending health, strength etc.) are supposed to fit in the final ranking. A. E. Taylor and R. Hackforth speculate that the reference to a sixth class at 66c–d is meant to encompass the necessary pleasures while Gosling explains the omission by pointing out that the prize-giving is not between all elements of the good life but only those which contribute to its goodness. (See Taylor, *Plato: Philebus and Epinomis,* ed. R. Klinbansky, G. Calogero, and A. C. Lloyds [London: Thomas Nelson and Sons, 1956], 91; Hackforth, *Plato's Examination,* 139, 140 n. 3; and Gosling, *Plato: Philebus,* 224.] Perhaps Taylor and Hackforth are right but it is still puzzling why there is no explicit reference to what constitutes the sixth class. I find Gosling's suggestion unsatisfactory because the necessary pleasures include those that promote fitness, health, and virtue (62e–63a, 63e), and these elements, (especially virtue), surely contribute to the goodness of the mixed life.

52. As Hackforth notes (*Plato's Examination,* 124 n. 1), Plato does not always restrict the meaning of the terms *nous, phronesis,* and *episteme.* But the context strongly suggests that the first two terms refer to a specially elevated form of knowledge. The reference to "contemplation" simply means knowledge of the Forms, which includes intuiting them (that is, *nous*), but also involves knowing how to embody them in our lives (that is, *phronesis*). I shall discuss this in greater detail later.

Concerning the use of the Greek term for knowledge, *episteme,* it is used in the *Philebus* in a general sense as something roughly equivalent to "cognition," the term I use above. In this general sense, it is sometimes used in conjunction with *techne* (craft, skill, or art). Roger

Shiner in his monograph, *Knowledge and Reality in Plato's Philebus* (Assen: Koninklijke Van Gorcum, 1974), 55, points to the interchangeability of the terms *episteme* and *techne* as evidence of the radical shift in the *Philebus* from the epistemology in the *Republic.* But as Richard Mohr has pointed out (in "*Philebus* 55C–62A and Revisionism," in *New Essays on Plato,* ed. Francis Jeffry Pelletier and John King-Farlow [Guelph: Canadian Association for Publishing in Philosophy, University of Calgary Press, 1983], 166), Plato does not consistently use technical language even in the *Republic.* Note *Republic* 533b1–6 where the dialectic is called a *techne.* In response to Mohr, Shiner claims (in "Knowledge in *Philebus* 55C–62A; A Response," *New Essays on Plato,* 172) that the language in the *Republic* suggests that the dialectic is the only way to knowledge whereas the *Philebus* does not. But it seems to me that in both dialogues, the dialectic is the highest form of cognition and hence knowledge in the full or true sense, and the lower forms, including *techne,* presuppose it. But to settle this question here would take us too far afield.

53. "Cognitively dependable" is a phrase used by Gregory Vlastos. See his "Degrees of Reality in Plato," in *Platonic Studies,* 2d ed. (Princeton: Princeton University Press, 1981), 64.

54. See my "Pleasure, Truth, and Being in Plato's *Philebus,*" 256–57.

55. See the Divided Line passage in the *Republic* at 509d–511c.

56. A similar reason might also help explain the use of the Divine Artisan or Demiurge in *Republic* Book X and in the *Timaeus.*

57. Plato, both in the *Phaedrus* and his seventh letter, notes the limitations of written language for conveying truth. See *Phaedrus* 274c ff. and seventh letter, 341b–344d.

58. Although Plato's philosophy is holistic, I hesitate to call it mystical. As I pointed out above, direct communion with ultimate reality, *nous,* is supposed to be coupled with the ability to realize this intuition in action through *phronesis.* In other words, rational intuition and practical reasoning are two moments or aspects of the same capacity. Intuition is not "superrational," much less irrational. Instead, *nous* is part of the highest type of reasoning or knowledge.

12

The Presence and Absence of the Feminine in Plato's Philosophy

Nancy Tuana and William Cowling

Preface

(Problematically, in the voice of a WOMAN PHILOSOPHER *whose work in feminist theory has placed her on the margins of philosophy)*[1]

I was trained into dissonance. The image of the philosopher as the rational man dazzled me with its seeming strength and virility. Beneath I could feel the tensions of being a woman placing myself into the guise of a man so that I could achieve the ideal, be accepted as real, a real philosopher. But even so I remained other, shadow—always the woman philosopher. The qualifier marking my difference/dissonance.

I was distressed by the paternal metaphor encompassing the tradition. Always the father's rule. I was to accept the paternal figure as emblem of authority. Was I expected to deny maternity, to make myself into the image of the father? Or did they rather intend for me to remain always marginal, when the margins of philosophy were viewed as a place for outcasts, misfits, outlaws. Dissonance.

I was held captive by their words. How long it took me to see that the image of reason I clasped so lovingly was a sword designed to sever me in two! The celebration of abstract thought misplaces the body. When mind is defined over against the body, the body becomes a lack, not a void but an impediment. I aspired to an ideal destined to undo me. The very air I breathed coursed through a body socially constructed as female. I/we had been subject of an unrelenting training: she is body; she is passion; she is desire; she is emotion. How to place the man of reason into my female body? Dissonance.

My/our only hope is to return, to search beneath and behind the images that hold us captive. To understand anew the path between real and image so that we can see the multiplicity of their connections and weave them together anew.

(*Problematically, in the voice of a* MAN PHILOSOPHER *whose work in feminist theory has placed him on the margins of philosophy and feminist theory*)

If I speak alone I risk losing the power of connection that arises from the interplay of voices. If I speak alone I risk hearing only myself. By joining my voice with hers I begin to hear the rhythms of difference that too often remain obscured by the dominance of the singular male voice, my voice. But I discover very quickly that combining my voice with hers is difficult. I have not been trained to work with *her*; my training has reinforced the many guises of autonomy. I had to learn everything again just to sit and write a sentence or a paragraph with her. No part of my training prepared me to write with a woman philosopher; I was only trained to be a man philosopher.

But when man philosophers speak alone they run the great risk of forgetting the power of difference; they risk hearing only those voices that are already so familiar. I no longer wish to take that risk. Too much is lost when I/we speak alone, when I/we risk the conceit of soliloquy. Speaking alone I stand firmly in the tradition of voices that excludes difference, that ignores the feminine, that privileges the Platonic *logos* while forgetting the real mystery of the cave.

When the man philosopher leaves the cave, he does so reluctantly. His body is bruised by the rough ascent. Long years of sitting chained to the floor of the cave have taken their toll on his body. The man philosopher (this man philosopher) has forgotten the deeper embodied connections that fuse thought with action. I have forgotten my body and I must learn how difficult/dangerous it is to do philosophy while moving about the space of a conference hall. I often remark that my most comfortable moments in this performance occur when I, speaking in the voices of other man philosophers, am allowed to stand behind a podium, to remain motionless and hidden from view. The difficulties of performing philosophy almost overwhelm me.

I work at setting aside my discomfort. I desire to engage the more complex, richer, conversation that emerges from the performance. I want to speak with her as we attempt to grapple with the problems of exclusion of the feminine in Western thought. The strangeness of performance seems less important to me now than the risk of speaking alone, of standing alone behind a podium like a proper man philosopher. I begin to sense the power of the conversation that is engendered by the performance. I begin to remember more clearly the presence of the feminine.

(*Unproblematically, in the voice of* NANCY *and* WILLIAM)

The ideas embodied in this presentation arose out of many years of conversation. Our mutual interests in feminist philosophies engendered a plethora of dialogues and discussions. This performance piece originated out of our investigations of the Platonic views of woman and the location of the feminine within the Platonic corpus. Our work in feminist theory had made us sensitive to the complexities of the problem of gender. We were particularly concerned with the gendering of language and of the central concepts of philosophy. The Platonic texts seemed crucial to this investigation in that there is good evidence for viewing the Platonic metaphysic as providing a foundation for the evolution of Western philosophy. Furthermore, Plato's relations to the feminine were particularly challenging because of their ambiguity. Many of our discussions focused on the Platonic conception of rationality as we began to recognize the ways in which Plato excluded the feminine from the rational.

The particular structure of this presentation arose out of our desire to create an alternative style and method for performing philosophy that would problematize the style and methods of the "traditional" conference/journal paper. We did not want to reinforce the Platonic conception of rationality within our discourse, while fully recognizing how embedded it is in our worldview. The use of multiple voices in the dialogue format is well suited to this endeavor in that it questions the linearity and univocality of the more traditional narrative. Ironically we found ourselves mimicking the Platonic dialogue form.

The decision to cast this as a performance piece was a result of our desire to assist the audience in questioning traditional philosophical narratives. We wanted to inhibit the inclination to privilege the authorial voice, as well as reject the denigration of the bodily and emotional aspects of rationality. Though we emphasize voices over movements, our goal is to use the dialogue to create tensions between discourse and embodiment. We believe that in problematizing the conditions under which philosophical presentations are made, we have embraced the power of marginalization. Given our intent, we encourage you to develop a performance of our piece whenever possible. Whenever it is read, the reader should be careful to attend to the multiplicity of voices within the text, which might be more easily accomplished by reading the text aloud.

I

(*The stage should be empty except for a podium located toward the front of the stage, one third of the distance from the left wing. If the space will be in use prior to the performance, then the two* PHILOSOPHERS *should empty the space of everything else prior to beginning the dialogue but as part of the performance.*

The PHILOSOPHERS *enter from stage left side by side, the* FEMALE *closest to the audience. They walk together until they are even with the podium. The* MALE *stops at that point, and remains standing sideways to the audience; the* FEMALE *continues walking until she reaches a point two-thirds of the distance from the left wing. The* FEMALE *turns to face the* MALE, *creating a mirror image. Each* PHILOSOPHER *holds her/his script at her/his side.*)

IN THE VOICE OF EURYDICE (*From memory, in a confident, conversational tone*): I am the world under you. The descent is difficult and fraught with dangers. My darkness is filled with wisdom. The courageous desire my embrace—Inanna, Persephone, Ishtar—for I hold the key of the ever-flowing rhythms of birth and death, the sacred marriage, the cycles of nature. I speak with the hiss of the serpent's tongue, my song giving rise to the cadence of time. I have been heard by the many, but understood by the few—Metis, she who tends Delphi, Demeter, Ananta, Isis. I am Eurydice, mother of the underworld, she who knows.[2]

II

IN THE VOICE OF PLATO (*Both* PHILOSOPHERS *raise scripts, but* FEMALE PHILOSOPHER *continues to gaze at* MALE): There is a cave that is inhabited by men. The long passageway out is rough and steep. Some of the men have been shackled from birth, forced to stare straight ahead at the wall of the cave. Behind them, behind a wall, on a raised path, other men walk, carrying images. These men are hidden by the wall, the images raised above the wall. Behind is a fire whose light casts shadows of the images onto the wall seen by the shackled men. The men sometimes speak and are sometimes silent. There is an echo in the cave. The sounds bounce off the walls, so the prisoners think that these voices come from the shadows that they cannot help but see as reality. Plato says that the prisoner is to be freed from his shackles. Plato commands that the prisoner be compelled to stand, to turn, to walk, to look at the fire. (*Turning to audience and speaking in a deliberate manner.*) The man is dazzled and distressed. He feels pain. He tries to flee. He is captured. Plato commands that he be "dragged away by force up the rough and steep incline of the cave's passageway, held fast until he is hauled out into the light of the sun." The man feels pain and anger. He resents his captors. With habituation the man comes to see that the action was for his own good. With habituation he comes to see the truths intended by those who forced him into the light. He thinks of those who were left behind. With habituation he feels pity for them and longs to return in order to lead them out of the cave. He descends. His vision is dimmed. He can no longer see in the darkness. The others mock his journey. Some wish to kill him.[3]

III

IN THE VOICE OF INANNA (*Remains facing stage left. With confidence and precision*): I, Inanna, the Queen of Heaven, visited the God of

Wisdom, who knows all things, and received from him the holy laws of heaven and earth. My wisdom was deep. My wisdom was broad. But my journey was not complete. To know the heart of the gods, to embrace the sacred connections between life and death, one must travel from the great above to the great below. I set aside my crown, abandoned my temples, and set out for the underworld. To enter the gates of the great below one must surrender the possessions of the above, entering naked and alone into death. To understand anew, I set aside all knowledge. The wisdom of the deep embraces me. I am complete. I return to the great above with my heart focused on the connection in between. The fullness of wisdom is to be found there. Life. Death. The path in between.[4]

IV

FEMALE VOICE IN ACADEMIC MODE (*Turns to audience. Pauses for fifteen seconds*): This presentation is constructed with the aim of locating the feminine within Platonic metaphors concerning the philosophical pursuit of knowledge. The thesis of this presentation is that the presence and absence of the feminine in this aspect of Platonic thought is an important, yet neglected component of Platonic scholarship. In one of the first studies of this topic, *Sowing the Body: Psychoanalysis and Ancient Representations of Women,* Page duBois argues that Plato engages in a mimesis of the female in which he relocates the female powers of generation and reproduction to the male philosopher, "whose experience in labor and birth is idealized and made to transcend that of women."[5] Philosophical reproduction is ascribed exclusively to men who will inseminate each other with ideas in a sexual act in which women are excluded. The philosopher's children are wisdom and truth. The ideal philosopher is Socrates, a man to whom Plato has transferred female powers. Socrates is thus a midwife who brings Theaetetus to bear ideas.

IN THE VOICE OF SOCRATES: "My art of midwifery is in general like theirs; the only difference is that my patients are men, not women, and my concern is not with the body but with the soul that is in travail of birth."[6]

FEMALE VOICE IN ACADEMIC MODE: Socrates, the ideal philosopher, feminizes young men.

IN THE VOICE OF SOCRATES: "And in yet another way those who seek my company have the same experience as a woman with child; they suffer the pains of labor and, by night and day, are full of distress far greater than a woman's, and my art has power to bring on these pangs or to allay them."[7]

FEMALE VOICE IN ACADEMIC MODE: It is our intention to add an additional perspective to the insights of duBois by focusing on the nature of Plato's appropriation of the feminine in his account of the ascent to wisdom in the *Symposium* and in the myth of the cave.

V

FEMINIST PHILOSOPHER (*Walks diagonally to front center to a point closer to the audience than the* MALE PHILOSOPHER. *Faces audience*): Plato tells us to imagine men living in a cave. Plato asks us to further imagine men behind the wall. He asks us, "Do you not think those men would see only shadows?" The cave is full of men.[8]

PATRIARCHAL VOICE (*one step forward*): Sex unspecified.

FEMINIST PHILOSOPHER: Women are absent. The men . . .

PATRIARCHAL VOICE: Sex unspecified . . .

FEMINIST PHILOSOPHER: . . . do not choose to leave the cave. They are content.

IN THE VOICE OF PLATO (*Stares at point above and beyond audience*): He is compelled to stand up.

FEMINIST PHILOSOPHER: There is no longing.

IN THE VOICE OF PLATO: He is compelled to look directly at the light.

FEMINIST PHILOSOPHER: There is no desire to look away from the shadows.

IN THE VOICE OF PLATO: He is dragged away by force . . .

FEMINIST PHILOSOPHER: His refusals are not acknowledged.

IN THE VOICE OF PLATO: . . . up the rough and steep incline of the cave's passageway . . .

FEMINIST PHILOSOPHER: His cries of pain are not heeded.

IN THE VOICE OF PLATO: . . . held fast until he is hauled out into the light of the sun.

FEMINIST PHILOSOPHER (*Slowly and with emphasis*): The memory of this rape will forever change his perception of the world.

IN THE VOICE OF PLATO (*Walks in arc behind* FEMALE PHILOSOPHER, *pacing movement so that end of statement coincides with end of arc*): "In the beginning he would most easily see shadows; next, see reflections in the water of men and other objects. Then he would see the objects themselves. From there he would go on to behold the heavens . . . in the intelligible world the last thing to be seen—and then only dimly—is the idea of the good. Once seen, however, the conclusion becomes irresistible that it is the cause of all things right and good."[9]

FEMINIST PHILOSOPHER: According to Luce Irigaray "Woman's desire does not speak the same language as man's desire. In this logic, the prevalence of the gaze . . . is particularly foreign to female eroticism. Women find pleasure more in touch than in sight."[10] Plato's visual metaphors for knowledge are pervasive in his philosophy. He employs images of the eye, the sun, and light to establish the characteristics of intelligibility.

IN THE VOICE OF PLATO (*Begins arc back to original point, ending arc at end of statement*): "The sun furnishes to visibles the power of visibility . . . in like manner . . . the objects of knowledge receive from the presence of the good their being known, but their very existence and essence is derived from it."[11]

FEMINIST PHILOSOPHER: Visual imagery is prevalent in Plato's description of the original state of pure knowledge.

IN THE VOICE OF PLATO (*Stares at point above and beyond audience*): "Every human soul has, by reason of her nature, had contemplation of true being. . . . Beauty it was ours to see in those days when, amidst that happy company, we beheld with our eyes that blessed vision, our selves in the train of Zeus."[12] We who were originally a part of the divine structure can see into it again with the eye of our mind.

FEMINIST PHILOSOPHER: The association of knowledge and vision provides a model of knowledge as disembodied. In touch, the body is always present. As one reaches out to feel an object, the sensation is clearly connected to one's physical movements. But vision, being the most detached of the senses, occludes the action of the body. The world appears to my gaze without any apparent movement or action on my part. The action of the body in vision disappears into the background. Furthermore, vision, the sense least corporeal, places the world at a distance from the observer, thereby dematerializing knowledge. The perceived scene appears physically unaffected by one's gaze. Nor does the observer experience any physical impact from the outside world. Unlike touch, where the body is a place of action and interchange of affect with the world, vision provides a model of knowledge disembodied from the physical world, including the body of the perceiver. This lends itself to a perception of the senses and the passions as an unreliable source of knowledge and an emphasis on cognition.

IN THE VOICE OF PLATO: This part of such a soul, if it had been hammered from childhood, and had thus been struck free of the leaden weights, so to speak, of our birth and becoming, which attaching themselves to it by food and similar pleasures and gluttonies turn downward the vision of the soul—if, I say, freed from these, it had suffered a conversion toward the things that are real and true, that same faculty of the same men would have been most keen in its vision of the higher things.[13]

FEMINIST PHILOSOPHER: The association of the eye with the eye of the mind, the sun to the good allows for a transcendent knowledge, a blessed vision, a communion with the good, but a communion that remains disembodied.[14]

IN THE VOICE OF PLATO: "Without taint of that prison within which we are now encompassed, and call a body."[15]

VI

IN THE VOICE OF DIOTIMA (*There is a fifteen-second pause. The* FEMALE PHILOSOPHER *turns away from audience and walks back to original location. She turns to face the* MALE PHILOSOPHER *and as she begins to turn, the* MALE PHILOSOPHER *steps back to his original location and turns to face* FEMALE PHILOSOPHER *in mirror position. Timed so that both* PHILOSOPHERS *face each other at the same moment*): His song, like that of Orpheus is beautiful. Listening to it we forget and forgetting begin to follow him up the steep incline. But we must not forget those who have been left behind. Plato's city is barren. Do not forget. Remember love and desire. Plato has banned them from the city. Remember mating in sweet love.[16]

IN THE VOICE OF PLATO: I will select proper mates from amongst the most fit. "Those men who excel in war will be bestowed honors and prizes, and, in particular, the opportunity of more frequent intercourse with the women."[17]

IN THE VOICE OF DIOTIMA: Remember the sensuous sucklings.

IN THE VOICE OF PLATO: Children will be removed at birth, raised by nurses who will prevent anyone from recognizing her own infant and will take care that the mothers themselves shall not suckle too long.[18]

IN THE VOICE OF DIOTIMA: Remember the gentleness of our caring.

IN THE VOICE OF PLATO: The women will go forth to war with the men, keep guard together and hunt together, as it were, like hounds.[19]

IN THE VOICE OF DIOTIMA: Remember the women, whether slave or free, guardian or worker. Woman is present in the city, the manly guardian woman, but absent in the cave, even the manly guardian woman. Remember.

MALE VOICE IN ACADEMIC MODE (*Walks to podium. From behind it with formal demeanor*): According to Terrence Irwin in his book *Plato's Moral Theory* (FEMALE PHILOSOPHER *turns back to audience*) "The method of ascent prescribes the pursuit of first-order ends chosen by the rational part of the soul. The rational part, on this view, will have independent rational desires: they will not be confined to concern for the existing ends of the non-rational parts, but will consider a man's capacities and needs as a whole, whether or not he already has non-rational desire to satisfy them. Plato's views are not free of obscurity. But at least he could argue plausibly that someone who follows the method of ascent, trying to find the right plan for his life as a whole, will reject the solutions of deviant men, which concentrate on one narrow aspect of a man's aims and capacities . . . the philosopher who completes the ascent brings forth 'intelligence and reality.' "[20]

FEMINIST PHILOSOPHER: The cave thus is depicted as a stronghold of masculinity. It is inhabited by men. The ascent to knowledge is brutal and coerced. (*Turns to audience*) Knowledge is divorced from the body, from the passions, from desire.

VII

MALE VOICE IN ACADEMIC MODE: According to F. M. Cornford (FEMALE PHILOSOPHER *looks down*) in his article, "The Doctrine of Eros in Plato's *Symposium*," "[t]here is a higher education which might end in perfect knowledge and fashion the only type of man who ought to take control of human society—the philosopher-king. But the process is not purely intellectual; it involves the education of desire. This aspect is developed in the *Symposium*, in the theory of Eros, the name for the impulse of desire in all its forms."[21]

FEMINIST VOICE (*Looks at audience. While walking to center to a point closer to audience than* MALE PHILOSOPHER): We women are beginning to speak in many voices to find an answer to Socrates.

IN THE VOICE OF SOCRATES: "No, no, (*Moves to side of podium*) dear Agathon. It's the truth you find unanswerable, not Socrates. And now I'm going to leave you in peace, because I want to talk about some lessons I was given, once upon a time, by a Mantinean woman called Diotima"[22]

FEMINIST PHILOSOPHER: The women are absent, left in another room. Even the flute girl was ordered out.

IN THE VOICE OF SOCRATES: "[L]et her play to herself or to the women inside there, whichever she prefers, while we spend our evening in discussion of a subject."[23]

FEMINIST VOICE: We are the women inside, placed on the margin. We look both from the outside in (*Looks at* MALE PHILOSOPHER) and from the inside out (*Looks at audience*). From our location we subvert the manly discourse, creating new languages through which we give voice to our desires.

MALE VOICE IN ACADEMIC MODE (*Returns to position behind podium*): According to Stanley Rosen in his book *Plato's Symposium*, "Diotima is not a thinly disguised Plato, but a purified Agathon, generated by the bisexual dialectic of Socrates. Instead of a womanly man, we are presented with a masculine woman, who dominates Socrates, prefers children of the psyche to those of the body, and herself aspires to synoptic vision."[24]

FEMINIST PHILOSOPHER (*Looks at* MALE PHILOSOPHER): Socrates, through his bisexual (MALE PHILOSOPHER moves to side of podium) dialectic (*Looks at audience*) evokes Diotima. Woman enters the symposium, but is not present. Diotima is not there. She does not speak. She is spoken for.[25]

IN THE VOICE OF SOCRATES: ". . . a woman who was deeply versed in this and many other fields of knowledge. It was she who brought about a ten years' postponement of the great plague of Athens on the occasion of a certain sacrifice, and it was she who taught me the philosophy of Love. And now I am going to try to connect her teaching—as well as I can without her help—with the conclusions that Agathon and I have just arrived at."[26]

FEMINIST PHILOSOPHER: Diotima is well-credentialed, the mannish woman, whose speech is directed toward men. Her voice bounces off the walls separating the rooms, preventing the women from hearing her. She assists men in giving birth to their own knowledge. Plato depicts Socrates speaking Diotima so well that we do not even notice that she is absent.[27]

IN THE VOICE OF SOCRATES: Diotima teaches us that Love is a very powerful spirit, halfway between god and man. Diotima teaches us that spirits are "the envoys and interpreters that ply between heaven and earth, flying upward with our worship and prayers, and descending with the heavenly answers and commandments, and since they are between the two estates they weld both sides together and merge them into one great whole."[28]

FEMINIST PHILOSOPHER: Diotima, the mannish woman, explains that Love was engendered through female agency.

IN THE VOICE OF SOCRATES: "On the day of Aphrodite's birth the gods were making merry, and among them was Resource. . . . Need came begging at the door because there was good cheer inside. . . . Resource, having drunk deeply of the heavenly nectar . . . wandered out into the garden of Zeus and sank into a heavy sleep, and Need, thinking that to get a child by Resource would mitigate her penury, lay down beside him and in time was brought to the bed of Love. So Love became the follower and servant of Aphrodite because he was begotten on the same day that she was born."[29]

FEMINIST PHILOSOPHER: Thus it was Need's deficiency that causes her to act, thinking that a child of Resource would relieve her poverty. Her ignorance led her astray.

IN THE VOICE OF SOCRATES: "Love is a lover of wisdom, and being such, he is placed between wisdom and ignorance—for which his parentage also is responsible, in that his father is full of wisdom and resource, while his mother is devoid of either."[30]

FEMINIST PHILOSOPHER: The son can offer his mother only love—of that which is lovely, of wisdom—but she, being deficient, can appreciate neither. Her poverty remains unaltered. Need who acted from ignorance disappears. Love remains.

IN THE VOICE OF PLATO: Diotima enjoins Socrates to be Love's follower, to pursue Love's principles.

FEMINIST PHILOSOPHER: Diotima, the mannish woman, is summoned by Socrates. After reminding us of the depth of her knowledge, he employs her voice to create a male principle, Love, which is to be followed by all. All except Need, the female agent, who personifies the ignorant.

IN THE VOICE OF SOCRATES: Those who follow Love long "not for the beautiful itself, but for the conception and generation that the beautiful effects." "When the procreant is big with child, he is strangely stirred by the beautiful, because he knows that beauty's tenant will bring his travail to an end."[31]

FEMINIST VOICE: With these new languages we can break apart and break out of the definitions that have left us room only as other, reclaiming our bodies, our desires, our wisdoms.

MALE VOICE IN ACADEMIC MODE (*Returns to position behind podium.* FEMALE PHILOSOPHER *continues to gaze at audience*): According to Stanley Rosen in his book *Plato's Symposium,* "[a]s both prophet and woman, Diotima is passive with respect to the gods. She cannot rebel against them, but neither can she explain them. Her function is to receive and deliver their revelations. Her activity is directed toward man; like Socrates, who is a midwife who assists others in giving birth to their own divine revelations."[32]

FEMINIST PHILOSOPHER: Agency now is given to the male. The first step in the appropriation of the generative power of the feminine.[33]

DIOTIMA IN PLATO'S VOICE (*Moves to side of podium*): "Well then . . ."

FEMINIST PHILOSOPHER: She went on . . .

DIOTIMA IN PLATO'S VOICE: ". . . those whose procreancy is of the body turn to woman as the object of their love . . ."

FEMINIST PHILOSOPHER: The women remain outside . . .

DIOTIMA IN PLATO'S VOICE: ". . . and raise a family . . . but those whose procreancy is of the spirit rather than the flesh . . . conceive and bear the things of the spirit. And what are they? you ask. Wisdom and all her sister virtues."[34]

FEMINIST PHILOSOPHER: The female power of generation is relocated on to the male and purified. The second step of appropriation.

DIOTIMA IN PLATO'S VOICE: "Now, by far the most important kind of wisdom . . ."

FEMINIST PHILOSOPHER: She went on . . .

DIOTIMA IN PLATO'S VOICE: ". . . is that which governs the ordering of society, and which goes by the names of justice and moderation. And if any man is so closely allied to the divine as to be teeming with these virtues even in his youth, and if, when he comes to manhood, his first ambition is to be begetting, he too, you may be sure, will go about in search of the loveliness—and never of the ugliness—on which he may beget."[35]

FEMINIST PHILOSOPHER: The subject of conversation has turned to the men. No women here. Women are allowed in only if they are manly, like Diotima. Such women can assist in the ordering of the city, if they are manly, like the guardian women. Otherwise they remain outside, bringing children up.[36]

DIOTIMA IN PLATO'S VOICE: "And what is more, he and his friend will help each other rear the issue of their friendship—and so the bond between them will be more binding, and their communion even more complete, than that which comes of bringing children up, because they have created something lovelier and less mortal than human seed."[37]

FEMINIST PHILOSOPHER: Not simply different. Better.

DIOTIMA IN PLATO'S VOICE: "And I ask you, who would not prefer such fatherhood to merely human propagation, if he stopped to think of Homer, and Hesiod, and all the greatest of our poets? Who would not envy them their immortal progeny, their claim upon the admiration of posterity."[38]

FEMINIST PHILOSOPHER: The third and final step of appropriation.

DIOTIMA IN PLATO'S VOICE: "And so, when his prescribed devotion to boyish beauties has carried our candidate so far that the universal beauty dawns upon his inward sight . . ."

FEMINIST PHILOSOPHER: The appropriation is completed with the complete banishment of women. Neither lover nor beloved remains female. The man, all men, must be . . .

DIOTIMA IN PLATO'S VOICE: ". . . saved from a slavish and illiberal devotion to the individual loveliness of a single boy, a single man, or a single institution."[39]

FEMINIST PHILOSOPHER: The masculine reigns.

DIOTIMA IN PLATO'S VOICE: ". . . he is almost within reach of the final revelation. And this is the way, the only way, he must approach, or be led toward, the sanctuary of Love . . ."

FEMINIST PHILOSOPHER: The imagery is no longer violent.

DIOTIMA IN PLATO'S VOICE: ". . . starting from individual beauties, the quest for the universal beauty must find him ever mounting the heavenly ladder, stepping from rung to rung . . ."

FEMINIST PHILOSOPHER: The ascent is now painless.

DIOTIMA IN PLATO'S VOICE: ". . . that is, from one to two, and from two to *every* lovely body, from bodily beauty to the beauty of institutions, from institutions to learning, and from learning in general to the special lore that pertains to nothing but the beautiful itself—until at last he comes to know what beauty is."[40]

FEMINIST VOICE: Our discourses disclose the multiplicity of our beauties, which had been hidden from us by his namings.

MALE VOICE IN ACADEMIC MODE (*Returns to position behind podium*): According to Stanley Rosen in his book *Plato's Symposium*, "[i]n anticipation of Diotima's teaching that Eros is born of need and cleverness, Socrates himself gives birth to the prophetess from the marriage of wisdom and the need to persuade."[41]

FEMINIST PHILOSOPHER: Diotima speaks once more (MALE PHILOSOPHER *moves to side of podium*) reinforcing the appropriation of the generative power of the female.

DIOTIMA IN PLATO'S VOICE: "And remember . . ."

FEMINIST PHILOSOPHER: She said . . .

DIOTIMA IN PLATO'S VOICE: ". . . that it is only when he discerns beauty itself through what makes it visible that a man will be quickened with the true . . ."

FEMINIST PHILOSOPHER: His child moving within him . . .

DIOTIMA IN PLATO'S VOICE: ". . . and not the seeming, virtue—for it is virtue's self that quickens him, not virtue's semblance. And when he has brought forth and reared this perfect virtue, he shall be called the friend of the god."[42]

FEMINIST PHILOSOPHER: And speaking, she is silenced.

SOCRATES IN PLATO'S VOICE: "This, Phaedrus—this gentlemen—was the doctrine of Diotima. . . . So you may call this my eulogy of Love, Phaedrus."[43]

FEMINIST PHILOSOPHER: Socrates speaking, silences Diotima, and is himself silenced by the arrival of the flutegirl.

MALE VOICE IN ACADEMIC MODE (*Returns to position behind*

podium): According to F. M. Cornford in his article "The Doctrine of Eros in Plato's *Symposium,*" "Diotima's words to Socrates on the threshold of the greater mysteries, where she doubts if he can follow her further, indicate that Plato is going beyond the historic Socrates . . . the best commentary . . ."

FEMINIST PHILOSOPHER: He continues . . .

MALE VOICE IN ACADEMIC MODE: ". . . on the *Symposium* is to be found in the *Divine Comedy.* Virgil . . ."

FEMINIST VOICE: A man . . .

MALE VOICE IN ACADEMIC MODE: ". . . stands for human wisdom or philosophy. . . . Dante's guide to the higher region is . . . the divine wisdom symbolized by Beatrice . . ."

FEMINIST VOICE: The faithful guide who is supplanted at the penultimate moment by a man, Saint Bernard . . . an act of appropriation.

MALE VOICE IN ACADEMIC MODE: "Virgil's farewell words exactly express the doctrine of Eros: This day the sweet fruit which mortals seek on so/many branches will set thy hunger at rest./The sweet fruit is happiness which men pursue under so many guises. At these words, / Desire upon desire of being (*Look at point above and beyond audience and recite remainder of quote from memory*) above so came to me/that at every step thereafter I felt my wings/grow for the flight."[44]

VIII

WOMEN FINDING VOICE (*Both* PHILOSOPHERS *turn and return to original mirror position.* FEMALE PHILOSOPHER *faces* MALE PHILOSOPHER. MALE PHILOSOPHER *faces audience*): The shape of a cave. Enveloped by darkness. Our voices echoing off the walls. We are afraid to speak. We see nothing. Nothingness spreads around us. But in this nothing we find what we did not know existed. In our bodies we begin to feel the rhythms, faintly at first. We tend to them and now we hear other voices, not our own, but of those who have come before. We feel the hunger deep within us. The melodies ancient, secret, buried, now pulsate within us. And we can feel those who came before us, and before them, and before. The hunger deepening. Back to the beginning. The shape of a cave. Space divided and not divided, space turning in on itself, transforming.[45]

IX

MALE VOICE TRANSFORMING[46] (MALE PHILOSOPHER *turns to face* FEMALE PHILOSOPHER. *Maintains eye contact except when reading from script*): It is decided that the prisoner must return to the cave, transformed.

VOICE OF THE OTHER WOMAN (*Turns at an angle between* MALE PHILOSOPHER *and audience. At times looks at* MALE PHILOSOPHER, *at other times looks at audience. Looks at* MALE PHILOSOPHER *when he speaks*): One of the voices speaking from the outside in is that of Luce Irigaray. Evoking her voice we reproduce the Platonic journey within and without the cave, gaze refocused.

MALE VOICE TRANSFORMING: Sitting on the floor of the cave, removing our shackles, our gaze initially reveals only the pervasiveness of the masculine. But with habituation, our eyes grow accustomed to the darkness, and we begin to see behind the appearances.

VOICE OF THE OTHER WOMAN: Plato has emptied the cave of women. The cave is full of men. But he cannot banish the female, the foundation behind, buried beneath. That which grounds *eidos.* Always inside: the womb, the cave, the home, the soul.[47]

MALE VOICE TRANSFORMING: As the numbness ebbs, our bodies begin to feel a maternal and silent ground.

VOICE OF THE OTHER WOMAN: The beneath is virgin, mute. The voices spoken by the men echo off the back of this silent matrix, which reflects their words back to them. This reflecting matrix is the silent womb which a man, an obstetrician, turned round, backward and upside down in order to craft a stage, a space, for the performance of representation.[48]

MALE VOICE TRANSFORMING: We begin to remember the presence

and power of the reproductive. A power causing fear and discomfort. A power controlled, a power thus appropriated.

VOICE OF THE OTHER WOMAN: "So some accomplice, some acolyte-obstetrician, some faceless, nameless hack, of whom we know only that he is male, will with a firm hand forcibly extract the prisoner-child, against his will, from his previous home. Will thrust him out of the den, forcing him along the rocky track full of obstacles that can tear and multilate flesh, up the steep slope, the vertical shaft, out of the place where he has always dwelled, and into the light of day."[49]

MALE VOICE TRANSFORMING: We are filled with longing. Having put aside the children of our bodies in order to rear the offspring of our minds, we are empty. We long to begin again.

VOICE OF THE OTHER WOMAN: We are told that the forms reveal true nature. The cave, the space of the mother, is revealed to be a simulacrum of that which is real. A space of imitations, phantoms, fakes. Plato tells us that "One must leave its circle in order to bear worthy children." We are told that the forms are the source of being, the material a mere shadow of the real, mimesis. What remains hidden is the identity between cave and form, the image of the one within the other. The shadow arises only out of the interplay between cave and fire; the Idea arises only out of the interplay between female and male—neither source, neither mirror.[50]

MALE VOICE TRANSFORMING: The longing intensifies. Shutting our eyes to the light we begin to feel the presence of the mother behind it. Always behind.

VOICE OF THE OTHER WOMAN: Plato turns our attention to the fire and from it to the shadow, explaining that the shadow is a slight of hand, created by images blocking the light of the fire. But little mention is made of the wall upon which the image is cast, and in his silence we forget that the wall of the cave is as much the source of the shadow as is the fire, for the projection arises out of the interplay of the light of the fire and the material of the cave.

MALE VOICE TRANSFORMING: We are initially confused by the sensations. After a considerable time we begin to feel the veiled wisdom of the cave which has been concealed from us for so long.

VOICE OF THE OTHER WOMAN: Whether outside or in Plato

directs us to attend to the "optics of Truth." We are required to lift our eyes to the light. We are instructed to contemplate reflections and images. We are ultimately compelled to gaze at the sun itself.[51] Forgotten is the material ground of the cave. By a slight of hand, Plato tricks us into desiring a Source, thereby turning our attention away from the connection between Idea and existence, between male and female, between offspring and mother.

MALE VOICE TRANSFORMING: Our bodies speak forth and we follow their urgings. Sensations spiral around us. Pain, pleasure, doubt, fear, love, desire, weave a complex melody that we begin to follow. Tentatively at first, our bodies moving awkwardly to the rhythm, the beauty of the dance embraces us.

VOICE OF THE OTHER WOMEN: Through repetition, Plato makes us captive. Matter is always presented as a fetter to be escaped. The prisoners are shackled; matter limits their ability to perceive. The cave is a prison; the walls of the cave impeding vision of the true. The physical body is to be rejected; the senses, the emotions, obstruct the philosopher's journey to the Forms. Through repetition, Plato makes men forget.

MALE VOICE TRANSFORMING: Our bodies burst forth.

VOICE OF THE OTHER WOMAN: Through repetition Plato makes us forget the ground that supports us; ignore the walls against which the representations appear; overlook the path that provides passage between; disregard the bodily basis of being. Repetition.

MALE VOICE TRANSFORMING: Knowledge exploding and imploding. Attempting to remember what has been severed.

VOICE OF THE OTHER WOMAN: Plato carefully directs our attention away from the path in between, but cannot deny it. Remember there is within the cave a road, a path, without which Plato could not depict the play of shadows. Recall too the path between inside and out without which Plato could not describe the journey into the light and back down into the darkness. Plato carefully veils the paths lest we recall the necessity of the play in between: between darkness and light, between inside and out, between matter and form.

MALE VOICE TRANSFORMING: Attempting to speak the silent, words, *logos*, fail us.

VOICE OF THE OTHER WOMAN: "The mother's relation to the specular is an issue that cannot be spoken."[52] It is not the relation in between that creates the need for silence, but Plato's conception of a Source that makes us dumb. Having crafted an absolute against which all else is measured, Plato sets the stage for privilege: light over darkness, idea over existence, form over entity, reality over appearance. Then the path in between becomes a secret that must be carefully guarded lest one see the possibility of reversal and re-present the cave as the source of representation.

MALE VOICE TRANSFORMING: We lay down the Law, set aside Truth, open ourselves to the uncertainty, the multiplicity, to experience difference.

VOICE OF THE OTHER WOMAN: Plato recognizes the need to return: "If such a one should go down again and take his old place." We have been taught that the philosopher returns out of duty, but it is not duty that calls him back but some dim recognition of his own need. For the connection to the mother cannot be broken and all of Plato's tricks cannot keep a man from some subterranean desire for her neglected wisdom. But Plato allows the man to reenter only "forewarned and forearmed, masked, furtive, behind a curtain," a prophylactic against reversal.[53]

MALE VOICE TRANSFORMING: Rejecting vision, embracing the pregnant body.

VOICE OF THE OTHER WOMAN: "Would it not be said of him that he had returned from his journey aloft with his eyes ruined and that it was not worth while even to attempt the ascent?" You who have journeyed with Plato know the "right" answer. But be careful of Plato's shackles. For he who has returned is "lost in contemplations that wall him in on every side, separating him from everything by projection screens; and he can no longer even perceive that they are playing a part."[54]

MALE VOICE TRANSFORMING: Re-fusing the outside and in, undoubling the doubling, our multiplicities dislocating sameness.

VOICE OF THE OTHER WOMAN: And when the philosopher goes back in order to free the "prisoners," Plato tells us that they will want to kill him. We are told that this desire arises out of their ignorance. And this is the final inversion. The philosopher can no longer see that those who remained in the cave remember more of the wisdom of the connection in-between. They will kill anyone who threatens to take it from them.

X

IN THE VOICE OF EURYDICE (*Script down. Both* PHILOSOPHERS *deliver remainder of dialogue from memory.* FEMALE PHILOSOPHER *turns to audience*): I am the world under you. The descent is difficult and fraught with dangers . . .

MALE VOICE TRANSFORMED (*Turns to audience*): The dangers of the hidden mother.

IN THE VOICE OF EURYDICE: My darkness is filled with wisdom . . .

MALE VOICE TRANSFORMED: The wisdom of the hidden mother.

IN THE VOICE OF EURYDICE: The courageous desire my embrace—Inanna, Persephone, Ishtar—for I hold the key of the ever-flowing rhythms of birth and death . . .

MALE VOICE TRANSFORMED (*Quick echo*): rhythms of birth and death . . .

IN THE VOICE OF EURYDICE: . . . the sacred marriage, the cycles of nature. I speak with the hiss of the serpent's tongue, my song giving rise to the cadence of time.

MALE VOICE TRANSFORMED (MALE VOICE *one beat later than* FEMALE VOICE, *so voices overlap*): . . . my song giving rise to the cadence of time.

IN THE VOICE OF EURYDICE (*In unison*): I have been heard by the many, but understood by the few . . .

MALE VOICE TRANSFORMED (*In unison*): I have been heard by the many, but understood by the few . . .

IN THE VOICE OF EURYDICE: Metis, she who tends Delphi, Demeter, Ananta, Isis. I am Eurydice, mother of the underworld, she who knows.

(PHILOSOPHERS *turn to face one another.* FEMALE PHILOSOPHER *walks to join* MALE. *He turns and they walk off together, stage left.*)

Notes

1. Our use of voices in the preface is inspired by the model developed by Maria C. Lugones and Elizabeth V. Spelman, in "Have We Got a Theory for You!: Feminist Theory, Cultural Imperialism, and the Demand for 'The Woman's Voice,' " *Hypatia Reborn: Essays in Feminist Philosophy,* ed. Azizah Y. Al-Hibri and Margaret A. Simons (Bloomington: Indiana University Press, 1990), 18–33.

2. Eurydice is the Orphic name for the underworld goddess who received the soul of Orpheus. In ancient mythologies the goddess of the underworld possessed wisdom unattainable by those who did not successfully complete and return from a descent into her realm. Such a descent was seen as very dangerous, often requiring a passage through death. However, it was also believed to be necessary for complete wisdom. Inanna, for example, did not complete her evolution into full power and understanding until she had given herself to her sister, Ereshkigal, Queen of the Underworld.

Eurydice was originally one of the Furies of Demeter, the threefold goddess. The Furies were charged with punishing the most heinous of all sins, matricide. In the underworld, with the snake as her sacred animal representing the secrets of rebirth, the wisdom of the divine, Eurydice was Persephone, the death goddess. The wisdom of the connection of the great above and the great below, of life and death, was enacted each year in the ceremony of the sacred marriage in which the new births of the spring were regenerated from the death of the winter.

Sacred caves, such as that at Delphi, were originally identified with the underworld, with the womb of the goddess, and were seen as a source of divine inspiration, particularly concerning the mysteries of the cycles of birth, death, and rebirth. Porphyry claimed that prior to the erection of temples, all religious rites took place in caves. The original guardians of the caves, like the Oracle of Delphi, were women.

With the evolution to patriarchal religions, the ancient symbols were modified. Eurydice was demoted into Orpheus's wife who had been sent to the land of death by a serpent's bite. Demeter was reduced to a goddess of fertility. The Oracle of Delphi became a man. The serpent became a symbol of evil. Wisdom was transmuted from an understanding of the cycles of change to insight into universals. And the sacred descents of Inanna, Ishtar, and Persephone, were replaced by an emphasis on the descents of Odysseus, Aeneid, and Jesus. See Joseph Campbell, *The Masks of God,* 4 vols. (New York: Viking, 1959–70); Joseph Campbell and Charles Muses, *In All Her Names: Explorations of the Feminine in Divinity* (San Francisco: Harper, 1991); Pamela Berger, *The Goddess Obscured: Transformations of the Grain Protectress from Goddess to Saint* (Boston: Beacon, 1985); Miriam Robbins Dexter, *Whence the Goddesses: A Source Book* (New York: Pergamon, 1990); Riane Eisler, *The Chalice and the Blade: Our History, Our Future* (San Francisco: Harper and Row, 1987); Tikva Simone Frymer-Kensky, *In the Wake of the Goddesses: Women, Culture, and the Biblical Transformations of Pagan Myth* (New York: Free Press, 1992); Marija Gimbutas, *The Civilization of the Goddess:*

The World of Old Europe (San Francisco: Harper, 1991); Marija Gimbutas, *The Goddesses and Gods of Old Europe, 6500–3500 B.C.* (Berkeley and Los Angeles: University of California Press, 1982); Marija Gimbutas, *The Language of the Goddess: Unearthing the Hidden Symbols of Western Civilization* (San Francisco: Harper and Row, 1989); Naomi Goldenberg, *The Changing of the Gods* (Boston: Beacon, 1979); Diane Wolkstein and Samuel Noah Kramer, *Inanna: Queen of Heaven and Earth: Her Stories and Hymns from Sumer* (New York: Harper and Row, 1983).

3. This section was paraphrased or directly quoted from Plato's *Republic,* trans. Richard Sterling and William C. Scott (New York: Norton, 1985), 514a–517a.

4. This passage is based on the myth of Inanna as translated by Diane Wolkstein and Samuel Noah Kramer, *Inanna: Queen of Heaven and Earth: Her Stories and Hymns from Sumer* (New York: Harper and Row, 1983).

5. Page duBois, *Sowing the Body: Psychoanalysis and Ancient Representations of Women* (Chicago: University of Chicago Press, 1988), 181.

6. Plato, *Theaetetus,* trans. F. M. Cornford, *The Collected Works of Plato (including the Letters),* ed. Edith Hamilton and Huntington Cairns, Bollingen Series 71 (Princeton: Princeton University Press, 1961), 845–919.

7. Plato, *Theaetetus* 151a–b1.

8. Plato, *Republic* 514a–515b.

9. Plato, *Republic* 516a–517c.

10. Luce Irigaray, *This Sex Which Is Not One,* in *New French Feminisms,* ed. and with intro. by Elaine Marks and Isabelle de Courtivron (Amherst: University of Massachusetts Press, 1980), 101.

11. Plato, *Republic* 509b.

12. Plato, *Phaedrus* 250a–c.

13. Plato, *Republic* 519a–b.

14. For an interesting discussion of the importance of the visual metaphor for knowledge, see Drew Leder, *The Absent Body* (Chicago: University of Chicago Press, 1990) and Evelyn Fox Keller and Christine R. Grontkowski, "The Mind's Eye," in *Discovering Reality,* ed. Sandra Harding and Merrill B. Hintikka (Dordrecht: D. Reidel, 1983), 207–24.

15. Plato, *Phaedrus* 250c.

16. For feminist discussions and critiques of the role of desire in Plato's thought, see Wendy Brown, " 'Supposing Truth Were a Woman': Plato's Subversion of Masculine Discourse," *Political Theory* 16, no. 4 (1988): 594–616 (repr. Chapter 8, this volume); Monique Canto, "The Politics of Women's Bodies: Reflections on Plato," in *The Female Body in Western Culture: Contemporary Perspectives,* ed. Susan Rubin Suleiman (Cambridge, Mass.: Harvard University Press, 1986), 339–53 (repr., Chapter 3, this volume); Luce Irigaray, "Sorcerer Love: A Reading of Plato's *Symposium,* Diotima's Speech," *Hypatia: A Journal of Feminist Philosophy* 3, no. 3 (1989): 32–44 (repr. Chapter 9, this volume); Christine Pierce, "Eros and Epistemology," in *Critical Feminist Essays on the History of Western Philosophy,* ed. Bat Ami Bar-On (New York: State University of New York Press, 1993); Caroline Whitbeck, "Love, Knowledge, and Transformation," *Women's Studies International Forum* 7, no. 5 (1984): 393–405.

17. Plato, *Republic* 460b.

18. Plato, *Republic* 460c–d.

19. Plato, *Republic* 451d–452c.

20. Terrence Irwin, *Plato's Moral Theory: The Early and Middle Dialogues* (Oxford: Clarendon Press, 1977), 114. Substitute at will: "he [Socrates] proves this from the experimental fact that not only is Reason in man in many ways at strife with Desire, but that Courage, on the one hand acts blindly without rational intelligence, and on the other, when in the service

of Reason, combats Desire." Eduard Zeller, *Plato and the Older Academy*, trans. Sarah Frances Alleyne and Alfred Goodwin (New York: Russell, 1962), 415. Or, " 'the virtue of intelligence seems to belong to something altogether more divine, something which never loses its force, but is made serviceable or unserviceable, helpful or harmful, according as it is turned to the light or not.' The power of mental insight still remains active in the warped soul of the clever scoundrel; it is the divine and immortal part of the soul, that which makes it 'capable of bearing all good things,' but capable also of bearing 'all evil things'; it may be 'buried in the mud' of ignorance or overgrown with the 'incrustations' of passion, but it is never so lost that it cannot be lifted up, purged, and re-illumined, or so negative that anything else can be substituted for it." R. L. Nettleship, *The Theory of Education in Plato's Republic* (London: Oxford University Press, 1969), 124.

21. Cornford, *Collected Works of Plato,* 121. Substitute at will: "In the power he called *Eros,* Plato saw the dual (yet united) movement toward the beautiful person and the idea of beauty. Erotic experience and knowledge of *Ideas* are indissolubly united." Paul Friedlander, *Plato: An Introduction,* trans. Hans Meyerhoff (Princeton: Princeton University Press, 1969), 54. Or, "Love aims at happiness, which is the aim of all men. Men love the good, and they wish to possess it always, whether in the body or the soul. That is its final object . . . [t]he way up, Socrates repeats, is step by step . . . the lover knows indeed 'what beauty is,' and in this contemplation he will create not semblances of excellence, but excellence itself. He is the true philosopher in love." G. M. A. Grube, *Plato's Thought,* intro. Donald J. Zeyl (Indianapolis: Hackett, 1980), 101.

22. Plato, *Symposium,* trans. Michael Joyce, *The Collected Dialogues of Plato, including the Letters,* ed. Edith Hamilton and Huntington Cairns (Princeton: Princeton University Press, 1973), 201d.

23. Plato, *Symposium* 176e.

24. Stanley Rosen, *Plato's Symposium* (New Haven: Yale University Press, 1987) 203. No substitutions allowed.

25. Susan Hawthorne, "Diotima Speaks Through the Body," in *Critical Feminist Essays,* ed. Bat Ami Bar-On (Albany: State University of New York Press, 1993); Luce Irigaray, "Sorcerer Love," Andrea Nye, "Irigaray and Diotima at Plato's Symposium," *Hypatia* 3, no. 3 (1989): 45–61 (repr. Chapter 10, this volume); Eleanor Kuykendall, "Introduction to 'Sorcerer Love' by Luce Irigaray," *Hypatia* 3, no. 3 (1989): 28–31; Barbara Freeman, "(Re)writing Patriarchal Texts: *The Symposium,*" in *Postmodernism and Continental Philosophy,* ed. Hugh Silverman (Albany: State University of New York Press, 1988), 170–77; David Halperin, "Why Is Diotima a Woman?" in *One Hundred Years of Homosexuality and Other Essays on Greek Love* (New York: Routledge, 1990), 113–51; Barbara Freeman, "Irigaray at *The Symposium*: Speaking Otherwise," in *Sexual Difference,* ed. Robert Young (South Hampton: Oxford Literary Review, 1986), 170–77.

26. Plato, *Symposium* 201d.

27. In referring to Diotima as manly we do not intend to imply that the historical Diotima or her philosophy was androcentric, but rather to emphasize that Plato's appropriation of her voice and his transfiguration of her philosophy results in a denial of the feminine. David Halperin, in "Why Is Diotima a Woman?" also denies Diotima's femininity. His analysis differs from ours, however, in that he argues that Socrates constructs Diotima's femininity according to a male paradigm in order to legitimate male cultural reproduction.

28. Plato, *Symposium* 202e.

29. Plato, *Symposium* 203b–c.

30. Plato, *Symposium* 204b.

31. Plato, *Symposium* 206d–e.

32. Rosen, *Plato's Symposium,* 225.

33. See duBois, *Sowing the Body*: We have made extensive use of duBois's thesis that Plato "appropriates the female powers of reproduction to the male philosopher (and that) the philosophical tradition after him stress the autonomy of that male, his self-sufficiency, his privileged access to the divine and the one, and that tradition describes the female as a defective male, a creature distanced from the absolute presence and union with the divine" (173).

34. Plato, *Symposium* 208e–209a.

35. Plato, *Symposium* 209a–b.

36. For a discussion of feminist reading of Plato's views on guardian women, see Lorenne M. G. Clark and Lynda Lange, eds., *The Sexism of Social Political Theory: Women and Reproduction from Plato to Nietzsche* (Toronto: University of Toronto Press, 1979); Elizabeth Spelman, *Inessential Woman: Problems of Exclusion in Feminist Thought* (Boston: Beacon, 1988). See also Natalie Harris Bluestone, *Women and the Ideal Society: Plato's Republic and Modern Myths of Gender* (Amherst: University of Massachusetts Press, 1987). Bluestone also examines Platonic scholarship over the last hundred years and traces what she labels an "anti-female" bias. She argues that there has been a "systematic bias against women philosophers," but that recent trends in feminist scholarship reveal the absolute necessity in any "ideal commonwealth" for "philosopher-queens" as well as "philosopher-kings."

37. Plato, *Symposium* 209c.

38. Plato, *Symposium* 209c–d.

39. Plato, *Symposium* 210d.

40. Plato, *Symposium* 211b–d.

41. Rosen, *Plato's Symposium* 226. Substitute at will: "We thus get a series of speeches on Love, culminating in the famous speech of Socrates which he modestly attributes to the Mantinean priestess Diotima." G. M. A. Grube, *Plato's Thought* 96. Or, "He [Socrates] pretends that he himself had spoken of Eros in similar terms to Diotima, a wise priestess of Mantinea, and represents the criticism as administered by Diotima to himself. This is sufficient reason for the invention of Diotima." F. M. Cornford, "The Doctrine of Eros in Plato's *Symposium*," in *Plato: A Collection of Critical Essays*, ed. Gregory Vlastos (Garden City, N.Y.: Doubleday, 1971), 2:122.

42. Plato, *Symposium* 212a–b.

43. Plato, *Symposium* 212b–c.

44. Cornford, "Doctrine of Eros," 129. Substitute at will: "we are haunted by the feeling that we have 'seen the mysteries'—by that Transcendental Feeling which Dante finds language to express in the twenty-fifth sonnet of the *Vita Nuova*, and in the last canto of the *Paradiso*: —'O grace abounding, in which I presumed to fix my gaze upon the eternal light, for so long that I wore away my sight in it. Within its depths I saw, gathered and bound by love into one volume, that which is scattered throughout the universe." G. R. Levy, ed., *The Myths of Plato* (Carbondale: Southern Illinois University Press, 1960), 47.

45. My voice and the images contained in this section are highly influenced by the voices of Susan Griffin in *Woman and Nature: The Roaring Inside Her* (New York: Harper and Row, 1978).

46. Sandra Harding, in *Whose Science? Whose Knowledge?: Thinking from Women's Lives* (Ithaca: Cornell University Press, 1991), argues that "feminists are made, not born" (279); that biology is not, in itself, sufficient to determine whether a person will be a feminist. Moreover, men and women are the products of "biological, cultural, and political differences" that may predispose either sex to sexism, racism, or classism (278–80). It does not seem to Harding that being a man necessarily disqualifies one from becoming a "feminist." Harding shows that the logic of standpoint theory, which focuses on "gender differences, on differences between men and women's situations . . . (and) an objective location—women's lives—as the

place from which feminist research should begin," seems to require that "feminist analysis and feminist politics (can) clarify men's lives for men" (280–83). Just as "white . . . European American (women)" must accept responsibility for their "identity (and) racial, social location," men too must relocate their own rhetoric outside of the "appropriating, directing, judging" discourse that tends to dominate Western culture (280–83). Harding explains that "(women) cannot learn and generate less distorting explanations and understandings out of an identity and a social location that are half or two-thirds repressed. If we take the stance that we can separate or ignore these dimensions of our lives, how are we different from the men in the dominant social groups who claim that they can separate the authority of *their* knowledge claims from the social situations that generated their claims? . . . His destiny appears to be linked to ours" (284).

47. Luce Irigaray, *Speculum of the Other Woman,* trans. Gillian C. Gill (Ithaca: Cornell University Press, 1974).

48. Irigaray, *Speculum* 263.

49. Irigaray, *Speculum* 278.

50. Irigaray, *Speculum* 300–301.

51. Plato, *Republic* 516b–c.

52. Irigaray, *Speculum* 308.

53. Plato, *Republic* 516e; Irigaray, *Speculum* 309.

54. Plato, *Republic* 517a; Irigaray, *Speculum* 363.

Select Bibliography

Allen, Christina Garside. "Can a Woman Be Good in the Same Way as a Man?" *Dialogue* 3 (1971): 534–44.

———. "Plato on Women." *Feminist Studies* 2, nos. 2–3 (1974): 131–38.

Allen, Prudence. "Aristotelian and Cartesian Revolutions in the Philosophy of Man and Woman." *Dialogue* [Canada] 26 (1987): 263–70.

———. *The Concept of Woman: The Aristotelian Revolution 750 B.C.–A.D. 1250*. Montreal: Eden, 1985.

Annas, Julia. An Introduction to Plato's "Republic." Oxford: Oxford University Press, 1981.

Bluestone, Natalie Harris. "Why Women Cannot Rule: Sexism in Plato Scholarship." *Philosophy of Social Science* 18 (1988): 41–60.

———. *Women and the Ideal Society: Plato's* Republic *and Modern Myths of Gender*. Amherst: University of Massachusetts Press, 1987.

Brown, Wendy. " 'Supposing Truth Were a Woman . . .' Plato's Subversion of Masculine Discourse." *Political Theory* 16, no. 4 (1988): 594–616.

Calvert, Brian. "Plato and Equality of Women." *Phoenix* 29, no. 3 (1975): 231–43.

Canto, Monique. "The Politics of Women's Bodies: Reflections on Plato." In *The Female Body in Western Culture: Contemporary Perspectives*, edited by Susan Rubin Suleiman, 339–53. Cambridge: Harvard University Press, 1986.

Cohen, David. "The Legal Status and Political Role of Women in Plato's *Laws*." *Revue internationale des droits de l'antiquité*, 3d ser., 34 (1987): 27–40.

Croix, G. E. M. D. "Plato on Women." *Times Literary Supplement*, issue 4488 (7–13 April 1989): 382.

Darling, John. "Are Women Good Enough: Plato's Feminism Re-examined." *Journal of the Philosophy of Education* 20, no. 1 (1986): 123–28.

Deleuze, Gilles. "Plato and the Simulacrum." *October* 27 (1983): 46–51.

Dickason, Anna. "Anatomy and Destiny: The Role of Biology in Plato's View of Women." *Philosophical Forum* 5 (1973): 45–53.

duBois, Page. "On the Invention of Hierarchy." *Arethusa* 15, nos. 1–2 (1982): 203–20.

———. *Sowing the Body: Psychoanalysis and Ancient Representations of Women*. Chicago: University of Chicago Press, 1988.

Elrod, Eleanor. "Plato's Argument for Equal Opportunity." *Journal of the West Virginia Philosophy Society* 9 (1978): 9.

Elshtain, Jean B. *Public Man, Private Woman*. Princeton: Princeton University Press, 1981.

Fortenbaugh, W. W. "On Plato's Feminism in *Republic* V." *Apeiron* 9 no. 2 (1975): 1–4.

Freedman, Barbara. "(Re)Writing Patriarchal Texts: The *Symposium*." In *Postmodernism and Continential Philosophy*, edited by Hugh J. Silverman, 170–77. Albany: State University of New York Press, 1988.

Fuss, Diana. "Essentially Speaking: Luce Irigaray's Language of Essence." *Hypatia* 3, no. 3 (1989): 62–80.

Geddes, Anne. "The Philosophic Notion of Women in Antiquity." *Antichthon* 9 (1975): 35–40.

Genova, Judith. "Feminist Dialectics: Plato and Dualism." In *Critical Feminist Essays*, edited by Bat Ami Bar-On, 41–52. Albany: State University of New York Press, 1993.

Grimshaw, Jean. *Feminist Philosophers: Women's Views on Philosophical Traditions*. Brighton: Wheatsheaf, 1986.

Gunkel, Ann Hetzel. "Writing Women: Of Technology and the (Im)possibility of Philosophy." Unpublished manuscript.

Halperin, David. "Platonic 'Eros' and What Men Call Love." *Ancient Philosophy* 5 (1985): 161–204.

———. "Why Is Diotima a Woman?" In his *One Hundred Years of Homosexuality*, 113–51. New York: Routledge, 1990.

Hawkesworth, Mary E. "Re/Vision: Feminist Theory Confronts the Polis." *Social Theory and Practice* 13 (1987): 155–86.

Hawthorne, Susan. "Diotima Speaks through the Body." In *Critical Feminist Essays*, edited by Bat Ami Bar-On, 83–96. Albany: State University of New York Press, 1993.

Irigaray, Luce. "Sorcerer Love: A Reading of Plato's *Symposium*, Diotima's Speech." Trans. Eleanor H. Kuykendall. *Hypatia* 3, no. 3 (1989): 32–44.

———. *Speculum of the Other Woman*. Trans. Gillian C. Gill. Ithaca: Cornell University Press, 1985.

Jacobs, William. "Plato on Female Emancipation and the Traditional Family." *Apeiron* 12 (1978): 29–31.

Keller, Evelyn Fox. *Reflection on Gender and Science*. New Haven: Yale University Press, 1985.

Kuykendall, Eleanor H. "Introduction to 'Sorcerer Love,' by Luce Irigaray." *Hypatia* 3, no. 3 (1989): 28–31.

Lange, Lynda. "The Function of Equal Education in Plato's *Republic* and *Laws*." In *The Sexism of Social and Political Theory: Women and Reproduction from Plato to Nietzsche*, edited by Lorenne M. G. Clark and Lynda Lange, 3–15. Toronto: University of Toronto Press, 1979.

Lefkowitz, Mary. "Only the Best Girls Get To." *Times Literary Supplement*, issue 4492 (5–11 May 1989): 484.

Lesser, Harry. "Plato's Feminism," *Philosophy* 54 (1979): 113–17.

Lloyd, Genevieve. *The Man of Reason: "Male" and "Female" in Western Philosophy*. Minneapolis: University of Minnesota Press, 1984.

Martin, Jane Roland. *Reclaiming a Conversation: The Ideal of the Educated Woman*. New Haven: Yale University Press, 1985.

———. "Sex Equality and Education in Plato's Just State: A Case Study." In *"Femininity," "Masculinity," and "Androgyny": A Modern Philosophical Discussion*, edited by Mary Vetterling-Braggin, 279–300. Totowa, N.J.: Littlefield, Adams, 1982.

Nails, Debra. "The Erotic Education of the Slave." *South African Journal of Philosophy* 4, no. 1 (1985): 1–7.

———. "Let All Be Virtuous: Radical Socrates and the Concept of Democracy." In

Socratic Philosophy, edited by K. J. Boudouris, 244–52. Athens: International Association for Greek Philosophy, 1991.

———. "The Shrewish Wife of Socrates." *Echoes du Monde Classique*. 19th ser., vol. 4, no. 1 (1985): 97–99.

Nye, Andrea. "Irigaray and Diotima at Plato's Symposium." *Hypatia* 3, no. 3 (1989): 46–61.

O'Brien, Mary. "Creativity and Procreativity." In her *The Politics of Reproduction*, 116–39. Boston: Routledge and Kegan Paul, 1981.

Okin, Susan Moller. "Philosopher Queens and Private Wives: Plato on Women and the Family." *Philosophy and Public Affairs* 6 (1977): 345–69.

———. "Plato." Part 1 of her *Women in Western Political Thought*, 15–70. Princeton: Princeton University Press, 1979.

Osborne, Martha Lee. "Plato's Unchanging View of Women: A Denial that Anatomy Spells Destiny." *Philosophical Forum* 6, nos. 2–3 (1975): 447–52.

Pierce, Christine. "Equality: *Republic* V." *Monist* 57, no. 1 (1973): 1–11.

———. "Eros and Epistemology." In *Critical Feminist Essays*, edited by Bat Ami Bar-On, 25–40. Albany: State University of New York Press, 1993.

Pomeroy, Sarah B. "Feminism in Book V of Plato's *Republic*." *Apeiron* 8, no. 1 (1974): 32–34.

———. "Plato and the Phemale Physician (*Republic* 454d2)." *American Journal of Philology* 99 (1978): 496–500.

Ragland-Sutherland, Ellie. "Plato's Symposium and the Lacanian Theory of Transference: Or What Is Love?" *South Atlantic Quarterly* 88 (1989): 725–55.

Reeve, C. D. *The Naked Old Women in the Palaestra: A Dialogue on Plato's Views on Women*. Indianapolis: Hackett, 1992.

Rosenthal, Abigail. "Feminism Without Contradictions." *Monist* 57, no. 1 (1973): 29–42.

Salkever, S. G. "Women, Soldiers, Citizens: Plato and Aristotle on the Politics of Virility." *Polity* 19, no. 2 (1986): 232–53.

Saxonhouse, Arlene W. "Eros and the Female in Greek Political Thought: An Interpretation of Plato's *Symposium*." *Political Theory* 12, no. 1 (1984): 5–27.

———. "The Philosopher and the Female in the Political Thought of Plato." *Political Theory* 4, no. 2 (1976): 195–212.

———. *Women in the History of Political Thought*. New York: CBS Educational and Professional Publishing, 1985.

Scaltsas, Patricia Ward. "Is There Time to Be Equal?: Plato's Feminism." *APA Newsletter on Feminism and Philosophy* 90, no. 1 (1990): 108–10.

———. "Virtue Without Gender in Socrates." *Hypatia* 7, no. 3 (1992): 126–37.

Schott, Robin May. *Cognition and Eros: A Critique of the Kantian Paradigm*. Boston: Beacon, 1988.

Senter, Nell W. "Plato on Women." *Southwestern Philosophical Studies* 2 (1977): 4–13.

Smith, Janet Farrell. "Plato, Irony, and Equality." *Hypatia / Women's Studies International Forum* 6, no. 6 (1983): 597–607.

Smith, Nicholas D. "The Logic of Plato's Feminism," *Journal of Social Philosophy* 11 (1980): 5–11.

———. "Plato and Aristotle on the Nature of Women." *Journal of the History of Philosophy* 21, no. 4 (1983): 467–78.

Spelman, Elizabeth V. *Inessential Woman: Problems of Exclusion in Feminist Thought*. Boston: Beacon, 1988.

———. "Woman as Body: Ancient and Contemporary Views." *Feminist Studies* 1 (1982): 109–31.

Tuana, Nancy, and William Cowling. "Plato and Feminism: A Review of the Literature." *APA Newsletter on Feminism and Philosophy* 90, no. 1 (1990): 110–16.

Vlastos, Gregory. "Was Plato a Feminist?" *Times Literary Supplement*, iss. 4485 (17–23 March 1989): 276, 288–89.

Wender, Christine Pierce. "Equality: *Republic* V." *Monist* 57, no. 1 (1973): 1–11.

Wender, Dorothea. "Plato: Misogynist, Paedophile, and Feminist." *Arethusa* 6, no. 1 (1973): 75–90.

Whitbeck, Caroline. "Love, Knowledge, and Transformation." *Women's Studies International Forum* 7, no. 5 (1984): 393–405.

Wider, Kathleen. "Women Philosophers in the Ancient Greek World: Donning the Mantle." *Hypatia* 1, no. 1 (1986): 21–62.

Willitts, R. F. "Plato on Women." *Times Literary Supplement*, issue 4490 (21–27 April 1989): 423.

Notes on Contributors

NATALIE HARRIS BLUESTONE teaches philosophy at the Radcliffe Seminars, Radcliffe College. She received her Ph.D. from The Johns Hopkins University and has taught epistemology, ethics, and aesthetics in the United States and England. She has published articles on literature and film, and is the author of *Woman and the Ideal Society: Plato's* Republic *and Modern Myths of Gender.* She is editor of and a contributor to *Double Vision: Perspectives on Gender and the Visual Arts,* which appeared earlier this year.

WENDY BROWN teaches at the University of California, Santa Cruz, in the Women's Studies, Legal Studies, and History of Consciousness programs. She is the author of *Manhood and Politics: A Feminist Reading in Political Theory* (1988) and *Political Timing: Essays on Power and Freedom in Late Modernity,* forthcoming.

MONIQUE CANTO teaches philosophy at the University of Amiens. She has published essays on Plato and the Sophists. Her current research is on the problem of the dramatization of thought.

WILLIAM COWLING is a graduate student at the University of Texas at Dallas. He is currently working on the manuscript *Body, Gender, and Rationality in Plato's* Symposium *and* Republic.

PAGE DUBOIS teaches in the Literature Department at the University of California at San Diego. She is author of *History, Rhetorical Description and the Epic* (Cambridge, 1982), *Centaurs and Amazons* (Ann Arbor, 1982), *Sowing the Body* (Chicago, 1988), *Torture and Truth* (New York, 1991), and of the forthcoming *Sappho Is Burning.*

CYNTHIA HAMPTON specializes in Ancient Greek Philosophy at

Ohio University, where she is an associate professor. She is the author of articles and a book on Plato, *Pleasure, Knowledge, and Being: An Analysis of Plato's Philebus* (SUNY, 1990). She is currently pursuing a degree in theology at Yale.

LUCE IRIGARAY is a leading French feminist and psychoanalyst. She holds doctorates in both linguistics and philosophy and is a director of research at the Centre National de la Recherche Scientifique. Her books in English include *Speculum of the Other Woman* (Cornell, 1985), *This Sex Which Is Not One* (Cornell, 1985), and *Marine Lover* (Columbia, 1993).

ANDREA NYE teaches philosophy and feminist theory at the University of Wisconsin–Whitewater. Her books include *Feminist Theory and the Philosophies of Man, Words of Power: A Feminist Reading of the History of Logic,* and *Philosophia: The Thought of Rosa Luxemburg, Simone Weil, and Hannah Arendt.* She is just finishing a study of the effect of feminism on the discipline of philosophy.

ARLENE W. SAXONHOUSE is James Orin Murfin Professor of Political Science at the University of Michigan. She is author of *Fear of Diversity: The Birth of Political Science in Ancient Greek Thought* (Chicago, 1992), *Women in the History of Political Thought: Ancient Greece to Machiavelli* (Praeger, 1985), and numerous articles in the area of ancient political thought.

JANET FARRELL SMITH is Associate Professor of Philosophy at the University of Massachusetts at Boston. She has taught philosophy at Smith College and has taught the ethics of property at the Harvard Divinity School. Her current work includes the subjects of abortion, property, and the methods of discourse ethics.

ELIZABETH V. SPELMAN is Professor of Philosophy at Smith College. She is author of *Inessential Woman: Problems of Exclusion in Feminist Thought* (Beacon, 1988) and is at work on a new book, *Unworthy Subjects: Suffering and the Economy of Attention.*

NANCY TUANA teaches philosophy and women's studies at the University of Oregon. She is author of *The Less Noble Sex: Scientific, Religious, and Philosophical Conceptions of Woman's Nature* (Indiana, 1993) and *Woman and the History of Philosophy* (Paragon, 1992).

GREGORY VLASTOS was a professor of philosophy at Princeton

University and at the University of California at Berkeley. His publications in the area of classical philosophy include *Socrates: Ironist and Moral Philosopher* (Cornell, 1991), *Philosophy of Socrates* (Notre Dame, 1971), *Plato's Universe* (Washington, 1975), and *Platonic Studies* (Princeton, 1973).

ktesis (possession), 15, 21, 53, 70

Lacan, Jacques, 204, 205, 208, 210, 211
Lambert, Helen, 39
language and linguistics, 205–6, 225–26, 245
laughter, 29, 78, 85 n. 13, 182, 187
Laws
- interpretations in scholarship, 122
- second-best society, 12
- soul/body distinction, 92, 93, 98, 100
- women and politics, 52–53, 56–65
- women's rights, 22

Lee, Desmond, 126
legal capacity, 13, 22
- *Letters*, 110
- *Seventh Letter*, 164, 167, 169

liberty, 16, 17
libidinality, 155
Lloyd, Genevieve, 218, 223
location of the female, 145, 171, 245, 248. *See also* appropriation of female powers
logocentrism, 140, 141, 163, 170
love, 63, 98, 252. *See also* eros; desire
- Diotima's philosophy, 153–54, 181–95, 198–99, 208–9
- Form of, 93
- loving intercourse, 199, 201
- and wisdom, 169, 170, 255

Lydia, queen of, 69
Lysias, 144, 145, 146, 148
Lysistrata, 74, 75

Maccoby, E., 32, 37, 38
madness, 168–70
male as object of beauty, 23, 179 n. 9
manly soul / female body, 8, 101–2
manly soul / male body, 8, 101–2
Mantinean priestess, 153, 154, 207, 253
marriage, 53–54, 57, 70, 114, 117
- arrangement of, 21, 40, 78, 112
- group, 15
- laws, 60, 62
- "sacred," 73

measure. *See* proportion (measure)
Medea, 152
Medea, 19, 152
mediator. *See* intermediary, intermediate
Medusa, 153
Meletus, 152–53
Memory, Muses' mother, 151
Meno, 97, 163–64
Meno, 90
metaphysics, 19, 20, 140, 202
Metis, 265
midwife, Socrates as, 77, 150, 151–52, 164, 248, 256
military service, 13, 123. *See also* war; warrior class
Mill, John Stuart, 30, 129 n. 38
mimesis (imitation) of the female, 55, 142, 149, 154, 261. *See also* appropriation of female powers
Minoan culture, 207
Minos, 148
misogyny, 212
- in Greek culture, 127 n. 2, 141, 145, 173
- in Plato's works, 22–23, 45, 99, 142, 162

Moira, 199
Morris, Jan, 102
mortality. *See* immortality
mousike, 69, 73
Muses, 147, 151, 207
Mycenaean dominance, 207
Myrrha, 149

Nagler, Michael, 146
Namasonians, 15
natural vs. unnatural, 27, 30, 42–46, 116
nature
- capability and performance, 33–37, 88, 91, 112
- *phusis*, 18, 78, 81, 84, 123
  - female equality, 70, 71, 72
  - politics, 74–75, 76
- sex differences, 30–31, 37

need, 83, 233, 255, 258
Nietzsche, Friedrich Wilhelm, 163, 203
nomos (convention), 70, 123
nous (intellectual intuition), 227, 230–31, 234, 235–36
nudity in athletics, 12–13, 30, 53, 73, 78
Nye, Andrea, 223
Nymphs, 147

objectification of women, 44, 45
Odysseus, 19, 153
oikos, 171, 175
oligarchy, 139
one
- as the Good, 223, 224–25, 227
- and the many, 221, 222

Opposites, Pythagorean Table of, 217, 222
Oracle of Delphi, 207, 265 n. 2
Orpheus, 252, 265 n. 2
Oschophoria, 148
other, otherness, 149, 155, 191, 210, 218
  and desire, 56, 57, 60, 63–65
  and the same, 51, 59
Ouranos, 219–21, 227

paideia (education), 18, 20
pain, 50, 51, 53, 55, 56, 60, 61, 232
palaestrae, 12, 53, 73, 78
Pandora, 142
para phusin (contrary to nature), 42
Parmenides, 147, 222, 224
Pater, Walter, 119–20
Pausanias, 205
pedagogy, 167, 168, 177
pederasty, 78, 150, 156 n. 8
Peloponnesian War, 139
Penelope, 19, 81
Penia (need), 83
Pentheus, 148
performance and capability, 33–37
Pericles, 74, 79, 81, 122, 160
Persephone, 246, 264, 265 n. 2
Persians, 147
Phaedo
  soul / body distinction, 91, 92, 223, 230
  supremacy of mind, 162, 163
  women in, 75, 97
Phaedrus, 23, 140–50, 162, 200, 201, 207
  wisdom, 163–64, 168, 169–70
Phaedrus, 83, 144, 145, 146, 149, 170, 258
Phaenarete, 152
phallic, phallus, 203, 204, 205, 208
phallocentrism, 141, 142, 143
Philebus, 92, 217–37
philosopher-queens, 87–105. *See also* guardians; philosopher-rulers
  in Plato scholarship, 111, 114
philosopher-rulers, 31, 83, 94–97, 105, 253. *See also* guardians
  women as, 67, 74, 87, 89, 99
philosophy, philosophers. *See also* dialectic
  Diotima's definition, 184–86
  and the female, 67–84
  female/male discourse, 157–78
phronesis (practical reasoning), 228, 231, 234, 235, 236
phusis (nature), 76, 78, 81, 84, 123
  equality, 70, 72
  female, 18, 71, 74–75
Piraeus, 81
Plato / Socrates distinction, 178 n. 2, 180 n. 22, 239 n. 34
pleasure, 228, 230–33, 234, 235
  city and, 50, 51, 53, 55, 56, 60, 61
  sexual, 199, 208, 209, 210, 250
plenty, 83, 183, 223
polis, 21, 71, 94, 146. *See also* city
  ideal city, 111–12, 113
politics, 96, 167, 168. *See also* power: political
  political office, 13, 14
  women and philosophers in, 74–76, 78–84
  of women's bodies, 49–65
power
  and authority, 105
  of Diotima, 181, 194
  political, 20, 158–63, 173–78
Politics, Aristotle, 19
Politicus, Plato, 19, 80, 81
Pomeroy, Sarah, 15
Pontus, 220
Pope, Alexander, 41
Popper, Karl R., 115
Poros (plenty), 83
possession, common (*ktesis*), 15, 21, 53, 70
poverty and wealth, 181, 183–84, 185
Praxagora, 14, 15, 75
procreation, 50–51, 53–54, 59, 70. *See also* reproduction
  appropriation of, 170–71, 173, 189–92
Prometheus, 142, 227
property
  abolition of private, 14, 21, 36, 104, 113
  right to own, 22
proportion (measure), 228–31, 235
prostitution, 13
Protagoras, 150
psychic traits, 39, 40
psychology, contemporary, 37–41
puberty, 148
purity, 233, 234, 235
Pythagoras, 105 n. 1
Pythagorean Table of Opposites, 217, 222

rationalism, 157, 163, 166, 170
reality
  Form of, 93
  and knowledge, 182

reasoning
  dialectical, 163, 164, 165, 166, 167
  practical (*phronesis*), 228, 231, 234, 235, 236
reconstruction, 218. *See also* deconstruction
recovery
  of truth, 169
  of wisdom, 163–64
reincarnation, 98, 100, 107 n. 18, 107 nn. 21, 22
representation of women
  cave as source, 260, 263
  in the city, 56, 58, 59, 62
  and procreation, 50–51
reproduction, 51, 57, 58, 72. *See also* procreation
  appropriation of, 139–55, 248–49, 254, 256, 257
Republic
"burden of proof" argument, 30–32
dramatic presentation, 29–30
female de-sexed, 68–76
guardian-women, 87, 88–90
interpretations in scholarship, 110–13, 115, 117, 118, 121–23, 125, 126
masculine discourse, 158–61, 163–67, 170–72, 173–74, 176–77
"natural" vs. "unnatural," 42–46
philosopher-rulers, 95–96
philosophy and the female, 78–84
position and traits of women, 12–22, 28, 36, 40, 67–68
sexual female, 76–78
soul / body distinction, 91–92
womanly soul / female body, 103
women's bodies in the city, 52–57, 62, 65
resource and need, 255
rhythms of life, 244, 246, 259, 264
rights
  vs. duties, 103–4
  of guardian women, 12–14, 21
Rosen, Stanley, 254, 256, 258
Ruddick, Sara, 218
ruling class. *See* guardians; philosopher-rulers

Sappho, 148–49
Saxonhouse, Arlene W., 160, 161, 162
Schleiermacher, Friedrich, 110, 114
second-best society, 4, 12
seduction, 62, 140, 143, 144
seeing vs. feeling, 226, 247, 250–51, 259, 260, 262
self-sufficiency (*autarkeia*), male, 143, 144, 268 n. 33
sensibles and Forms, 194, 222–23, 225
Seventh Letter, 164, 167, 169
  sex differences, 25, 31, 32, 45, 64, 244
  contemporary psychology, 37–41
  individual variation, 33–37
  interpretations in scholarship, 115, 116–18, 120–21
  sexuality, 208–9
sexism, 3, 97, 203. *See also* misogyny
  in scholarship, 109–27
sexual. *See also* desire; eros; intercourse; love
  choice, 13–14, 40, 113, 120
  desire, 142, 148, 169–70
  equality, 109–10, 113–14
  female, 76–78
  identity, 102, 145–49
Shakespeare, William, 19
Sherman, Julia, 37, 38, 41
sibyl, 147, 207
skill (*techne*), 72
slavery, 13
social
  intercourse, right to, 13
  justice, 21–22
socialization, 35, 39, 40
Socrates / Plato distinction, 178 n. 2, 180 n. 22, 239 n. 34
Sophist, 158
Sophists, 75, 158–61, 173. *See also* agonistic expression
Sophocles, 69, 150, 151
soul / body distinction, 91–100, 230
Sparta, Spartan, 29, 56, 139
spatial abilities, 32, 37, 38, 47 n. 18
sperma (seed), 149–50
spiritual life and sex, 120
statesmanship and weaving, 80–81
stones, metaphor of, 150, 153
Strauss, Leo, 28, 84 n. 7, 115, 123–24
Symposium, 23, 181–95, 197–212
  Alcibiades, 80
  appropriation of female powers, 140, 142, 145, 147, 153–55
  Diotima, 98, 254, 256, 258
  Eros, theory of, 82, 83, 253, 259
  knowledge, 92

masculine discourse, 165, 169, 170, 171–72
need for women, 52, 63, 64
wisdom, 249
symposium, women's, 62–63
synagogē, synousia (collection), 144, 145

Taylor, A. E., 120–22
techne (skill), 72
Teiresias, 148
Telemachus, 19
Terpsion, 82, 150
Theaetetus, 82
appropriation of reproduction, 150–53
dialectical inquiry, 164, 166
language and imagery, 77, 140
Sophistic discourse, 159
Theaetetus, 82, 150, 248
Theages, 84 n. 7
Thebes, 150
thēlus (female), 146
Theodorus, 150
Theogony, 219–20, 222
Theseus, 148
Thesmophorian rituals, 207
Thrasymachus, 160, 161, 168
Thucydides, 12, 74, 79
Timaeus, 75, 92, 98, 100, 142
time
and desire, 56, 61–62, 63, 64
force of, 58, 59–60
timocracy, 160
Titans, 227
Trachiniae, 146
training. *See* education and training
transsexualism, 102
transvestism, 145, 147, 148, 149, 156 n. 10
trophe, 121. *See also* childrearing
true being, 172, 234, 235, 239 n. 32, 240 n. 45
truth, 165, 167, 168, 170, 172, 173, 248
as intermediate of the Good, 228–31, 233, 234, 235
recovery of, 164, 169
Typhon, 146

verbal abilities, 32, 37, 38
Vernant, Jean-Pierre, 148
Virgil, 259
virtue, 70, 90, 168, 201, 258
vision. *See* seeing vs. feeling
vocational opportunity, 13, 22

war, 73, 121, 123, 252
masculine world of death, 81–82
women in, 28, 64–65, 79–80
warrior class, 69, 70, 72, 74
waves, three, 29, 47 n. 12, 85 n. 18, 111–13
wax, mind's likeness to, 151
weakness, 28, 29, 38, 45, 67, 72
physical, 36, 71
wealth and poverty, 181, 183–84, 185
weaving and statesmanship, 80–81
Wender, Dorothea, 15
Whitbeck, Caroline, 218
wings metaphor, 146, 169–70
wisdom, 162, 190, 192–93, 259. *See also* knowledge
darkness and, 246, 248, 261, 264
dialectic and, 165
ignorance and, 182, 184–85, 263
love and, 169–70, 172, 255
recovery of, 163–64
womanly soul/female body, 8, 101–2
womanly soul/male body, 8, 101–2
women, absence of, 243–57
women as rulers. *See* guardians; philosopher-queens; philosopher-rulers
work-allocation, 14–15, 43

Xerxes, 147–48

Zeus, 143, 145, 221, 224, 227, 250, 255